Catholicity and Emerging Personhood

Catholicity in an Evolving Universe
Ilia Delio, General Editor

This series of original works by leading Catholic figures explores all facets of life through the lens of catholicity: a sense of dynamic wholeness and a conscious awareness of a continually unfolding creation.

Making All Things New: Catholicity, Cosmology, Consciousness
Ilia Delio

A New Heaven, A New Earth: The Bible and Catholicity
Dianne Bergant

The Source of All Love: Catholicity and the Trinity
Heidi Russell

The Image of the Unseen God: Catholicity, Science, and Our Evolving Understanding of God
Thomas E. Hosinski

And God Created Wholeness: A Spirituality of Catholicity
Edwin E. Olson

Christian Ministry in the Divine Milieu: Catholcity, Evolution, and the Reign of God
Donald C. Maldari, SJ

Church as Dynamic Life-System: Shared Ministries and Common Responsibilities
Joseph A. Bracken, SJ

Catholicity and Emerging Personhood

A Contemporary Theological Anthropology

DANIEL P. HORAN, OFM

ORBIS BOOKS
Maryknoll, New York 10545

Founded in 1970, Orbis Books endeavors to publish works that enlighten the mind, nourish the spirit, and challenge the conscience. The publishing arm of the Maryknoll Fathers and Brothers, Orbis seeks to explore the global dimensions of the Christian faith and mission, to invite dialogue with diverse cultures and religious traditions, and to serve the cause of reconciliation and peace. The books published reflect the views of their authors and do not represent the official position of the Maryknoll Society. To learn more about Maryknoll and Orbis Books, please visit our website at www.maryknollsociety.org.

Library of Congress Cataloging-in-Publication Data

Names: Horan, Daniel P., author.
Title: Catholicity and emerging personhood : a contemporary
    theological anthropology / Daniel P. Horan, OFM.
Description: Maryknoll, New York : Orbis Books, [2019] | Series:
    Catholicity in an evolving universe | Includes bibliographical
    references and index.
Identifiers: LCCN 2019010042 (print) | LCCN 2019013564 (ebook) |
    ISBN 9781608338009 (e-book) | ISBN 9781626983366 (print) |
    ISBN 9781608338009 (ebk.)
Subjects: LCSH: Theological anthropology—Catholic Church.
Classification: LCC BT701.3 (ebook) | LCC BT701.3 .H67 2019
    (print) | DDC 233—dc23
LC record available at https://lccn.loc.gov/2019010042

Contents

Preface

This book is the product of years of thinking about what it means to be human in theological terms. I am thankful for the communities of faith and learning that have made this process of research, reflection, dialogue, and articulation possible. In addition to the many university and conference lectures that I have had the privilege to deliver on themes included in this book, and after being refined somewhat in the fire of academic and pastoral conversations, special thanks is owed to the faculty and doctoral students in the Theology Department of Boston College as well as my students and colleagues at Catholic Theological Union in Chicago, where I have the honor of serving as a faculty member.

Many friends, family members, and brother Franciscan friars have supported and encouraged me in ways too numerous to name here. I am especially grateful for the feedback offered to me by my CTU colleagues during our regular faculty seminar in 2018, where I shared early drafts of some chapters. Additionally, I am particularly indebted to two of my friends and theological colleagues, Robert J. Schreiter and Jessica Coblentz, who graciously read the manuscript at various points throughout its development and offered me helpful comments and suggestions.

The idea for this book originated with an invitation from Ilia Delio, OSF, for me to contribute this volume in a new and important series on theology and catholicity published by Orbis Books. I am grateful to her for the opportunity and the occasion to develop this line of thinking about the Catholic theological tradition in light of catholicity and the world today. I am also thankful for Robert Ellsberg and Paul McMahon of Orbis Books, the publisher and my editor respectively. Ilia and the whole team at Orbis have been nothing but supportive and patient with me, particularly when teaching loads, other writing projects, and speaking commitments inevitably delayed my original completion estimation.

It is not my intention to present this book as a complete answer to the question of the human in the Christian theological tradition. Such a formidable task may very well be beyond any of us. Instead, it is my hope that this volume might serve as a contribution to a conversation that is still very much in process, because the meaning of human personhood is still very much emerging.

❖ ❖ ❖

Portions of Chapters 2, 3, and 4 appeared in previously published essays and have been revised and expanded in this book. I am grateful to Bloomsbury Academic for permission to include parts of my forthcoming essay "Creation," in the *T & T Clark Companion to Theological Anthropology,* ed. Mary Ann Hinsdale and Stephen Okey (New York: Bloomsbury Academic); to Rowman and Littlefield for permission to include selections that appeared in earlier form in my *All God's Creatures: A Theology of Creation* (Lanham, MD: Lexington Books/Fortress Academic, 2018); and to Paul Crowley, SJ, editor of Theological Studies for permission to reprint and expand parts of my article "Beyond Essentialism and Complementarity: Toward a Theological Anthropology Rooted in Haecceitas," *Theological Studies* 75 (2014): 94–117.

Foreword

ILIA DELIO

The scientific technological matrix of the twenty-first century invites new ways of human interaction, evoking new forms of human identity and new patterns of knowledge. Despite the rapid technological advances surrounding us, however, we never question to what effect they are changing us. We treat the human person as a fixed entity, as one who is created immediately by God. But science tells us otherwise and sobers our anthropocentric views. In his new book Dan Horan asks the question, What exactly is the human person? He addresses this question from a multidisciplinary perspective. He points out from the start that we think we know what the human person is (in the same way we think we know what God is), but we need to step back in a spirit of humility and reevaluate the meaning of personhood in light of modern science and the wider ecological framework. Christian anthropology defines the human person in particular ways: as image of God, as male and female, as body and soul. Much of our theology of the human person, however, is still based on patristic and medieval ideas, despite advances in modern science such as evolutionary biology, neuroscience, cognitive psychology, and physics. By humbly seeking wisdom from the scientific, philosophical, and social-scientific communities, Horan argues, we can gain new insight on personhood and a wider perspective of where the human stands in the overall sphere of nature itself.

In his encyclical letter *Laudato Si'*, Pope Francis claims that science and religion need to be brought into fruitful dialogue if we are to have a realistic understanding of human personhood, one that corrects a notion of superiority over nature. Drawing on a broad scope of environmental studies and evolutionary biology, the pope laments the Western notion of the hegemonic individual and affirms the interdependence of all creation. In this respect he situates human personhood within the ecological network of living systems. Similarly, Horan begins his discussion of the human person from the point of ecology and notes that the stewardship model still places the human person in a superior position over nature, as principal caretaker and not as brother or sister. He examines the distinction of the human person as image of God and questions whether or not this isolates humankind from the ecological whole and if nonhuman nature also reflects the glory of divine Life. I find his perspective refreshingly Franciscan because he is asking: Is creation truly a family or not? Do we belong to creation or are we simply caring for creation? Does not creation care for us insofar as nature provides our food, our clothes, and all that sustains life? Thomas Berry pointed out years ago that the earth is primary and humans are children of (mother) earth. Evolution is a sober realization that we emerge from the dynamism of nature; human personhood is a long process of development in which environmental factors, including climate change, play a significant role in the selection of factors for the optimal emergence of human life. Situating the human person in the context of big history is no longer a task for the sciences but for theology as well.

We realize today that a new theology is needed to support a new understanding of the human person in a world of interdependence and complexity. Horan takes up this challenge in a thoughtful and capacious manner, drawing on a variety of sources from medieval theology and philosophy to current scientific understandings of evolution and ecology. He enfolds the Franciscan concept of the human person in a way that is true to the core of Christian identity and the Scotistic notion of individuation, which reflects the ineffable love of God.

Horan's ability to harness varied and complex ideas on the human person lends to a rich discussion and a contemporary view that rightly contextualizes personhood within the broad scope of catholicity. This book is a valuable contribution to understanding the human person in the twenty-first century, and I am grateful to him for taking up this challenge in a timely and provocative manner.

Introduction

The history of Christian theological anthropology has been marked by incompleteness, by partial answers to questions in search of wholeness in meaning. Much of the way we discuss what it means to be human has been cast in an oppositional or binary frame. Human beings are *neither* animals *nor* divine; human beings are composed of matter *and* spirit. For centuries our quest to understand what is most fundamental about ourselves—What are we exactly?—has been governed by an uncritical, and at times unconscious, agenda to establish and maintain the superiority of our species. That we dare to claim for ourselves the title *Homo sapiens sapiens*—our collective name according to the binomial nomenclature used by modern taxonomists—represents a kind of hubris: modern humans are not merely wise, but "the wisest." Human intelligence has been the standard by which creaturely valuation has taken place for millennia. Aristotle claimed that humans were "rational animals," that rationality is what distinguishes us from all other creatures, thereby securing for us a sense of uniqueness and superiority, and not many people disagreed with the premise.[1] In time, the Book of Genesis would be read through a Hellenistic lens—as the influential Jewish philosopher Philo of Alexandria (d. 40 CE) did so well—and the concept of dominion understood as domination and lordship over nonhuman creation would emerge as one of our greatest eisegetical errors. In asking a simple question—What are we?—we provided a partial, yet self-serving answer for ourselves. We are the best. We are the pinnacle of God's creation.

---

[1] For example, see Aristotle, *Nicomachean Ethics*, Book I, Ch. 13, trans. Terence Irwin (Indianapolis: Hackett Publishing, 1999), 16–18.

1

We, and we alone, are created in God's own image and likeness. And, perhaps most important, we are *not* like other creatures. Whereas nonhuman creatures are merely material—fleshy "machines," as Rene Descartes put it—we are matter *and* spirit, the former subordinated to the latter, and the latter is how we can account for our special rationality.[2]

That this brief outline (admittedly oversimplified) would strike most Christians as uncontestable or at least noncontroversial gives me great pause. Statements about what the human person is from a Christian perspective that begin and end with doctrinal platitudes such as "we are created *imago Dei*" without further inquiry and qualification are a problem. And that views of the human person that rely on prescientific understandings of the cosmos, biology, and metaphysics to explain contemporary phenomena, human experience, and reality writ large go uncritically appropriated is troublesome. What I am describing here is the hermeneutical context of theological anthropology that has been a mainstay of our Christian tradition. Whereas the Copernican revolution has been accepted by people of faith and biological evolution declared compatible with Christian doctrine within magisterial teaching, the doctrinal foundations for theological anthropology in our catechetical instruction, moral theology, and pastoral ministry have not kept pace with the scientific "signs of the times."

To understand what it means to talk about the human person within the Christian tradition, to develop a theological anthropology that is both faithful and intelligible, we must critically reflect on the sources of our tradition while also humbly seeking wisdom from the scientific, philosophical, and social-scientific communities. If we take seriously Pope Francis's encyclical letter *Laudato Si'*, which states that "science and religion, with their distinctive approaches to understanding reality, can enter into an intense dialogue fruitful for both" (no.

---

[2] For more on this, see Daniel P. Horan, *All God's Creatures: A Theology of Creation* (Lanham, MD: Lexington Books/Fortress Academic, 2018).

62), then we have nothing to fear from such an intellectual and spiritual path of inquiry.[3]

This book contributes to moving the theological conversation about what it means to be human from the repetition of antiquated and incomplete perspectives of ages past to a place where discussion about the Christian tradition's view of humanity takes seriously what we have learned about the world, ourselves, and the rest of creation in conversation with what we rightly call tradition (from the verb *tradere*, "to hand on"). If theology is, as Saint Anselm in his *Prosologion* famously describes, *fides quaerens intellectum* ("faith seeking understanding"), then we should strive always to deepen our knowledge of and appreciation for the faith that has been handed on to us. The way we proceed in seeking greater knowledge and understanding of, and appreciation for, the human person within the Christian tradition is by way of *catholicity*.

The Hermeneutic of Catholicity

In recent years the notion of *catholicity* has received renewed attention.[4] Traditionally, the term has been associated in colloquial English with concepts like "universality" or "all-encompassing." As the late Jesuit scholar Walter Ong noted in a now classic

---

[3] In *Laudato Si'* Pope Francis continues to name explicitly the necessary dialogue that the faith tradition must have with philosophy and social sciences in addition to the natural sciences mentioned above: "The Catholic Church is open to dialogue with philosophical thought; this has enabled her to produce various syntheses between faith and reason. The development of the Church's social teaching represents such a synthesis with regard to social issues; this teaching is called to be enriched by taking up new challenges" (no. 63). All papal texts are available in multiple translations at vatican.va.

[4] See, for example, Robert J. Schreiter, who proposes a renewed sense of catholicity as both a constructive and heuristic response to the challenges globalization poses to theological reflection today. See *The New Catholicity: Theology between the Global and the Local* (Maryknoll, NY: Orbis Books, 1997), esp. 116–33.

article, the correspondence between *catholic* and *universal* does not quite work when one examines the etymological roots of the word, especially within a theological context. Ong explains:

> If "universal" is the adequate meaning of "catholic," why did the Latin church, which in its vernacular language had the word *universalis*, not use this word but rather borrowed from Greek the term *katholikos* instead, speaking of the "one, holy, catholic and apostolic church" (to put it into English) instead of the "one, holy, universal and apostolic Church"? The etymological history of *universalis* is not in every detail clear, but it certainly involves the concepts of *unum*, "one," and *vertere*, "turn." It suggests using a compass to make a circle around a central point. It is an inclusive concept in the sense that the circle includes everything within it. But by the same token it also excludes everything outside it. *Universalis* contains a subtle note of negativity. *Katholikos* does not. It is more unequivocally positive. It means simply "through-the-whole" or "throughout-the-whole"—*kata* or *kath*, through or throughout; *holos*, whole, from the same Indo-European root as our English "whole."[5]

This insight, minor as it may seem at first, presents the kernel of wisdom that has since germinated into the robust theological series of which this book is a part. For too long catholic, catholicism, and catholicity have been concepts governed by the logic of *universalis*, which was seemingly inclusive but—to borrow Ong's apt description of the terminology—nevertheless contain "a subtle note of negativity." This logic of *universalis*, with its clearly etched line of exclusion, has cast a shadow over much of the Christian theological enterprise and has shaped the way we have reflected on discrete doctrines within the tradition.

---

[5] Walter Ong, "Yeast: A Parable for Catholic Higher Education," *America* (April 7, 1990), 347.

In a complementary fashion the theologian Avery Dulles, in his classic text *The Catholicity of the Church*, explores how diverse theological loci—Trinity, Christology, ecclesiology, and so on—ought to reflect this sense of catholicity, albeit at times unrealized or too-often stilted. Setting the stage for a project such as this book on theological anthropology or the other volumes in this series, Dulles observes that the term *catholicity* implies a "qualitative wholeness" that should have a direct bearing on how we understand Catholicism and the content of our faith.[6] In summarizing its meaning, Dulles echoes Ong: "Unlike universality, catholicity is a concrete term: it is predicated not of abstract essences but of particular, existing realities. Furthermore, it always implies intensity, richness, and plenitude. Unlike fullness, it implies a unitive relationship among things that are diverse."[7]

When we return to the example of the Christian understanding of the human person, much of the classical attempts to articulate a theological anthropology have started with presuppositions of exclusion: human beings are defined by what we are not (such as nonhuman animals or angels; the latter was occasionally employed as a metaphysical foil in Scholasticism for precisely this purpose). With this history of theological reflection in mind, a few questions begin to surface. What might it look like to renew our understanding of a truly *catholic* theology? How can we proceed to develop a theological anthropology that is faithful to our tradition and yet avoids some of the longstanding pitfalls of the *universalis* logic? The answer begins with the deliberate appropriation of a hermeneutic of catholicity.

Setting the stage for this series of theological renewal, Ilia Delio draws on the kind of insights proffered by Ong and Dulles, amplifying the call for reconsideration of the terms *catholic* and *catholicity*, arguing that they are essentially about "wholeness" and "wholemaking." A hermeneutic of catholicity, then, "is the

---

[6] Avery Dulles, *The Catholicity of the Church* (Oxford: Clarendon Press, 1985). See, for example, page 8.

[7] Dulles, *The Catholicity of the Church*, 167.

orientation of all life toward making wholes."[8] It is a mode of interpretation that looks beyond the ostensibly axiomatic principles of radical distinction, separateness, exclusivity, and isolation to recognize an intrinsic connectivity present throughout the whole of God's creation. A hermeneutic of catholicity takes as its starting point the presupposition of an evolutionary cosmos, which, originating from the one God who is Creator, seeks an ever-greater unity in its journey through salvation history back to the very same God. As Irenaeus of Lyons stated in *Adversus Haereses* during the second Christian century, creation and salvation, protology and eschatology, are two sides of the same coin of the one divine Will.[9] Wholemaking is inherent to creation because, although it may not always be visible to us from a quotidian perspective, God's intention remains the salvation of all creation—human and nonhuman alike. This means that the harmony and mutuality envisioned by the Creator from the beginning is the *telos* of salvation history as attested to by the New Testament (for example, Romans 8) and articulated in the twentieth century by luminaries such as Pierre Teilhard de Chardin, Karl Rahner, and others.[10] Dulles likewise addresses this dynamic of catholicity, stating that it "designates a fullness of reality and life, especially divine life, actively communicating itself. This life, flowing outwards, pulsates through many subjects, draws them together, and brings them into union with their source and goal."[11]

For too long the true catholicity of our theological foundations have been supplanted by an anthropocentrism that has

---

[8] Ilia Delio, *Making All Things New: Catholicity, Cosmology, Consciousness* (Maryknoll, NY: Orbis Books, 2015), xi.

[9] See Matthew C. Steenberg, *Irenaeus on Creation: The Cosmic Christ and the Saga of Redemption* (Leiden: Brill, 2008).

[10] For example, see Pierre Teilhard de Chardin, *Christianity and Evolution: Reflections on Science and Religion*, trans. René Hague (New York: Harcourt Brace, 1971); and Karl Rahner, "Christology within an Evolutionary View of the World," in *Theological Investigations*, vol. 5, trans. Karl-H. Kruger (Baltimore: Helicon Press, 1966), 157–92.

[11] Dulles, *The Catholicity of the Church*, 167.

distorted our understanding of ourselves and of the world. Keeping in mind the salvific significance of wholemaking, this book is governed by a desire to examine the Christian tradition of theological reflection on the human person through the lens of catholicity. It will require a consideration of the well-worn tropes of patristic and medieval philosophical and theological anthropology that have for too long gone uncritically accepted. Concurrently, such a survey and analysis allow for what scripture scholar Dianne Bergant has recognized as the aim of a hermeneutic of catholicity, namely, "a retrieval of the realization that a form of wholeness is already present, though often overlooked or forgotten. This form of wholeness is the most fundamental dimension of our reality."[12] In other words, while much of the "standard" accounting of what it means to be a human person from the Christian tradition is in need of faithful interrogation and critical examination, the process not only unveils what must be reconsidered but also reveals resources always already present that support a truly *catholic* theological anthropology. Bergant also alludes to the importance of starting such an inquiry within the broader community of creation, noting that, "humankind's participation within and oneness with all other members of this community [of creation] is the ultimate experience of catholicity, a catholicity that is universal in extent and encompassing all."[13]

The Development of Doctrine

In order to articulate a theological anthropology according to a hermeneutic of catholicity, we must first address the reality of the development of doctrine. Critics of constructive systematic theology often claim that such an activity is incongruous with the tradition that has preceded it, that theologians concerned with taking seriously the developments of human inquiry—natural

---

[12] Dianne Bergant, *A New Heaven, A New Earth: The Bible and Catholicity* (Maryknoll, NY: Orbis Books, 2016), 4.

[13] Bergant, *A New Heaven, A New Earth*, 4.

and social sciences, philosophy, psychology, and so on—leave behind orthodox Christianity so as to pursue a contemporary fad or intellectual experiment. While such criticisms may rightly be leveled against some scholars, the premise of this present study follows no such course. The operative presupposition behind criticism of this sort is that Christian doctrine is static and unchanging, that it has always been understood and expressed the way we have it today. What follows here is an effort to remain faithful to the Christian tradition while also acknowledging that Christian doctrine has and continues to develop.

Saint John XXIII remarked at the opening of the Second Vatican Council in October 1962 that the task of contemporary theological inquiry is to express better and more clearly the core of the apostolic faith handed on from one generation to the next. In a manner reminiscent of the Anselmian axiom that theology is always understood as the activity of *faith seeking understanding*, John XXIII acknowledged in *Gaudet Mater Ecclesia* the urgency and complexity of the theological enterprise at hand:

> As all sincere promoters of Christian, Catholic, and apostolic faith strongly desire, what is needed is that this doctrine be more fully and more profoundly known and that minds be more fully imbued and formed by it. What is needed is that this certain and immutable doctrine, to which loyal submission is due, *be investigated and presented in the way demanded by our times.* For the deposit of faith, the truths contained in our venerable doctrine, are one thing; the fashion in which they are expressed, but with the same meaning and the same judgment, is another thing. This way of speaking will require a great deal of work and, it may be, much patience: types of presentation must be introduced which are more in accord with a teaching authority which is primarily pastoral in character. (no. 5)

The core foundations of Christianity remain consistent, but ongoing inquiry into their meaning and consideration of their contemporary articulation are perennial responsibilities of the church and of its theologians. When we talk about the development of doctrine, this distinction expressed by the pope between the "core truths" that are *contained* in doctrines and the manner of their expression is a useful heuristic.

In addition to John XXIII's instruction to the participating bishops and *periti* of the Second Vatican Council, several major figures over the last two centuries articulate this fact about the development of Christian doctrine. Foremost among these theologians and scholars is Blessed John Henry Newman (1801–90), whose now-classic text *An Essay on the Development of Christian Doctrine* expertly addresses the reality and simple truth of the development of doctrine. In a strikingly succinct statement Newman remarks that doctrine must be consistently engaged with new and ever-emerging knowledge that humanity attains, noting that an idea (under which the concept of "doctrine" falls) changes with these various developments "in order to remain the same," for "in a higher world it is otherwise, but here below to live is to change, and to be perfect is to have changed often."[14] Given that orthodox Christian theology of revelation makes clear that neither sacred scripture nor creedal statements are delivered "from above" by God complete and verbatim, the quest to understand more fully the faith is a necessary task within the life of the church. Newman provides several examples of how doctrines have developed over time, which any student of history could easily recognize: the formation of the New Testament canon, the doctrine of original sin, and the concept of *homoousios* in Christology, to name a few.

It is important to include a brief discussion of the development of doctrine at the beginning of this book because it pertains directly to the constructive systematic exploration of what it means to be a human person from a Christian theological perspective. Newman anticipated this task and the necessity of reminding theologians and others of doctrinal development. Newman notes that ideas are very much alive and shaped by

---

[14] John Henry Newman, *An Essay on the Development of Christian Doctrine* (Notre Dame, IN: University of Notre Dame Press, 1989), 40.

context, culture, and increasing knowledge. He holds that it is precisely the complexity, nuance, and richness of doctrinal expression that require time for fuller understanding of this or that tenet of faith:

> And the more claim an idea has to be considered living, the more various will be its aspects; and the more social and political is its nature, the more complicated and subtle will be its issues, and the longer and more eventful will be its course. And in the number of these special ideas, which from their very depth and richness cannot be fully understood at once, but are more and more clearly expressed and taught the longer they last—having aspects many and bearings many, mutually connected and growing one out of another, *and all parts of a whole*, with a sympathy and correspondence keeping pace with the ever-changing necessities of the world, multiform, prolific, and ever resourceful—among these great doctrines surely we Christians shall not refuse a foremost place to Christianity.[15]

It is indisputable that one of the most complex, complicated, and subtle issues in Christian faith is our understanding of the human person. There is, perhaps, no other idea that could claim to be more "living," to put it in Newman's terms. Who we are, what we are intended to be, what it means to be human—these questions continue to fascinate and perplex Christians and non-Christians alike.

Keeping in mind Newman's insightful reminder about the reality of doctrinal development, we can return to our own time and context, aware of what theologian Bernard Lonergan called the "transition from a classicist world-view to historical-mindedness" in Catholic Christian theology in the twentieth century.[16]

---

[15] Newman, *An Essay on the Development of Christian Doctrine,* 56, emphasis added.

[16] Bernard Lonergan, "The Transition from a Classicist World-View to Historical-Mindedness," in *A Second Collection: Papers by Bernard*

In other words, with an appreciation for Newman's insights and John XXIII's exhortation, we have to resist the tendency merely to repeat doctrinal expressions or theological explanations that we have received in a propositional manner. A "classicist world-view" is a black-and-white approach to reality, seeking timeless, simple, and static answers to complex questions that deserve a more catholic response. "Historical-mindedness," on the other hand, denotes recognition of the world's complexity, the need for nuance in scholarly inquiry, and an appreciation for the full-ness of understanding of our faith toward which we seek but of which we may never master.[17]

This book contributes to our collective responsibility as Christians to seek a fuller understanding of our faith, which is another way of saying that we are tasked with the ongoing development of doctrine. To borrow a description of the task of theology from the Lutheran theologian Paul Tillich, the primary role of systematic theology is not intended to be merely historical but is always *constructive*. He explains that systematic theology, such as this project, "does not tell us what people have thought the Christian message to be in the past; rather it tries to give us an interpretation of the Christian message which is relevant to the present situation."[18] To proceed in this task we must not only be willing to presuppose the development of Christian doctrine but also that forms of its previous articulation may now be inadequate. Far too much of the manner in which Christian discussions of the human person have proceeded, even in recent decades, have relied on antiquated philosophical anthropologies

---

J. F. Lonergan, ed. William F. J. Ryan and Bernard J. Tyrrell, 1–9 (Toronto: University of Toronto Press, 1974).

[17] More recently, Eleazar S. Fernandez gives an account of the problem of what he calls "totalizing discourse," which reflects the attitudinal focus of Lonergan's "classicist world-view" and the need to overcome the limitations of that hermeneutical outlook. See *Reimagining the Human: Theological Anthropology in Response to Systemic Evil* (St. Louis: Chalice Press, 2004), esp. 11–30.

[18] Paul Tillich, *Systematic Theology*, 3 vols. (Chicago: University of Chicago Press, 1951), 1:53.

and prescientific conceptions of the human person, nonhuman creation, and cosmology writ large. One symptom of this limited understanding of the world, and therefore of the human person, is the persistence of theological and colloquial reliance on binary and oppositional discourse, as mentioned at the opening of this introduction. While one-for-one distinctions do exist in some contexts, nevertheless we have been wedded to Greek metaphysical frames—at first Platonic and then, with the rediscovery of "The Philosopher" and the Arabic commentaries on his texts in the Middle Ages, Aristotelian—to the exclusion of information and truths that did not fit our limited and preconceived notions. Again, it is worth stating from the outset that my claim is not that real distinctions do not exist and should not be accepted in any form. Instead, my invitation in the spirit of a more *catholic* theological anthropology is the need for openness to reality as it presents itself to us, and which is more complex and nuanced than the philosophical, theological, and scientific frameworks of our medieval predecessors could allow.

The call to move beyond the binary of so much of Christian theological reflection and articulation is not novel, but it is one to which I join my thought and voice. This book is tentative and exploratory. It is neither a complete doctrinal explication of theological anthropology nor is it an attempt to reject outright what has come before. Rather, it is a contribution to the ongoing effort to clarify and understand more deeply the faith that Christians profess, especially as it pertains to those who are making this same profession of faith: human beings. Furthermore, in an attempt to understand better the human person from the Christian tradition, the primary lens through which we will view and approach scripture, tradition, experience, and human reason—the sources of theological reflection—is that of *catholicity*.

The Meaning of Emergence

The term *emergence* is important and yet polyvalent. Generally, it refers to some entity that is not just more but is also distinct from the sum of its constitutive parts. Something emergent is more complex than what preceded it. This term describes the appearance or advent of something novel and coherent, which accounts for the presence of something radically new.[19] As Ilia Delio explains, "Emergence is produced by a combination of causes or events but cannot be regarded as the sum of their individual effects."[20] Elsewhere, she provides the following succinct summary: "Emergence is irreducible novelty of increasing complexity, a combination of holism with novelty in a way that contrasts with both physical reductionism and dualism."[21]

The concept of emergence became especially popular among evolutionary theorists in the early twentieth century as scientists and philosophers sought to understand better the natural world in light of the recent biological and historical discoveries.[22] It is tied to a worldview that is hierarchical or "leveled." Over eons, the process of evolution produces "continually more complex realities in a process of ongoing creativity," with more complex entities emerging from less-complex ones while at the same time remaining tied to that which is "beneath" or has come before.[23] Consequently, evolutionary theorists can begin to provide an accounting for extremely complex and differentiated creatures appearing over time in a system of emergence that remains open-ended and evolving.

---

[19] For a summary, see Peter A. Corning, "The Re-Emergence of 'Emergence': A Venerable Concept in Search of a Theory," *Complexity* 7 (2002): 18–30.

[20] Delio, *Making All Things New*, 49.

[21] Ilia Delio, *The Emergent Christ: Exploring the Meaning of Catholic in an Evolutionary Universe* (Maryknoll, NY: Orbis Books, 2011), 20.

[22] For some pioneering works in this area, see George H. Lewes, *The Problems of Life and Mind*, vol. 2 (New York: Houghton, Mifflin, 1891); Samuel Alexander, *Space, Time, and Deity: The Gifford Lectures at Glasgow*, 2 vols. (London: MacMillian Publishing, 1920–27); and C. Lloyd Morgan, *Emergent Evolution: The Gifford Lectures* (London: William and Norgate Publishing, 1927).

[23] Philip Clayton, *Mind and Emergence: From Quantum to Consciousness* (New York: Oxford University Press, 2004), 42.

Theologians who have been particularly interested in engaging with process philosophy have been drawn to this use of emergence in evolutionary theory.[24] But the meaning of the term *emergence* in this book is far more expansive and used in a less-narrowly conceived or specialized way. While recognizing its importance in the discourse of evolutionary theory—as will be explored further in Chapter 2—this project is not focused on science and theology as such. As the subtitle of this book suggests, I am primarily interested in exploring how we understand key loci within the Christian tradition as it concerns reflection on the human person; in other words, I am interested in theological anthropology. The driving theme of this book is that we can consider these key loci through the lens of catholicity or wholemaking, which reveals a general sense of an evolving understanding of human personhood. What *emerges* from such a reflection are new insights about the role of evolutionary biology in our theological consideration of humanity; alternative approaches to explicating the doctrine of *imago Dei*; new resources discovered in the Christian tradition for grounding our theology; novel trajectories that allow us to understand how previous anthropologies have harmed certain populations or erased them altogether, while offering us new paths forward for a holistic understanding of human diversity; reconsiderations and expansions of our understanding of sin; and explorations of the reality of God's grace and lived-out response to that gift.

The use of *emergence* in this book conveys a capacious sense that in some instances signals the presence of novelty and

---

[24] For example, see Joseph A. Bracken, *Christianity and Process Thought: Spirituality for a Changing World* (Philadelphia: Templeton Foundation Press, 2006); Catherine Keller, *On the Mystery: Discerning Divinity in Process* (Minneapolis: Fortress Press, 2008); Mikael Leidenhag, "The Relevance of Emergence Theory in the Science-Religion Dialogue," *Zygon* 48 (2013): 966–83; Joseph A. Bracken, "Actions and Agents: Natural and Supernatural Reconsidered," *Zygon* 48 (2013): 1001–13; and Joseph A. Bracken, *The World in the Trinity: Open-Ended Systems in Science and Religion* (Minneapolis: Fortress Press, 2014).

increased complexity, but in other senses gestures toward an overlooked wholeness always already present in the theological tradition but too frequently overlooked, silenced, or ignored.

Cultural Location

Before providing a summary overview of the book, it is imperative that I identify my cultural location, for it has an inevitable bearing on my reception, interpretation, engagement, and articulation of the sources I draw upon in the chapters that follow. Regarding the requisite social markers that locate me within the complex matrix of relationship in our contemporary setting, I am a white-identified, cisgender male who is a Franciscan friar and an ordained Roman Catholic presbyter. As someone born, reared, and educated primarily in the context of the East Coast of the United States during the late twentieth and early twenty-first centuries, the cultural formation most familiar to me is one that might be described generally as Euro-American or, alternatively, North Atlantic. These labels, while useful in a limited sense, are nonetheless inadequate to situate me fully in relation to every source engaged and each reader of this project. However, I believe it is important for me to name from the outset that I unwittingly occupy a location at the nexus of a tremendous amount of privilege and power: racial, gender, and clerical. In what follows, I am mindful of my location and the various dynamics that accompany it. This plays a particularly important role in the way my relationship to various theological interlocutors shifts throughout my theological reflection in this book.

I have found the work of theologian Robert Schreiter on intercultural hermeneutics helpful in naming these dynamics at work. The starting point for Schreiter's hermeneutic reflection is a concern with the possibility of "intercultural communication," which "might be defined as the ability to speak and to understand across cultural boundaries. It is a matter of speaking and hearing in a situation where a common world is not shared by speaker and hearer."[25] This is an especially relevant matter for a constructive theological project articulated from one cultural context that draws from insights, sources, and perspectives articulated in other cultural contexts. Within the context of an intercultural communication event there are two sets or pairs of distinctions that provide four locations "from which one can locate oneself and one's dialogue partner within the communication event. These are inner/outer and speaker/hearer."[26] An interlocutor is able to understand a given culture from within or outside—inner/outer—and as a speaker or a hearer, a sender or a receiver in the communication event. When engaging in an intercultural communication event, it is important to note and give an account of one's cultural location so as to be as aware as possible of the complex dynamics under way in the dialogue.

At times throughout this project I recognize my cultural location as an inner-speaker or inner-hearer, particularly when the theological source originates from within a context proximate to my own. Such is the case when engaging the thought of other white, cisgender male Roman Catholic theologians. Nevertheless, there are numerous times when my location is more accurately described as an outer-hearer; that is, as someone who is in a position outside the cultural context of my interlocutor and seeks to receive and interpret the message communicated within the intercultural communication event. Such is the case when I am engaging the thought of, for example, indigenous people, transgender women and men, or black theologians, each of whom occupies a place as an inner-speaker in relationship to my location as an outer-hearer in that respective context. My intention as an outer-hearer is always to receive with a hermeneutic of generosity the insights, experiences, and challenges of interlocutors whose social and cultural locations differ from my own, aiming to receive and engage a relatively adequate understanding

---

[25] Schreiter, *The New Catholicity*, 28.

[26] Kevin P. Considine, *Salvation for the Sinned-Against: Han and Schillebeeckx in Intercultural Dialogue* (Eugene, OR: Pickwick Publications, 2015), 89.

of what the inner-speakers are expressing in the intercultural communication event.

I take seriously the caution that Kevin Considine expresses in his work as an outer-hearer engaging Korean and Korean American theological reflection, that it is "intellectually problematic, if not culturally arrogant, to assume that the surplus of meaning . . . is immediately apparent and easily accessible to a cultural outsider."[27] And yet, following the guidance of Alejandro Garcia-Rivera, I believe that the risk of misunderstanding does not outweigh the necessity of *both* inner and outer perspectives. Such a risk has, as Garcia-Rivera states, "led some to call for abandonment of any outsider perspectives. Only Hispanics can speak for Hispanics, for example. This is misguided. The outsider perspective is vital to the insider. It protects the cultural insider from the demands and pressures of a more powerful outsider by providing understanding and communicating worth."[28] In the sense briefly described here, I understand the following constructive work to be at times a small contribution in intercultural theological communication, attempting as an outer-hearer to engage what is presented by inner-speakers and following their lead in my reception and interpretation.

Overview

This book is organized into two major parts. Part I, which argues for a broader theology of creation as the starting point for any theological reflection on the human person, is composed of three chapters. Chapter 1 examines the manner in which we must understand our own species as part of creation alongside all else that exists in the cosmos. Drawing on the natural sciences, the wisdom traditions of indigenous peoples, and the creation accounts of the Book of Genesis, this chapter argues for a renewed

---

[27] Considine, *Salvation for the Sinned-Against*, 160–61.

[28] Alejandro Garcia-Rivera, *St. Martin de Porres: The "Little Stories" and the Semiotics of Culture* (Maryknoll, NY: Orbis Books, 1995), 35.

sense of our human animality as the starting point for reflection on human personhood.

To articulate a theological anthropology in the key of catholicity or wholemaking, we must take developments in the natural sciences seriously. Chapter 2 explores the meaning, challenges, and promises of evolutionary biology. Opening with an explication of the meaning of evolution, this chapter goes on to highlight important insights from Charles Darwin and Pierre Teilhard de Chardin, as well as contemporary theologians that have previously engaged the theory of evolution in theological reflection. Such engagement refers to deep incarnation and resurrection, evolutionary theodicy and suffering, and the meaning of the human person as it continues to develop and emerge in an evolutionary view of the world.

Chapter 3 takes up the task of considering what the Christian doctrine of *imago Dei* means within a cosmic vision of humanity's place within the broader community of creation. This chapter opens with an examination of recent theological and scriptural scholarship that has unsettled the uncritically received view of the *imago Dei*, which finds little textual support in scripture and yet has played a significant role in Christian articulations of human personhood and theological ethics. In response to the ambiguity of the meaning of *imago Dei*, this chapter surveys three general approaches to engaging the doctrine that have surfaced in recent years, which include arguments for rejecting, redefining, or expanding the concept of *imago Dei*. The chapter concludes with a constructive proposal that seeks an understanding of *imago Dei* that maintains a sense of inclusivity as well as distinction.

Part II, which is composed of four chapters, shifts focus from humanity within the broader community of creation to the human person as such. Chapter 4 introduces the philosophical theology of John Duns Scotus (d. 1308) as an alternative foundation for theological anthropology to the nearly hegemonic thought of Thomas Aquinas (d. 1277) in Catholic theology. Beginning with a stark examination of the meaning of human nature, this chapter provides an overview of Scotus's principle of individuation *(haecceitas)* and its significance for theological anthropology in the key of catholicity.

Chapter 5 examines what I am calling illustrative subjects, which can be understood as a set of case studies or investigations into how a theological anthropology rooted in *haecceitas* might provide a more capacious understanding of the human person that can accommodate the experiences and realities of women and men that do not fit comfortably into the relatively inadequate theological anthropology grounded in an Aristotelian-Thomistic philosophical anthropology. Among the themes considered here are the sexism of gender complementarity, the reality of transgender persons, and the dehumanization of racism.

Chapter 6 takes up the theme of sin. Recognizing the inherent goodness of all God's creation, this chapter opens with a look at the inherent capacity for sin that appears as a universal human experience. Next, we explore the ways in which catholicity challenges simplistic understandings of personal sin and instead look at how the experience of sin varies among individuals and communities. We then consider structural sin and seek to understand its persistence and relationship to personal sin. Finally, this chapter draws on the work of Korean and Korean American theologians who have called for the need to pay more attention not only to the sinners or victimizers in our theology of sin, but also to consider the sinned-against or victims—a truly catholic theology of sin can only become whole when both sides of the relationship of sin are included.

Chapter 7 considers grace, the classic central focus of Christian theological anthropology. It opens with an explication about the meaning of *grace,* a term that is often used colloquially (and at times theologically) with little awareness of the nuances tied to the term throughout the tradition. From there we look at the inherent capacity of every person to receive grace, known in Latin as *capax Dei* ("the capacity for God"), and how this reality calls all persons to a life of "everyday mysticism." Drawing on the work of the twentieth-century German theologian Karl Rahner, we develop the notion of *capax Dei* in terms of what

Rahner called the "supernatural existential." This chapter closes with a call to reconsider the world in which we live in light of the gift of God's self as grace.

Finally, we conclude with a brief chapter that brings together the various themes explored by offering a reflection on the spirituality of theological anthropology articulated by this project of catholicity.

Part I

Creation as Starting Point

Chapter 1

We Are Creation Too

Any theological reflection on the human person that hopes to be *wholemaking*, that is, any theological anthropology that bears true catholicity, can only begin with the recognition that human beings are first and foremost a part of creation. Despite the widespread acceptance of human exceptionalism—or what David Clough has called "human separatism"[1]—the biological sciences have largely disabused us of the anthropological ruse that any singular trait or attribute unequivocally sets the human species apart from the rest of the nonhuman world. That we are animals, material creatures made up of the same elements as all other creatures and as interdependent and interrelated as any of God's other animals, should not detract from the inherent dignity and value of each person. It is only when we look at Christianity through a fragmented, zero-sum-game perspective of creation and the human person that such a specious threat arises. And yet, this is the sad state of so much Christian theological reflection on the human person up to now.[2] The operative hermeneutic

---

[1] See David L. Clough, *On Animals: Volume 1, Systematic Theology* (London: T & T Clark, 2012).

[2] The examples of this fact are too numerous even to sample here. By way of illustration, one only has to look to the otherwise insightful dictionary entry by Michael J. Scanlon, who early in his lengthy essay states: "As image and likeness of God, the human being is graced with a *unique nobility*. Different from the cosmocentrism of Greek anthropology wherein the human being is understood as the highest grade of finite

has been one of absolute uniqueness and therefore separation, wherein theologians have read the Christian tradition and sacred scripture for any reason to justify the presupposition of a radical break between humanity and other creatures.

The aim of this chapter is to provide an alternative yet entirely orthodox grounding for theological anthropology by resituating theological anthropology within a theology of creation. Instead of presuming absolute uniqueness and human separatism, we shall instead return to a more fundamental notion of the creatureliness of humanity that will be the starting point and unifying factor that helps us to recall our intrinsic kinship within God's expansive community of creation.

Ecological Consciousness and Remembering Our Origins

What is required of us, the members of the human species, is an increased awareness of who God created us to be and an honest reckoning with our creaturely origins. In her aptly titled essay "Losing and Finding Creation in the Christian Tradition," theologian Elizabeth Johnson observes that Christians have periodically suffered from a demented perspective about the place of humanity within the broader community of creation. While this forgetfulness of divinely intended creaturely kinship shared among humans and nonhumans alike has been especially prevalent over the last half millennium, Johnson reminds us that "looking back over the whole two thousand years of Christian tradition, however, leads to a surprise, namely, that such amnesia about the cosmic world has not always been the case."[3] In

---

being within the cosmic order, the bible relates humanity directly to God" ("Anthropology, Christian," in *The New Dictionary of Theology*, ed. Joseph A. Komonchak [Collegeville, MN: Liturgical Press, 1990], 29, emphasis added). On the topic of the doctrine of the *imago Dei* as such, see the third chapter of this book.

[3] Elizabeth A. Johnson, "Losing and Finding Creation in the Christian Tradition," in *Christianity and Ecology: Seeking the Well-Being of*

fact, there has always been something of an ongoing "minority tradition" of Christian theologians, philosophers, and biblical exegetes that has not entirely forgotten the inherent interrelatedness of the cosmic family and has striven to call the faithful to remembrance of this truth.

We see this forgotten memory of our origins and interrelatedness illustrated in the ecological consciousness of the early Christian apologists such as Justin Martyr and Irenaeus of Lyons, both of whom defended the emergent doctrine of God's *creatio ex nihilo* and the goodness of God's creation from the singular divine source in the face of manifold iterations of Platonic Gnosticism.[4] We find in other Patristic thinkers an often overlooked appreciation for the place of nonhuman creation alongside human creatures in the treatises on resurrection and salvation of, for example, Athanasius and Gregory of Nazianzus.[5] Glimpses of this memory appear in the writings of Augustine, who struggles to respond to the threats of Manichaeism while also remaining steeped in the anthropocentrism of his time, as well as in the mystical writings of Hildegard of Bingen some centuries later.[6] We see further examples of this persistent Christian memory in

---

Earth and Humans, ed. Dieter T. Hessel and Rosemary Radford Ruether (Cambridge, MA: Harvard University Press, 2000), 4.

[4] For more on this, see Ian A. McFarland, *From Nothing: A Theology of Creation* (Louisville: Westminster John Knox Press, 2014); and Brian D. Robinette, "The Difference Nothing Makes: *Creatio Ex Nihilo*, Resurrection, and Divine Gratuity," *Theological Studies* 72 (2011): 525–57.

[5] See Denis Edwards, "The Redemption of Animals in an Incarnational Theology," in *Creaturely Theology: On God, Humans, and Other Animals*, ed. Celia Deane-Drummond and David Clough (London: SCM Press, 2009), 81–99; Denis Edwards, *Christian Understandings of Creation: The Historical Trajectory* (Minneapolis: Fortress Press, 2017), esp. 21–64; and Eric Daryl Meyer, "'Marvel at the Intelligence of Unthinking Creatures!': Contemplative Animals in Gregory of Nazianzus and Evagrius Ponticus," in *Animals as Religious Subjects: Transdisciplinary Perspectives*, ed. Celia Deane-Drummond, Rebecca Artinian-Kaiser, and David L. Clough (London: Bloomsbury Academic, 2013), 191–208.

[6] See Edwards, *Christian Understandings of Creation*, 65–108.

the face of a temptation for creational amnesia in the medieval period during the rise of the first universities. Scholastic and vernacular theologians alike bore witness to this minority view, which is seen in the writings and lived testimony of Francis of Assisi, Bonaventure of Bagnoregio, Angela of Foligno, John Duns Scotus, and others from the Franciscan tradition.[7] Even the trenchantly anthropocentric schoolman Thomas Aquinas provides us with rare moments of trace remembrance that it is in the diversity of creatures that God's loving harmony and beauty is found.[8]

While it is admittedly a chronological oversimplification, we can generally state that it was over the last five-hundred years that the minority tradition of recognizing our shared origin in God and therefore maintaining a continual, if at times dim, consciousness of our shared creatureliness, began to be lost. By the time of the reformations during the sixteenth century, "individual human consciousness thus becomes *the* place of encounter with God, who consoles terrified consciences with the promise of mercy in Christ. The center of gravity shifts to the human subject."[9] What begins with a determined shift to the human subject as it concerned contentious debates about justification and grace develops into rampant anthropocentrism and creational amnesia with striking momentum during the Italian Humanism movements of the European Renaissance period and reached something resembling its zenith with the development of modern natural sciences and philosophy illustrated in the work of Francis Bacon and René Descartes, respectively.[10] By the rise

---

[7] See Daniel P. Horan, *All God's Creatures: A Theology of Creation* (Lanham, MD: Lexington Books/Fortress Academic, 2018), esp. 143–80.

[8] This is something highlighted in Johnson, "Losing and Finding Creation in the Christian Tradition," 7, although it should be noted that other scholars have strongly critiqued the utility of resourcing Thomas Aquinas for a contemporary theology of creation. See, for example, Ryan Patrick McLaughlin, "Thomas Aquinas's Eco-Theological Ethics of Anthropocentric Conservation," *Horizons* 39 (2012): 69–97.

[9] Johnson, "Losing and Finding Creation in the Christian Tradition," 9.

[10] See Horan, *All God's Creatures*, 3–23.

of the Industrial Revolution of the nineteenth and twentieth centuries, it seemed that the Christian community had largely forgotten its cosmic ancestry, its creational interdependence, and its shared common source as creatures of God.[11]

In seeking to develop a theological anthropology marked by a commitment to wholemaking, and therefore *catholicity*, we must deliberately work to develop what biologist Christopher Uhl has called an ecological consciousness.[12] Uhl shares his own experience of ongoing scientific and ethical conversion to authentic ecological consciousness that takes seriously the significance of our creaturely origins in responding to the manifold ecological crises of our age. For much of his professional scientific and educational career Uhl embraced what we might theologically describe as a stewardship model of humanity's relationship to the rest of creation. We are, in effect, called to be good *stewards* or *caretakers* of the resources we have received in the form of nonhuman creatures and all that exists in the cosmos. Translated into scientifically friendly discourse, this amounts to participating in "sustainability movements" that promote environmental practices that seek to preserve our habitats, nonhuman creatures, and the land for future generations (of human beings). In time Uhl came to realize "that sustainability, insofar as it seeks to figure out ways to sustain our current way of life, is profoundly problematic."[13] He realized that the narrative told by those primarily concerned with sustainability, including Christian believers and other women and men of faith, centered on strategies that sought maintenance of the status quo without any noticeable shift in self-understanding or consideration of a larger ecological or cosmological picture. He states:

---

[11] This diagnostic sensibility is expressed in Lynn White, Jr.'s now-classic article "The Historical Roots of our Ecologic Crisis," *Science* 155 (1968): 1203–7.

[12] Christopher Uhl, *Developing Ecological Consciousness: The End of Separation*, 2nd ed. (Lanham, MD: Rowman and Littlefield Publishers, 2013).

[13] Uhl, *Developing Ecological Consciousness*, xi.

> The problem, I now see, is that sustainability, for all its good intentions, is part of our old story—the story that tells us that we can keep growing (as long as it's smart growth) and keep consuming (as long as we recycle) forever. It's a story that tells us that technology—so long as it's green—will solve our problems; and that happiness resides in *having* belongings, not in *the experience of* belonging. . . . Something bigger and deeper and more soulful than the shortsighted notion of sustainability is needed if humankind is to flourish in partnership with Earth. . . . This new story challenges us to wake up and, in so doing, to see ourselves, not as *apart from* Earth (as we now tend to do), but instead, as *a part of* Earth—literally a *part of* the body of Earth![14]

Ironically, the call for sustainability, which is essentially the secular analog of the Christian call for environmental stewardship, cannot solve the primary problem we face today. At its core the notion of sustainability is a principle or set of practices intended to perpetuate the status quo, to maintain the quality and experience of human life as it currently exists (at least from the perspective of wealthy inhabitants of the so-called Global North). What makes the embrace of this perspective ironic, as Uhl skillfully reminds us from the vantage point of his scientific worldview, is that it is founded on a false narrative of reality—a story about our absolute uniqueness and separatism from the rest of creation, a story that perpetuates anthropocentrism and speciesism.[15] We cannot simply correct the problems we are forced to recognize in the global creaturely community today with the discourse and narratives of sustainability and stewardship because this way of seeing reality is disingenuous and

---

[14] Uhl, *Developing Ecological Consciousness*, xi.

[15] *Speciesism* as a term was made popular in the late twentieth century by Richard D. Ryder and, shortly thereafter, Peter Singer. See Ryder, *Animal Revolution: Changing Attitudes Towards Speciesism* (Oxford: Blackwell Publishing, 1989); and Singer, *Animal Liberation* (New York: New York Review of Books, 1990).

unmoored from the truth of our actual origins. Another way of seeing is required; the development of an authentic ecological consciousness is necessary.

Passionist priest and theologian Thomas Berry long proclaimed the errancy of the narratives we have become accustomed to telling ourselves *about ourselves* both inside and outside of church.

> So completely are we at odds with the planet that brought us into being that we have become strange beings indeed. We dedicate enormous talent and knowledge and research in developing a human order disengaged from and even predatory on the very sources from whence we came and upon which we depend every moment of our existence.[16]

Like Johnson and Uhl, Berry called not for a *new* story, but what can only be described as a *renewed* story of our fundamental identity as creatures alongside God's other creatures within this vast cosmic family. There are many starting points toward this renewed story, or what the Trappist monk and mystic Thomas Merton called our "original unity," which he envisioned as God's intention for communion among the human family and between our species and the broader family of creation.[17] One such starting point can be for those situated within the Euro-American context, steeped as it is in anthropocentric cultures, to listen to the wisdom and stories of indigenous peoples that have for so long been oppressed, silenced, and destroyed by colonizing

---

[16] Thomas Berry, *The Great Work: Our Way into the Future* (New York: Three Rivers Press, 1999), 15.

[17] Thomas Merton, *The Asian Journal of Thomas Merton*, ed. Naomi Burton, Patrick Hart, and James Laughlin (New York: New Directions Publishing, 1973), 308: "And the deepest level of communication is not communication, but communion. It is wordless. It is beyond words, and it is beyond speech, and it is beyond concept. Not that we discover a new unity. We discover an older unity. My dear brothers, we are already one. But we imagine that we are not. And what we have to recover is our original unity. What we have to be is what we are."

forces. Identifying himself as one in need of embracing an epistemological humility in order to develop what Uhl would call an ecological consciousness, Berry contrasts his context with what he has come to learn from his Native American sisters and brothers.

> This experience [of intimate rapport with the surrounding universe] we observe even now in the indigenous peoples of the world. They live in a universe, in a cosmological order, whereas we, the peoples of the industrial world, no longer live in a universe. We in North America live in a political world, a nation, a business world, an economic order, a cultural tradition, a Disney dreamland. We live in cities, in a world of concrete and steel, of wheels and wires, a world of unending work. We seldom see the stars at night or the planets or the moon. Even in the day we do not experience the sun in any immediate or meaningful manner. Summer and winter are the same inside the mall. Ours is a world of highways, parking lots, shopping centers. We read books written with a strangely contrived human alphabet. We no longer read the Book of Nature.[18]

Berry is not presenting a naive or romantic vision of the traditions, wisdom, spirituality, practices, and worldviews of native peoples. That is a temptation that we must work hard to avoid.[19]

---

[18] Berry, *The Great Work*, 14–15.

[19] Furthermore, this caution implies also the conscious effort to avoid the twin pitfalls of cultural appropriation and religious syncretism. Regarding the former, there is a danger for those outside the tribal and national communities of indigenous peoples to misperceive and misappropriate elements or concepts from native traditions, cultures, or spiritualties, which in turn shifts an opportunity for humble learning and intercultural experience into a commoditized economy. Regarding the latter, there is a danger of oversimplification about the real differences in religious traditions and worldviews that must be respected. It is my intention in this chapter to avoid both pitfalls to the best of my ability and to instead occupy, as I am able, a location of epistemological humility such that I can learn—and in turn invite the reader to learn—

Instead, Berry is heeding the invitation felt also by Uhl for a greater awareness of what Merton called this "original unity." It is an invitation to reconsider the story of what it means to be human, it is a call to ecological consciousness, and it is the true story of our origin as members of the community of creation and a narrative that expresses the experience of emerging personhood, a process that is evolutionary, ongoing, and moving all of creation into the future. We do not need to create this story from scratch. Nor do we need to invent a new origin. There are numerous communities that have recounted this truth of our origins and interrelatedness from one generation to the next over thousands of years. In order for those of us who are accustomed to thinking primarily through Western philosophical and theological lenses, and therefore are in need of remembering the truth of our creaturely origins, it is helpful to look at what Native American theologians have been saying for a long time about the relations that make up our original creational unity as creatures who have emerged from the same source of divine love. The following consideration of Native American theological reflection on creation illustrates the often-overlooked diversity of imaginative starting points and resources outside the Euro-American Western Enlightenment context.

---

about the truth of human and nonhuman creation from perspectives not my own. As a Catholic theologian I do this in the spirit of the Second Vatican Council's teaching, which states: "The Catholic Church rejects nothing that is true and holy in these [non-Christian] religions. She regards with sincere reverence those ways of conduct and of life, those precepts and teachings which, though differing in many aspects from the ones she holds and sets forth, nonetheless often reflect a ray of that Truth which enlightens all men" (*Nostra Aetate* no. 2). Additionally, I wish to acknowledge the cautionary prelude that George E. "Tink" Tinker offers non-Indian readers of his work, namely, that those occupying Euro-American Christian locations need to be self-aware of the temptations I named above and still another danger in the form of inadvertent dispositions and efforts to protect white power and privilege, which often are manifest in defensiveness. For more, see George E. Tinker, "An American Indian Theological Response to Ecojustice," *Ecotheology* 3 (1997): 85–109, esp. 85–91.

Recognizing the Kinship of Creation

Theologian George Tinker, a member of the Osage Nation, has been a leading voice in American Indian liberation theology and the history of Euro-American colonization, genocide, and Christianity.[20] Among the various theological loci Tinker has studied and taught stands the Christian doctrine of creation. He explains, "A theology of creation must begin with a self-understanding of individuals and communities as a part of creation. We must understand that all things are related to one another and that human beings participate as one aspect of creation alongside the rest of creation."[21]

Over the years Tinker has raised questions about the fittingness of the standard Judeo-Christian reading of the Genesis accounts in which creation has been construed and "objectified as something quite apart from human beings and to which humans relate from the outside."[22] As noted earlier, his observation is one that highlights and critiques the classical "forgetting" (or, perhaps "ignoring" is more apt) of our true creaturely origins. In response to this all-too-common Christian tendency to use the term *creation* in contradistinction to *humanity,* Tinker points us to a Lakota phrase that he believes might be instructive for Christians in seeking to recall better the truth of our place within God's creation. The phrase is *mitakuye oyasin,* which, as Tinker

---

[20] See, among his works, George E. Tinker's "Spirituality, Native American Personhood, Sovereignty, and Solidarity," *Ecumenical Review* 44, no. 3 (1992): 312–24; *Missionary Conquest: The Gospel and Native American Cultural Genocide* (Minneapolis: Fortress Press, 1993); *Spirit and Resistance: Political Theology and American Indian Liberation* (Minneapolis: Fortress Press, 2004); and *American Indian Liberation: A Theology of Sovereignty* (Maryknoll, NY: Orbis Books, 2008).

[21] George E. Tinker, "The Integrity of Creation: Restoring Trinitarian Balance," *Ecumenical Review* 41, no. 4 (1989): 536.

[22] Tinker, "An American Indian Theological Response to Ecojustice," 90.

explains, translates as "a prayer 'for all my relations.'"[23] Tinker adds:

> As such it is inclusive not only of immediate or even extended family, but of the whole of a tribe or nation, of all nations of two-leggeds in the world, and particularly of all the nations other than two-leggeds: the four-leggeds, the winged, and the living, that is moving-things. It is this interrelatedness that best captures what might symbolize for Indian peoples what Euro-American peoples would call creation. More to the point, it is this understanding of interrelatedness, of balance and mutual respect among the different species of the world, that characterized what we might call Indian peoples' greatest gift to Euro-Americans and to the Euro-American understanding of creation at this time of ecological crisis in the world.[24]

Indeed, Tinker is correct on a number of fronts, especially as we explore what it means to consider the human person from within the Christian theological tradition. When Tinker and his fellow theologians of native descent critique the Euro-American Christian understanding of creation, he is rightly naming the errors of what Uhl describes as the wrong story and therefore adds voice to Johnson's call for a "finding" or "remembering" the forgotten true story. As Tinker states, it is a gift to those of

---

[23] Tinker, "An American Indian Theological Response to Ecojustice," 91. This Lakota expression is also used by Winona Laduke in *All Our Relations: Native Struggles for Land and Life*, 2nd ed. (Chicago: Haymarket Books, 2013). See also Stan McKay, "An Aboriginal Christian Perspective on the Integrity of Creation," in *Native and Christian: Indigenous Voices on Religious Identity in the United States and Canada*, ed. James Treat (London: Routledge, 1996), 51–55.

[24] Tinker, "An American Indian Theological Response to Ecojustice," 91. See also John A. Grim, "Indigenous Traditions: Religion and Ecology," in *The Oxford Handbook of Religion and Ecology*, ed. Roger S. Gottlieb (New York: Oxford University Press, 2006), 283–309.

us from Euro-American Christian backgrounds to be reminded
of an older, original unity reflected in our common creaturely
origins and inherent interrelatedness. Let's now consider briefly
this gift and its implications for theological anthropology.

As Tinker notes in an essay on the limitations of Latin American liberation theology for American Indian peoples, one of the
often-underappreciated dimensions of indigenous spiritualities
is the foundational importance of creation. Typically, Tinker
observes, Christians concerned about social justice and peace-
making see creation in terms circumscribed by a particular commitment to praxis, namely, environmental justice. While that is
certainly an admirable focus of faith-based action in the world,
Tinker is quick to point out that "a Native American Christian
theology must begin with the Native American traditional praxis
of spirituality that is rooted first of all in creation."[25] The argument is that theology of creation is not some subfield or esoteric
discipline alongside others for theologians to examine, but the
very foundation, centerpiece, and starting point for all Christian
theological reflection. This is best illustrated by Tinker's reflection on the key evangelical theme of Jesus's proclamation—the
reign of God *(basileia tou theou)*. Tinker explains: "While Euro-
cultural scholars have offered consistently temporal interpretations of this metaphor, any American Indian interpretation must
build on a spatial understanding rooted in creation."[26] Whereas
many Euro-American theologians and scriptural exegetes find
themselves temporally fixated on the proclamation—like the
early Christian community at Thessalonica before us—asking
questions like: *When is the kingdom going to appear?* Tinker
affirms that American Indian Christians are more interested in
exploring the *basileia* in spatial terms, asking questions like:

---

[25] Tinker, "Spirituality, Native American Personhood, Sovereignty,
and Solidarity," 320.

[26] Tinker, "Spirituality, Native American Personhood, Sovereignty,
and Solidarity," 320. See also George E. Tinker, "Native Americans and
the Land: 'The End of Living, and the Beginning of Survival,'" *Word &
World* 6 (1986): 66–75.

Where is the kingdom going to appear? The answer is, simply put, here in God's creation.[27]

There is a rich catholicity inherent within this interpretation of the *basileia* announced by Jesus Christ. The *where* of the *basileia* is here and now, in this created world, of which we are but one part and member. It is indeed God's saving action in the world, but how we conceive of the divine agency is the key. As Tinker notes, there needs to be a shift from a strict anthropocentric consideration of time and individual sense of God's salvific work in human history toward an inclusive appreciation for divine grace operative throughout the whole of creation. "We do see the hegemony of the Mystery (God?) in the *whole of existence*, but we see ourselves as *participants in that whole*, doing our part to help maintain harmony and peace."[28]

The implications for theological anthropology are manifold. First, if we recognize the central theme of Jesus's life to be the ministry and preaching of the *basileia* of God, then we Euro-American Christians would do well to embrace this American Indian perspective that affirms the centrality of creation as theological locus. Second, creation is understood as a community in which all God's creatures—including us—exist in relationship according to ties of kinship founded on God's loving act of creation. Therefore, the proclamation of the *basileia tou theou* is not a message reserved for humans alone but for the entire family of creation. Or, as Tinker puts it, "Thus no one can be left out of the *basileia*. In the spirit of the prayer *mitakuye ouyasin*, we all belong. The question is whether I will recognize God's hegemony over myself and all of creation."[29] And, third, we cannot proceed in any legitimate way to reflect theologically on the human person as absolutely separate

---

[27] This privileging of space over time is also seen in recent postcolonial theological work. For example, see Vitor Westhelle, *Eschatology and Space: The Lost Dimension in Theology Past and Present* (New York: Palgrave Macmillian, 2012).

[28] Tinker, "Spirituality, Native American Personhood, Sovereignty, and Solidarity," 320, emphasis added.

[29] Tinker, "Spirituality, Native American Personhood, Sovereignty, and Solidarity," 320.

from or entirely unique compared with nonhuman creatures that are also included in God's salvific plan.

Recognizing the kinship of creation by maintaining a focus on these three elements allows Christian theologians to reexamine the commonsense understanding of humanity's place within creation. What is needed is theological imagination that does not shy away from the wisdom of indigenous peoples and the truth that their traditions, interpretations, and experiences provide. The result of recognizing this inherent kinship is not only an increased reverence for nonhuman creation as such—though that is certainly important—but also a foundation for adequately considering humanity with an eye toward wholemaking, that is catholicity, which presents challenges to the status quo in both popular doctrinal articulations about the human person and various ways we structure our societies and politics. Tinker explains:

> If we imagine ourselves as fellow createds, mere participants in the whole of creation, functioning out of respect for and reciprocity with all of creation, then our relationships with each other as two-leggeds must also be grounded in respect and reciprocity. As fellow createds, acknowledging God's hegemony over all, there can no longer be any rationale for exploitation and oppression. The desire for or even the perceived necessity for exerting social, political, economic or spiritual control over each other must give way to mutual respect, not just for individuals but for our culturally integrous communities. . . . If we believe we are all relatives of this world, then we must live together differently than we have.[30]

How we understand and interpret the meaning of creation and think about ourselves in relationship to this theological locus shapes both our inter- and intra-human relationships.[31] Stan

---

[30] Tinker, "Spirituality, Native American Personhood, Sovereignty, and Solidarity," 321–22.

[31] See Tinker, "The Integrity of Creation," 536: "If our theology—and hence our human communities—can begin to wrestle seriously with the

McKay, a Christian minister and member of the Cree Nation, summarizes well the significance of this spiritual outlook: "The value that comes from the spirituality of my people is one of wholeness. It certainly is related to a view of life which does not separate or compartmentalize."[32] In this sense, what the Euro-American Christian community can receive as gift from our indigenous sisters and brothers is an integral sense of catholicity that grounds our understanding of ourselves as part of and dependent upon the broad community of God's creation. The gift is a call to develop our ecological consciousness, remember our origins, and recognize the kinship of creation. We can see in various ways the deleterious effects of our underdeveloped ecological consciousness and the forgetting or ignoring of our true origins. In addition to listening with renewed intention to our indigenous sisters and brothers, we can also return to our sacred scripture to ground ourselves anew.

Loving the Dust We Are

One of the effects of this collective forgetting of our true origins and diminished ecological consciousness has been an emergent discomfort with the truth of our materiality and creatureliness. A case in point can be found with the uneasiness I have witnessed some ministers exhibit in proclaiming clearly our materiality as exhibited by lay and ordained Christian ministers during

---

necessity of balance and harmony in all of creation, then our self-image as a part of creation must also be deeply affected. As our self-perception and self-understanding begin to be self-consciously centered in respect for all creation, we will begin to participate actively not in the exploitation of the earth but in the establishment of balance and harmony. Our participation in balance and harmony of all creation will then most naturally include other individuals and communities of human beings. And justice and then genuine peace will flow out of our concern for one another and all creation." Also see Eric Daryl Meyer, "The Political Ecology of Dignity: Human Dignity and the Inevitable Returns of Animality," *Modern Theology* 33 (2017): 549–69.

[32] McKay, "An Aboriginal Christian Perspective on the Integrity of Creation," 54.

the celebration of Ash Wednesday. What I mean is that over the decades since the liturgical reforms of the Second Vatican Council, it has become increasingly common that those distributing ashes at the beginning of Lent opt for the saying "Repent, and believe in the Gospel" over "Remember that you are dust, and to dust you shall return."[33] In itself, there is nothing wrong with this choice of the former over the latter saying. However, I am inclined to believe, given the anecdotal evidence, that part of the discomfiture ministers have with the dictum focused on dust includes a misunderstanding that, on the one hand, the theme is grim and death centered (though that is itself another problematic reaction) and, on the other hand, that it sounds too pedestrian, material, and creation focused in the literal face of the dignity and uniqueness ascribed to human beings. If the ancient adage *lex orandi, lex credendi* is remotely true, then we learn something about what we actually believe by the prayers we do and do not pray and, in this case, the proclamations we do and do not say.

Rather than avoid hearing or speaking about the fact that we are dust, we should embrace this fact, for it is supported both scientifically and—perhaps surprisingly to some—scripturally. As cosmologist Brian Swimme and religion scholar Mary Evelyn Tucker explain about the planet earth and everything on and within it, "It is remarkable to realize that over immense spans of time stellar dust became a planet. In the earliest time of the universe this stellar dust did not even exist because the elements had not yet been formed by the stars. Yet hidden in this cosmic dust was the immense potentiality for bringing forth mountains and rivers, oyster shells and blue butterflies."[34] In the next chapter we explore the broad theological implications that arise from the revelation that we live in an evolutionary universe such as

---

[33] International Commission on English in the Liturgy, *The Roman Missal*, trans. of the amended 3rd Latin Typical Edition (New York: Catholic Book Publishing Company, 2011), 72.

[34] Brian Swimme and Mary Evelyn Tucker, *Journey of the Universe* (New Haven, CT: Yale University Press, 2011), 36.

Swimme and Tucker describe here. For now, it is worth noting what Uhl recounts in reflecting upon this cosmological fact: "As for you and me—every part of our bodies contains stellar dust. Yes, we are stardust through and through."[35] *And to stardust we shall return.*

How can we come to love the dust that we are? Prescinding from further consideration of the scientific nature of this statement for now, I want to turn to examine some of the ways that Christian scripture grounds this claim. By way of illustration, let us turn to the Book of Genesis, which has served as the classical starting point for theological reflection on creation in general and the human person in particular. This text, sacred for Jews and Christians alike, offers striking resonances with what the Native American theologians have highlighted as insights about humanity's place within the community of creation grounded in both indigenous worldviews and Christian belief.

If we look at the first creation narrative found in Genesis 1, a common reading of this Priestly account argues that the linear development of the act of creation, which spans the course of six "days," suggests a progressive development or a clear trajectory toward culmination ending with the creation of human beings on the sixth day. From this perspective we can see how many Christians have convinced themselves of the theological veracity of the modern adage "the best for last." This interpretation would make sense if what is articulated by the oral tradition, authors, and final redactors of the narrative understood the sequence to be primarily chronological—marking the significance of each created element by its placement in temporal order. However, scripture scholar Richard Bauckham has noted that the actual structure of this creation narrative is not primarily chronological but *spatial*. He adds that there is no clear cumulative trajectory at work that ends with the creation of humanity as pinnacle of the cosmos; even if there were such a trajectory in the text, it would be the Sabbath that represents this culmination of God's

---

[35] Uhl, *Developing Ecological Consciousness*, 13.

creation, not the human creatures.[36] This spatial structure of the creation narrative bears a noticeable logic. Bauckham explains that "the work of the third day has to follow that of the second, and the environments have to be created before their respective inhabitants. What is absent here is any sense of a building towards a culmination. Humans, the last creatures to be created, have a unique role within creation, but they do not come last because they are the climax of an ascending scale."[37] This is an important observation often overlooked because of anthropocentric presumptions informing classical exegesis. Bauckham notes that "creeping things" such as reptiles and insects, which are also created on the sixth day, "are not higher, in some order of being, than the birds, created on the fifth day."[38]

Additionally, when we provide the text with a close reading, what we see is God's appreciation for all aspects of creation on each day ("God saw that it was good") irrespective of humanity created afterward on the sixth day. Such a reading of the text circumscribes the purely instrumental valuation of nonhuman creation and the absolute separation of humanity from the rest of creation commonly understood with regard to this text. Instead, what we see in the structure of the narrative is "an interconnecting and interdependent whole, and so the refrain is varied at the end of the work of the sixth day: 'God saw everything that he had made, and behold, it was very good' (1:31). The value of the whole is more than the value of the sum of its parts."[39]

While it is indisputable that misreadings of Genesis 1 have contributed to significantly distorted theologies of creation over the centuries, a renewed sense of the text actually provides an unexpected resource for recalling our origins and recognizing the kinship of creation. For example, there are numerous parallels presented and continuity seen between human beings and

---

[36] Richard Bauckham, *The Bible and Ecology: Rediscovering the Community of Creation* (Waco, TX: Baylor University Press, 2010), 13–14.

[37] Bauckham, *The Bible and Ecology*, 14.

[38] Bauckham, *The Bible and Ecology*, 14.

[39] Bauckham, *The Bible and Ecology*, 15.

nonhuman creation within the narrative. Just as God blesses and commands the human beings to "be fruitful and multiply, and fill the earth" in Genesis 1:28, God also blessed and commanded the water and air creatures to do likewise in Genesis 1:22: "God blessed them, saying, 'Be fruitful and multiply and fill the waters in the seas and let birds multiply on the earth.'" Scripture scholar Mark Brett has commented that this parallel between humanity and nonhuman creatures (including the earth, which God commands to "grow vegetation" [Genesis 1:11]) can be read as the divine bestowal of creative agency to all living things. Instead of being an object for manipulation by God or humanity, nonhuman creation is viewed also as co-creators with God, something Brett sees bolstered by God's universal covenant with all creation (vs. humanity alone) later in Genesis 9:8–17.[40] That the earth is later commanded again to "bring forth living creatures of every kind" in Genesis 1:24–25 suggests that, "the creation of these land animals is the result of the combined activity of the earth and the Deity," which connotes the co-creativity traditionally reserved for humanity.[41]

Whereas a renewed understanding of Genesis 1 offers the promise of helping us to develop a robust ecological consciousness, a close reading of the creation narrative found in Genesis 2 presents us with firm grounding for recognizing the kinship of creation and loving the dust that we are. In fact, it is precisely in the dirt, dust, ground, earth (*adama* in Hebrew) that we find our creaturely origins. We read: "the Lord God formed man from the dust of the ground *(adama)*, and breathed into his nostrils the breath of life; and the man became a living being" (Gen 2:7).[42]

---

[40] Mark G. Brett, "Earthing the Human in Genesis 1—3," in *The Earth Story in Genesis*, ed. Norman C. Habel and Shirley Wurst (Sheffield: Sheffield Academic Press, 2000), 77. Also see William P. Brown, *The Seven Pillars of Creation: The Bible, Science, and the Ecology of Wonder* (New York: Oxford University Press, 2010), 44–46.

[41] William P. Brown, *The Ethos of the Cosmos: The Genesis of Moral Imagination in the Bible* (Grand Rapids, MI: Eerdmans, 1999), 40–41.

[42] Though the NRSV and most English translations gender the *adam* ("human") as male (in both the sense of "Adam" as proper noun from

The formation of human beings out of the ground *(ha'adama)* is the same process by which God forms all the animals and other creatures: "Now the Lord God had formed out of the ground [*ha'adama*] all the beasts of the field and all the birds of the air" (Gen 2:19). There is an explicit semantic parallel in this creation account that bespeaks a richly theological observation, which is echoed elsewhere in the Old Testament, including in the Book of Job: "Your hands fashioned and made me; and now you turn and destroy me. Remember that you fashioned me like clay [*adama*]; and will you turn me to dust [*adama*] again?" (Job 10:9).[43] The relational dimension of this act of God's loving creation reveals an intimacy between the Creator and creation. God gets the "divine hands" dirty with the dust of the earth. The Creator molds or shapes the created world in a way akin to a potter *(yasar)* whose hands actualize the intentional design of God with the material of the earth. This image of God as potter will also appear variously throughout the Hebrew prophetic literature.

We are dust; we are creation too. Human beings and the entirety of God's creation are, according to the Genesis 2 account, made from the same material and have the same origin.[44] The same dust or clay of the ground physically constitutes humanity as well as other animals, plant life, and everything else in the cosmos. The nature of this originating source and material is reiterated in Genesis 3:19 when God declares the punishment for the man in the wake of the Edenic transgression stating, "By

---

the opening of Genesis 2 and the pronoun usage), the Hebrew is best rendered "humanity" in general. The word *adam* is in the original masculine, but the word *'iš* meaning "biological male" does not appear until after YHWH builds the woman. For more, see Phyllis Trible, *God and the Rhetoric of Sexuality* (Minneapolis: Fortress Press, 1978), 72–165; and David W. Cotter, *Genesis*, Berit Olam series (Collegeville, MN: Liturgical Press, 2003), 29–31.

[43] For more, see Horan, *All God's Creatures*, 90–96.

[44] As Alexander Sand notes, the primary term that appears in the Old Testament to describe the human person is *flesh,* which is also used to describe nonhuman animals (104 times) and humans (169 times). See "Person: B. Biblical," in *Sacramentum Mundi: An Encyclopedia of Theology*, 7 vols. (New York: Herder and Herder, 1968–70), 4:412.

the sweat of your face you shall eat bread until you return to the ground [*adama*], for out of it you were taken; you are dust, and to dust you shall return."

When we think about ourselves—as individuals and as a species—where do we begin our reflections? Do we consider the ways in which we share what we might call our "cosmic DNA," the very elemental structure and quantum matter that forms our material existence, with everything else that God has brought into this world? Or do we tend to think in divisive modes, opting instead to offer our self-justifying taxonomy of difference, which almost always results in a celebration of our self-perception as unique, superior, and separate? What resources do we draw from to justify our assessments and perspectives? Do we claim that scripture, tradition, or science justifies our views? Considering what we have examined so far, can such a claim ever be authentic?

To understand the human person theologically and with catholicity, we must learn to begin anew and love the dust that we are. The implications of that starting point are humbling, for they unsettle classical conceptions of human separatism and speciesism that we as humans have fabricated to distance ourselves from the rest of the community of creation. As we take seriously the catholicity of our tradition as it concerns our theological understanding of humanity, a renewed personhood emerges, one that is not threatened by our creatureliness or insecure about our animality. Rather, these truths of our existence as creatures of God form the foundation of all that follows in our Christian theological anthropology.

Animality and Human Personhood

To grasp the true meaning of personhood requires that one embrace humanity's animality, which is to say that we are creatures alongside and in some way like nonhuman animals. And to know, let alone fully embrace, our animality is to admit to ourselves the veracity of our interrelatedness as members of God's community of creation and recognize those aspects or characteristics we share in common with our nonhuman neighbors. For many Christians this step seems ludicrous or at least naive. So accustomed have we become to viewing ourselves as a species entirely separate from the animate world around us—masters over everything nonhuman—that it is often perceived as grossly offensive to state in any way that human beings are animals (and not merely in the antiquated-yet-quaint philosophical descriptor that over-determines us as "rational animals").[45] Furthermore, the reality that we are animals can also appear threatening to many because we have for hundreds of generations perpetuated a self-justifying narrative of human exceptionalism that defines humanity in contradistinction to nonhuman creatures.[46] Despite the discomfort some people may have when facing this truth, the simple fact remains that we are animals too. Not only is it important for us to recall this certainty when venturing to understand the human person theologically through the lens of catholicity but, as Eric Daryl Meyer has compellingly argued, it can also be important in addressing the myriad ecological crises we face today. Meyer claims that embracing the truth of our animality can have a positive impact on human efforts to restore balance and health within the broader community of creation. "Unraveling conceptions of humanity rooted in anthropological exceptionalism would simultaneously turn human attention

---

[45] For an overview of this reaction, see Eric Daryl Meyer, *Inner Animalities: Theology and the End of the Human* (New York: Fordham University Press, 2018), 1–14. This reaction is also cataloged in Tim Ingold, ed., *What Is an Animal?* (London: Routledge, 1994).

[46] This oppositional frame has been a locus of contemporary continental philosophy in recent decades, which has resulted in new and productive insights. For example, see Giorgio Agamben, *The Open: Man and Animal*, trans. Kevin Attell (Stanford, CA: Stanford University Press, 2004); Jacques Derrida, *The Animal That Therefore I Am*, trans. David Wills (New York: Fordham University Press, 2008); and Jacques Derrida, *The Beast and the Sovereign*, trans. Geoffrey Bennington, 2 vols. (Chicago: University of Chicago Press, 2009–11).

toward transforming our overwhelmingly exploitative role in earth's ecosystems, but also reconfigure the terrain of our moral sensibilities regarding nonhuman neighbors."[47]

How is that we can come to a better understanding of our animality and therefore embrace rather than reject it?

One proposal is that we consider the manifold ways our reality and experience of the world overlaps with various nonhuman animals.[48] The easiest way for most people to begin considering this creaturely Venn diagram is to recall the ways we share an experience of materiality.[49] For one, we can talk about our elemental composition. Earlier, we were reminded of the stardust that forms the material foundation of all cosmic bodies, from stars and meteors to squirrel and human bodies. At the molecular and sub-molecular level, *what* we are is notably similar to other animals, and even those fellow creatures we are quick to dismiss as non-sentient. The hydrogen, oxygen, carbon, nitrogen, and all the other elements that form and structure our existence in time and space are the same elements that form and structure the corporeality of all creatures. This is to say nothing about what creation looks like at the quantum level and how the strange principles of quantum mechanics shed light on our cosmic interconnectivity and interrelationships.[50]

---

[47] Meyer, *Inner Animalities*, 173.

[48] For a succinct overview of various approaches to this question in the field of critical animal studies, see Matthew Calarco, *Thinking through Animals: Identity, Difference, Indistinction* (Stanford, CA: Stanford University Press, 2015).

[49] As I hope to demonstrate in Chapter 3 when we consider the doctrine of the *imago Dei*, there are also other overlapping characteristics and experiences we can recognize that are shared between human and nonhuman creatures.

[50] For more on the implications of quantum mechanics for theology, see Heidi Ann Russell, *Quantum Shift: Theological and Pastoral Implications of Contemporary Developments in Science* (Collegeville, MN: Liturgical Press, 2015); and Heidi Ann Russell, "Quantum Anthropology: Reimaging the Human Person as Body/Spirit," *Theological Studies* 74 (2013): 934–59.

In the next chapter we explore the scientific grounding and familial biology that ties us to nonhuman animals and the rest of the community of creation according to evolutionary theory. For now, we simply raise some questions about our perception and experience of our animality. If we are to develop our ecological consciousness, recognize our creational kinship, and love the dust we are, then we need to move outside the sphere of the intellect as imagined apart from the phenomenological experience of embodied life in order to see, hear, feel, taste, and smell the cosmos in a new way. This is what ecologist and philosopher David Abram has argued in his book *The Spell of the Sensuous;* he invites us to reflect upon in terms of attuning ourselves to the reality of creaturely existence too often overlooked and ignored.[51]

As an ecologist, Abram is captivated (a word I use advisedly) by what humans tend to miss with our preconceptions of exceptionality and our refusal to embrace our inherent connections to the nonhuman world. As a philosopher, Abram is drawn to the continental field of phenomenology, which is the study not of ideas or concepts that somehow exist outside of the phenomenal world but of the reality of the world and existence as it discloses itself to us. Abram's writing is a poetic intertwining of these two interests that brings together wisdom ancient and modern, experiential and theoretical. As he states at the outset of his book, his "simple premise" is that "we are human only in contact, and conviviality, with what is not human."[52] To reach a place of such encounter and therefore existential reflection requires a rediscovery and embracement of our animality. Abram continually listens to the wisdom of aboriginal cultures that have better preserved a sense of human animality in spirituality, social ordering, and quotidian life than most industrialized Western communities and traditions. For him, this signals an ancient truth or logic that ought to be recovered. He writes:

---

[51] David Abram, *The Spell of the Sensuous: Perception and Language in a More-Than-Human World* (New York: Vintage Books, 1997).

[52] Abram, *The Spell of the Sensuous,* ix.

Only when we slip beneath the exclusively human logic continually imposed upon the earth do we catch sight of this other, older logic at work in the world. Only as we come close to our senses and begin to trust, once again, the nuanced intelligence of our sensing bodies, do we begin to notice and respond to the subtle logos of the land.[53]

At the heart of this worldview is a call to wholemaking. Abram invites us to think holistically about the human and nonhuman world without such a dichotomous or separatist mode of understanding ourselves in relation to the rest of the cosmos:

It is a way of thinking that strives for rigor without forfeiting our animal kinship with the world around us—an attempt to think in accordance with the senses, to ponder and reflect without severing our sensorial bond with the owls and the wind. It is a style of thinking, then, that associates *truth* not with static fact, but with a quality of relationship. Ecologically considered, it is not primarily our verbal statements that are "true" or "false," but rather the kind of relations that we sustain with the rest of nature. A human community that lives in a mutually beneficial relation with the surrounding earth is a community, we might say, that lives in truth.[54]

While Abram is not particularly concerned with the theological implications of his eco-philosophical reflection, we can identify this sense of relational truth about which he speaks with a theological commitment to catholicity. Just as the Western philosophical tradition has resisted empirical phenomena as a locus for reflection on the human person, preferring over the course of its history instead to stick to verbal statements that are "true" or "false," theological anthropology has likewise silenced

---

[53] Abram, *The Spell of the Sensuous*, 268.
[54] Abram, *The Spell of the Sensuous*, 264.

and forgotten the fundamental creaturely kinship that grounds our earthly existence.

It is as if we humans—particularly those of us in Western or Euro-American contexts—have only been listening to the song of creation in mono, according to a one-sided channel of information. Meanwhile, the song of creation exists in stereo, offering us a multidimensional experience of knowing and perceiving because nonhuman creation is simultaneously disclosing itself to us as we ourselves encounter it and make meaning along the way. Abram explains that there is "an intimate reciprocity to the senses; as we touch the bark of a tree, we feel the tree *touching us*; as we lend our ears to the local sounds and ally our nose to the seasonal scents, the terrain, in turn, gradually attunes us. The senses, that is, are the primary way the earth has of informing our thoughts and of guiding our actions."[55] When we cut off that other channel, when we dismiss the sensorial information that our nonhuman neighbors in creation communicate to us, we are left with an incomplete sense of the world and ourselves.

When we do not presume an absolute divide between our nonhuman creaturely neighbors and us, the possibility for integrative reflection on what it means for us to be part of the larger whole of creation opens. One of the most promising resources for such consideration is found in the phenomenological work of French philosopher Maurice Merleau-Ponty. Given his prioritization of the body—as opposed to, for instance, the mind or thought—as the site of philosophical reflection, Merleau-Ponty's thought allows for a different approach to considering the meaning of human personhood. For Abram and many others, Merleau-Ponty provides a rigorous philosophical framework that complements otherwise dismissed loci of knowledge arising from diverse sources such as empirical experiences or indigenous traditions. From the vantage point of catholicity, his philosophical reflection lends a constructive voice to our inquiry about the theological understanding of the human person.

---

[55] Abram, *The Spell of the Sensuous*, 268.

Merleau-Ponty, too, believes that there is an inherent kinship among human and nonhuman creatures.[56] This intrinsic familial tie is grounded for him not in some classic characteristic thought previously to be reserved to humans alone like reason or emotion—though he does not reject that possibility—but instead is found in shared *embodiment*.[57] Philosopher Kelly Oliver summarizes this point well:

> Merleau-Ponty identifies a type of continuity between animals and humans with shared embodiment, which entails perception and behavior or movement. It is crucial to note from the outset that this continuity or kinship is "strange" in that it contains a discontinuity at its heart. For Merleau-Ponty, this is not a body in repose or dissected by biologists. Instead, it is a living body, dynamic and full of movement. In different ways, living bodies perceive and act, sense and move, in reversible relations with their environments and other beings. Merleau-Ponty describes the differences between bodies and behaviors as differences in styles or themes. He finds no abyss separating the bodies of animals and the bodies of humans.[58]

This admittedly "strange kinship" is not understood according to a hierarchical dualism such as one often finds in the Christian theological attempt to reconcile simultaneously the incontrovertible truth of our material existence alongside our claim to absolute human exceptionalism. Instead, Merleau-Ponty notes that humans and nonhuman creatures (recognizing the myriad diversity of the latter) are all embodied, have some level of consciousness, some sense of desire, some series of behaviors,

---

[56] See Maurice Merleau-Ponty, *Nature: Course Notes from the Collège de France*, trans. Robert Vallier (Evanston, IL: Northwestern University Press, 2003), esp. 251.

[57] Merleau-Ponty, *Nature*, 201–84.

[58] Kelly Oliver, *Animal Lessons: How They Teach Us to Be Human* (New York: Columbia University Press, 2009), 218.

some relational capacity, and so on, but *not all in the same way*. The way this has been described by others has been in terms of a lateral relationship rather than a hierarchical one; no one form of embodied existence is necessarily better or higher than another, just different and simultaneous with the others within a broader community of creation.[59] As Oliver explains, "This kinship neither erases all differences between animals and humans, thereby making them identical, nor erases any similarities between them, thereby making them radically separate. Instead, strange kinship allows for an intimate relation based on shared embodiment without denying differences between lifestyles or styles of being."[60]

Admittedly in a brief and summary form, Merleau-Ponty's insights, here, provide us with a philosophical method for taking seriously what Oliver describes in the clearest and most succinct form when it comes to understanding ourselves in relationship to nonhuman animals: "We are neither the same nor radically different."[61] Too much emphasis within Christian theology has been placed on the latter clause over the centuries, a kind of self-consciously obsessive dismissal of our creatureliness and animality. We would do well to recall the salient point that philosopher Mary Midgley once made: "We are not the only unique species. Elephants, as much as ourselves, are in many ways unique; so are albatrosses, so are giant pandas."[62] Hopefully, conveyed here is the need for the restoration of Oliver's latter clause in our understanding of ourselves: that there is *no absolute divide* between human and nonhuman creatures. We are related, connected, and

---

[59] On the notion of Merleau-Ponty's description understood in terms of lateral relationship, see Robert Vallier, "The Indiscernible Joining: Structure, Signification, and Animality in Merleau-Ponty's *La Nature*," *Chiasmi International* 3 (2001): 187–212; and Oliver, *Animal Lessons*, 218–28.

[60] Oliver, *Animal Lessons*, 222.

[61] Oliver, *Animal Lessons*, 224.

[62] Mary Midgley, *The Myths We Live By* (London: Routledge, 2003), 152.

yet distinguishable within the broader community of creation. Keeping this in mind will allow us to pursue questions about what it means to be human with an eye toward the catholicity of our creaturely kinship and, therefore, develop a more catholic theological anthropology.

Chapter 2

The Challenge and Promise
of Evolution

One of the most striking aspects of Charles Darwin's masterful
theory of evolution from the perspective of catholicity is the way
in which its fundamental premise proclaims a sense of wholeness.
All creaturely life is joined in a multi-billion-year evolutionary
line of dynamic development and emergence. This reality is awe
inspiring. And deep consideration of the interconnectedness and
relationality among all creation can lead even the person most
incredulous about God and faith to grasp for religious language
to articulate the magnitude of evolution's significance.

Reflecting on the import of this scientific theory, biologist
Bernard Wood opens his introductory book on human evolution
with just such an allusion (even if he was unaware of the term's
Christian origins): "Many of the important advances made by
biologists in the past 150 years can be reduced to a single metaphor. All living, or extant, organisms, that is, animals, plants,
fungi, bacteria, viruses, and all types of organisms that lived in
the past, are situated somewhere on the branches and twigs of an
arborvitae or Tree of Life."[1] This fitting metaphor for creation's
interconnectedness within evolutionary history—the tree of life—
carries its own history of implicit religious valence. Generally
associated with the cross of Christ, the tree of life often redounds

---

[1] Bernard Wood, *Human Evolution: A Very Short Introduction*
(New York: Oxford University Press, 2005), 1.

to ancient christological hymns such as one finds in the Letter to
the Colossians. In this New Testament text we are reminded that
in Christ "all things in heaven and on earth were created, things
visible and invisible . . . all things have been created through
him and for him. He himself is before all things, and in him all
things hold together" (1:16–17). It does not take much imagination to identify the resonances between the insights revealed to
us by natural sciences and the truths expressed in Christian faith.

One can anticipate the promise that evolutionary theory
presents to theology in general and theological anthropology
specifically. And yet, there are challenges present as well. On
the one hand, a challenge emerges from evolutionary theory to
contest those Christians who insist on a literal or Biblicist reading of scripture.[2] Even the Roman Catholic Church maintained
a strict notion of monogenesis, which claims that all human
beings descended from an originating single pair of ancestors
("Adam" and "Eve"), up to the mid-twentieth century.[3] Sub-

---

[2] This is not a tenable method of scriptural interpretation for Roman Catholics, for a "fundamentalist interpretation" of the Bible is the
only hermeneutical approach that is considered invalid by the Pontifical
Biblical Commission. For more, see the Pontifical Biblical Commission,
"The Interpretation of the Bible in the Church," *Origins* (January 6,
1994), sec. I.F.

[3] See Pius XII, *Humani Generis* (*Acta Apostolica Sedis* 42 [1950]:
561–77): "When, however, there is question of another conjectural
opinion, namely polygenism, the children of the Church by no means
enjoy such liberty. For the faithful cannot embrace that opinion which
maintains that either after Adam there existed on this earth true men
who did not take their origin through natural generation from him as
from the first parent of all, or that Adam represents a certain number
of first parents. Now it is in no way apparent how such an opinion
can be reconciled with that which the sources of revealed truth and
the documents of the Teaching Authority of the Church propose with
regard to original sin, which proceeds from a sin actually committed
by an individual Adam and which, through generation, is passed on to
all and is in everyone as his own" (no. 37). For a historical overview
of the relationship between evolutionary theory and Catholic theology,
see Rafael A. Martínez, "The Reception of Evolutionary Theories in
the Church," in *Biological Evolution: Facts and Theories, A Critical*

sequently, John Paul II and his immediate predecessors, along with numerous theologians, have clarified the church's position toward evolutionary theory as accepting its veracity beyond a mere hypothetical proposal. Nevertheless, John Paul II qualified that the Christian notion of a "soul" is something that does not evolve from nature but is created directly by God.[4] Still, the longstanding interpretation of Genesis that rendered such an outlook casts a long shadow into our contemporary age and over the theological imaginations of many Christians.

On the other hand, there is a second challenge that emerges from the near-universal acceptance of evolution, namely, the temptation to slip into a form of "reductionism" or mere "physicalism" that seeks to account for human existence on a material plane alone. The fear associated with this challenge is that "what you see is what you get" in terms of that which is empirically verifiable and materially analyzable. Given that evolutionary theory makes clear that we have not been created apart from the rest of creation but emerge as the species we know ourselves to be today alongside the rest of creation, this challenge is to claim that we are merely equal to the sum of our parts. This perspective would appear to preclude the noumenal or transcendental and therefore threaten our capacity for and relationship with the Divine, if not appear to outright threaten belief in the existence of God altogether.

Acknowledging these challenges from the outset we apply our lens of catholicity to the reality of biological evolution. As John Paul II rightly admits, evolution is more than a theory. Therefore it is something to be engaged with and taken with utmost seriousness in our consideration of what it means to be a human person. In this chapter we explore evolution and its implications

---

Appraisal 150 Years after 'The Origin of Species', ed. G. Auletta, M. Leclerc, and R. A. Martínez (Rome: Gregorian and Biblical Press, 2011), 589–612.

[4] See John Paul II, "Message to the Pontifical Academy of Sciences: On Evolution" (October 22, 1996). Also, see Eugenie C. Scott, "Creationists and the Pope's Message," *The Quarterly Review of Biology* 72 (1997): 401–6.

for theological anthropology, drawing from insights found in the foundational texts for evolution, the wisdom of Jesuit Pierre Teilhard de Chardin, and the contributions of contemporary theologians.

The Meaning of Evolution

It is commonplace in our contemporary setting to assume that the concept of evolution began with the empirical research and later scientific publications of the British naturalist Charles Darwin. While Darwin is certainly to be credited with the most comprehensive and coherent *theory* of evolution, the concept of evolution as it pertains to the natural world generally and human beings specifically dates millennia before Darwin would set sail on the HMS Beagle in 1831. As Bernard Wood reminds us, there are intimations of something akin to evolution in the nascent philosophical theories of human origins posited by some Greek thinkers in the fifth and sixth centuries BCE. The two key components of the theory of evolution—common origin and gradual change over time—can be recognized in these ancient philosophical reflections. Concerning common origin, Wood notes, "These early Greek philosophers suggested that the entire natural world, including modern humans, forms one system."[5] One does not need to be a trained specialist to recognize commonalities among what would be called species in the world around us, the observation of which could likely lead to one considering a shared history or at least some sort of interconnectedness. Concerning gradual change over time, Wood points to a first-century BCE Roman philosopher, Lucretius, who "proposed that the earliest humans were unlike contemporary Romans. He suggested that human ancestors were animal-like cave dwellers, with neither tools nor language."[6] While neither the ancient Greeks nor Romans proposed anything as cogent or compelling as what would

---

[5] Wood, *Human Evolution*, 7.
[6] Cited in Wood, *Human Evolution*, 7.

be described in the nineteenth century CE, the point is well taken that evolution was a concept that predated any comprehensive scientific attempt to explain its veracity.

At the risk of utilizing a predictable pun, the theory of evolution has *evolved* over the course of millennia, reaching a point of notable clarity in the natural scientific articulation of researchers over the last century and a half. As popular scientist Carl Zimmer notes, the basic principles that compose the theory of evolution are surprisingly simple and straightforward. Essentially, they do not vary much from the ancient intimations found in the philosophical musings of the ancient philosophers Wood describes. Zimmer explains:

> Organisms inherit traits from their ancestors because they receive a molecule called DNA from them. Cells use DNA as a guide to building biological molecules, and, when organisms reproduce, they make new copies of DNA for their offspring. Living things do not replicate their DNA perfectly, sometimes introducing errors into its sequence. Such errors are referred to as mutations. A mutation may be lethal; it may be harmless; or it may be beneficial in some way. . . . Evolution takes place because mutated genes become more or less common over the course of generations.[7]

This process, commonly described in scientific shorthand as "descent with modification," does not happen merely between generations but spans the course of centuries and millennia. In fact, the evolution of living organisms has been taking place on earth for some 3.5 billion years and continues today. Over the course of these expansive periods of time developments from simple organisms to more complex forms of life have unfolded, resulting from genetic mutation and the preponderance of valuable or advantageous traits. Those organisms that are best

---

[7] Carl Zimmer, *The Tangled Bank: An Introduction to Evolution* (Greenwood Village, CO: Roberts and Co. Publishers, 2010), 4–5.

adapted for survival do precisely that, and those that are not so
suited do not typically survive or have an equal opportunity to
reproduce and pass along the less-apt traits. This is what is now
typically called *natural selection.*

Biologists Brian and Deborah Charlesworth summarize the
function of natural selection as first outlined by Charles Darwin
and Alfred Russel Wallace in three points:

- Many more individuals of a species are born than
  can normally live to maturity and breed success-
  fully, so there is a *struggle for existence.*
- There is *individual variation* in innumerable
  characteristics of the population, some of which
  may affect an individual's ability to survive and
  reproduce. The successful parents of a given generation may therefore differ from the population
  as a whole.
- There is likely to be a *hereditary component* to
  much of this variation, so that the characteristics
  of the offspring of the successful parents will differ
  from the characteristics of the previous generation,
  in a similar way to their parents.[8]

In time, organisms that once shared a common source, perhaps many millions of years earlier, become so differentiated that
they are no longer recognizable as belonging to the same species.
This is what evolutionary biologists refer to as *speciation.* While
admittedly more complex than this, in brief, one recognizable
marker of speciation is the inability to reproduce with organisms
of seemingly similar species (species with the ability to reproduce
asexually notwithstanding). The result is an incredible diversity
of species.[9] What we see evolve over the course of billions of

---

[8] Brian and Deborah Charlesworth, *Evolution: A Very Short Introduction* (New York: Oxford University Press, 2003), 7.

[9] Francisco J. Ayala notes that there are "more than two million
existing species of plants and animals" that have been named and

years is poetically described by Darwin in the conclusion of his 1859 book *On the Origin of Species by Means of Natural Selection*. He invites us contemporaries to consider the "entangled bank" of the world, "clothed with many plants of many kinds, with birds singing on the bushes, with various insects flitting about, and with worms crawling through the damp earth, and to reflect that these elaborately constructed forms, so different from each other, and dependent on each other in so complex a manner, have all been produced by laws acting around us."[10]

One of the promises for theology we can recognize immediately in this brief overview of evolution is the recognition of a common source and an intrinsic interrelatedness shared among all creatures. This fact echoes that which we examined in the last chapter about our need to recall our interdependence and corporeality. Indeed, like all other creatures—sentient and otherwise—found within Darwin's "entangled bank," we are *ha-adamah*, made "from the earth." And yet, while the seeming scientific affirmation of the second Genesis creation narrative presumed by evolution may be a comfort to many believers, a challenge concurrently arises for those committed to a strict teleological worldview.

Evolution does not account for the possibility of what is sometimes called *intelligent design*.[11] This concept, proposed by those who hold a literal or fundamentalist reading of Genesis (which, as noted above, precludes Roman Catholics as a rule), holds that even modern theories of evolution cannot account for

---

described, while there remain even more—perhaps as many as ten million—that have not yet been identified or classified (to say nothing of those species that have gone extinct). See Ayala, "The Evolution of Life: An Overview," in *God and Evolution: A Reader*, ed. Mary Kathleen Cunningham (London: Routledge, 2007), 59.

[10] Charles Darwin, *On the Origin of Species by Means of Natural Selection* (New York: Bantam Books, 2008), 478.

[11] For more on intelligent design, see Michael J. Behe, *Darwin's Black Box: The Biochemical Challenge to Evolution* (New York: The Free Press, 1996). For a good rebuttal, see Kenneth R. Miller, "Answering the Biochemical Argument from Design," in Cunningham, *God and Evolution*, 159–74.

every detail of the complexity of species, let alone the self-appropriated superiority of humanity, which therefore illustrates the existence of "design" (as opposed to the ostensible randomness of evolutionary theory). Proponents of this view describe the current state of advanced species, such as *Homo sapiens*, as necessitating a supplemental actor—an *intelligent designer*—who, in the case of many evangelical and fundamentalist Christians, is God. The pseudo-scientific hypothesis of intelligent design is really an effort to rebrand creationism for those who cannot square the overwhelming scientific evidence for biological evolution—including for the human species—with faith in a providential God.

What evolution requires of Christians is to hold two seemingly contradictory or paradoxical claims in creative tension: that God is the "Creator of heaven and earth, of all things visible and invisible" and that biological evolution operates according to what we might generally describe as *chance*. Such a tensive dynamic should not be unfamiliar to Christians, who profess faith in numerous seemingly paradoxical doctrines: the hypostatic union of Christ's fully human and divine natures; a God who is singular in divine being or substance yet triune; and the reality of life after death, to name just a few examples. Still, for some self-professed Christians, the simultaneity of biological evolution and God-as-Creator is too much to handle.

While we will examine some of the contributions of contemporary theologians as it pertains to the promise of evolution in the last section of this chapter, it is worth a brief mention of at least one response to this supposed impasse. It is here that Elizabeth Johnson's 1996 article "Does God Play Dice? Divine Providence and Chance" illumines at least a preliminary path beyond the perceived evolution-Creator divide.[12] Reiterating the issue at hand, Johnson summarizes:

---

[12] Elizabeth A. Johnson, "Does God Play Dice? Divine Providence and Chance," *Theological Studies* 57 (1996): 3–18. For another contemporary engagement with this tension, see Gordon D. Kaufman, *In the Beginning . . . Creativity* (Minneapolis: Fortress Press, 2004), in which he proposes the concept of "serendipitous creativity" as the means by which God operates with regard to creation.

Taken together, scientific understandings of the indeter-
minism of physical systems at the quantum level, the
unpredictability of chaotic systems at the macro level, and
the random emergence of new forms of life through the
evolutionary process itself undermines the idea that there
is a detailed blueprint or unfolding plan according to which
the world was designed and now operates.[13]

While creation does not come into existence in a singular, static
manner as proposed by so-called creationists or proponents
of intelligent design, it is also not entirely arbitrary or chaotic.
Johnson, drawing on the insight found in centuries of scientific
research, reminds us that there are such things as scientific laws.
What evolutionary theory on the macro level and quantum mechanics on the micro level reveal are the dynamics or interchange
between "chance and law"; it's a truly *catholic* "both/and" approach to reality.

Admittedly, nature is mysterious and the ultimate working
of the laws of nature are never comprehendible in their entirety.
Still, we can say that there are some principles of reality that
retain some kind of consistency but, as Johnson contends, "The
laws of nature require the workings of chance if matter is to
explore its full range of possibilities and emerge toward richness and complexity. Without chance, the potentialities of this
universe would go unactualized."[14] Rather than think of dichotomous possibilities, Johnson argues that there is merit—scientific
and theological—to thinking of God creating the universe precisely with the capacity for chance and possibility, an unfolding
of evolution, and the actualization of potential (to borrow a
traditional Hellenistic formulation). In other words, what if it
was God's plan not to work out each and every aspect of the
universe and its activity for all time as so many conceive divine
Providence to entail, but rather to empower creation to unfold
within a contingent frame guided and enabled by the working

---

[13] Johnson, "Does God Play Dice?" 7.
[14] Johnson, "Does God Play Dice?" 7.

of the Holy Spirit as the Christian doctrine of *creatio continua* entails?[15]

Johnson affirms this creational framework and draws from Thomas Aquinas's theory of divine causality (delineated in terms of primary and secondary causality) to provide a robust theological grounding:

> As God is the primary cause of the world as a whole and in every detail, endowing all created beings with their own participation in divine being (enabling them to exist), in divine agency (empowering them to act), and in divine goodness (drawing them to their goal), so too God graciously guides the world toward its end in and through the natural workings of the processes found in creation as a whole. Immanent in these processes, divine providential purposes come to fruition by means of purposes inherent in the creatures themselves.[16]

Basically, that the universe exists and unfolds within an evolutionary frame is precisely the way God creates and reflects the Creator's divine intention. God is truly the Creator of heaven and earth, but is so on God's own terms. As Creator, God remains the primary cause of the evolving universe but, as Thomas makes clear in his writing, God acts through secondary causes, including the apparent randomness of evolution and the dynamic that plays out between chance and law over billions of years.

---

[15] For more on the doctrine of *creatio continua*, see Arthur Peacocke, "Biological Evolution—A Positive Theological Appraisal," in Cunningham, *God and Evolution: A Reader*, 251–72; Herbert McCabe, *God, Christ, and Us*, ed. Brian Davies (New York: Continuum, 2003); and John C. Polkinghorne, "*Creatio Continua* and Divine Action," *Science and Christian Belief* 7 (1995): 101–8; among others.

[16] Johnson, "Does God Play Dice?" 13–14. It is worth stating clearly that while I am critical of Thomas Aquinas's approach to philosophical and theological anthropology in later chapters (especially his views on individuation and gender), I believe Thomas Aquinas offers numerous useful resources as well. Such is the case in distinguishing between primary and secondary causality noted here.

Here, the good news of the meaning of evolution is that God is not a micro manager, despite how much some people would love God to be such according to their own image and likeness. Rather than torpedo the Creator God of Christianity, the meaning of evolution offers the promise of a more catholic understanding of the human person situated within an evolving universe, connected to all other aspects of creation, and participating in an awe-inspiring history of becoming that is anything but antithetical to our faith. In fact, evolution is precisely the manner by which God desires to create.

Insights from Charles Darwin

Whereas Charles Darwin provides the fundamental grounding and arguments for the theory of evolution in *The Origin of the Species by Means of Natural Selection*, his most significant consideration of the human person and evolution appears in his 1871 book *The Descent of Man*.[17] It is here that the most direct implication from evolution for humanity emerges, which is our deeply interrelated existence as one creature among others. In the last chapter we looked at our inherent creaturely kinship, something that is affirmed by scripture and science alike. In *The Descent of Man* Darwin makes the case that this kinship is a natural phenomenon that does not take much advanced scientific analysis to begin to recognize in the world around us. Additionally, while our physical composition and genetic relatedness to other creatures is of interest to Darwin, *The Descent of Man* also presents his exploration of what biologist Michael Ghiselin describes as "a treatise on evolutionary psychology, especially social psychology."[18] Darwin was intrigued, as are so many scientists, theologians, and others, with what is distinctive about our being in the world while always already acknowledging that

---

[17] Citations of this text are from Charles Darwin, *The Descent of Man*, ed. Michael Ghiselin (New York: Dover Publications, 2010).

[18] Michael Ghiselin, "Introduction," in Darwin, *The Descent of Man*, ix.

the mechanism of evolution in human history is the same as that of other creatures, thereby accounting for "a fundamental unity due to descent from common ancestry."[19] Darwin affirms a sense of distinctiveness but does not go so far as to assert uniqueness.

Those characteristics that, over the centuries, have been typically reserved for human beings alone are also found in nonhuman creatures. Darwin states this plainly at the outset of the second chapter of *The Descent of Man*: "My object in this chapter is solely to show that there is no fundamental difference between man and the higher mammals in their mental faculties."[20] Here, Darwin anticipates the ethological discoveries that would follow in the decades after his presentation of anecdotal evidence for the shared characteristics above and beyond the physical structure, embryonic development, and the like easily recognized across species. He offers extensive descriptive detail about the presence of similar traits in human and nonhuman animals including instinct, intellect, agency, emotion, imagination, memory, attention, language, aesthetic appreciation or sense of beauty, self-consciousness, and others.[21] When it comes to religion or religious experience, Darwin notes—anticipating, to some extent, Teilhard de Chardin's insights—that this appears at first glance to be a trait uniquely human, but upon closer study, one recognizes the emergence of complex religiosity over time. The capacity for religious language, experience, practice, and organization seems to have evolved (at least when, following

---

[19] Ghiselin, "Introduction," ix.

[20] Darwin, *The Descent of Man*, 18.

[21] Nearly the entire second half of *The Descent of Man* develops Darwin's study of the role of aesthetic appreciation and what he terms "sexual selection" in both human and nonhuman animals, which has been an underappreciated element of his theory of evolution. Though outside the scope of this current project, it is a fascinating look into the ways a purely mechanistic understanding of evolution is inadequate and highlighting the need to account for subjectivity and choice in evolution. For an excellent overview of this element of his thought, see Richard O. Prum, *The Evolution of Beauty: How Darwin's Forgotten Theory of Mate Choice Shapes the Animal World—And Us* (New York: Doubleday, 2017).

Darwin's argument, one compares manifold aboriginal practices with those of more organized religions).[22] It's not that human beings are the only creatures *capable* of religion; rather, it's that our species may be the only one *so far* to have evolved to practice religion in this way.

One of the most significant insights Darwin presents to theologians thinking about the human person within an evolutionary view of the world is the stark reminder that, concurrent with our doctrinal claim that humans are created *imago Dei* (whatever that might mean),[23] we must never lose sight of the equally veracious claim that humans are created *imago mundi*—in the image of and from the earth. In fact, Darwin concludes *The Descent of Man* with a powerful paragraph that acknowledges the state of hubris we as a species have worked ourselves into over the centuries and cautions us not to lose sight of our inherent creatureliness and interrelatedness with all other creatures:

> Man may be excused for feeling some pride at having risen, though not through his own exertions, to the very summit of the organic scale; and the fact of his having thus risen, instead of having been aboriginally placed there, may give him hopes for a still higher destiny in the distant future. But we are not here concerned with hopes or fears, only with the truth as far as our reason allows us to discover it. I have given the evidence to the best of my ability; and we must acknowledge, as it seems to me, that man with all his noble qualities, with sympathy which feels for the most debased, with benevolence which extends not only to other men but to the humblest living creature, with his god-like intellect which has penetrated into the movements and constitution of the solar system—with all these exalted powers—Man still bears in his bodily frame the indelible stamp of his lowly origin.[24]

---

[22] See Darwin, *The Descent of Man*, 36–39.
[23] This is explored in greater detail in the next chapter.
[24] Darwin, *The Descent of Man*, 450.

Darwin's view, here, is not representative of natural scientists or atheists alone but is something compatible with a catholic outlook on the world in general and the human person in particular. This is something that Pope Francis restated in *Laudato Si'*: "We have forgotten that we ourselves are dust of the earth; our very bodies are made up of her [earth's] elements, we breathe her air and we receive life and refreshment from her waters" (no. 2).

In addition to recognizing our shared origins, thereby recalling our inherent interrelatedness with all of creation and the fact that we always already bear the indelible stamp of our earthly origins *(ha-adamah)*, Darwin offers us yet another insight and a practical one at that. Elizabeth Johnson holds Darwin up to theologians as a model for seeing and loving the world around us, the world of which we are a part. Noting his sharp observatory skills, Johnson notes of Darwin:

> The intensity of his observation registered the depth of his love for the world. I suggest that this quality of seeing the world with attentive and loving care is profoundly religious. In no way am I proposing that we project this interpretation onto Darwin as a person. His own religious odyssey which led him away from Christianity has its own integrity and is to be respected. But I am proposing that the sustained attention he lavished on the natural world models something of a keen religious value to those who approach his work from the perspective of faith.[25]

Admittedly, for those religious practitioners who have viewed Darwin and his work on the theory of evolution with suspicion or even trepidation, to claim Darwin as something of a mystic of the natural world might be startling. However, this sense of "beholding" is one that dates to the earliest centuries of Christianity. Darwin's quest to understand the origin of species arose from his ability to "read the book of creation," as Saint Augustine and

---

[25] Elizabeth A. Johnson, *Ask the Beasts: Darwin and the God of Love* (New York: Bloomsbury, 2014), 41.

Saint Bonaventure would put it. The world around us conveys truths not only about what it contains in itself but also points beyond itself to reveal insights about the Creator. For those who do not espouse a religious tradition (or may, in fact, even be hostile to religious belief) the narrative of "objective research" may suffice to permit the pursuit of scientific knowledge. However, for those who profess belief in a relational Creator, the insights Darwin presents serve as points of orientation when exploring the human person from a theological perspective. We must not lose focus on the inherent interrelatedness the theory of evolution calls us to attend, while at the same time, we remain beholders of the truth the natural world discloses to us about our origins and future. On this latter point Pierre Teilhard de Chardin offers us valuable perspectives.

Insights from Pierre Teilhard de Chardin

One of the challenges that faced Darwin's evolutionary theory was his lack of accounting for creativity or novelty in the natural process. His research led to a theory that provided insight into the mechanisms leading to diversity within nature and the emergence of different species from a common source but no means for describing why in this or that direction or to what end. In response, early twentieth-century French philosopher Henri Bergson, attracted to the truth of Darwin's evolutionary observations, offered a thesis that sought to account for creation's "creative impulse."[26] In his 1907 book *Creative Evolution* Bergson argued for a more teleological trajectory in the evolutionary process.[27] It was in this context that Bergson coined the term *élan vital* to

---

[26] See Magda Costa Carvalho and M. Patrão Neves, "The Bio-Philosophical 'Insufficiency' of Darwinism for Henri Bergson's Metaphysical Evolutionism," *Process Studies* 41 (2012): 133–49. For a survey of Bergson's thought, see G. William Barnard, *Living Consciousness: The Metaphysical Vision of Henri Bergson* (Albany, NY: SUNY Press, 2011).

[27] Henri Bergson, *Creative Evolution*, trans. Arthur Mitchell (New York: Dover Publications, 1998).

describe an inherent impulse or force that guided the evolutionary process of nature in particular directions. Bergson's orthogenetic evolutionary worldview set the stage for Teilhard de Chardin, serving as a kind of bridge that allowed the Jesuit to synthesize an evolutionary view of the world with a christologically focused telos for the whole cosmos. Consequently, we have to acknowledge that Bergson helped fill in some of the philosophical gaps in Darwin's work, so that theologians and philosophers of the twentieth century could begin the correlative work needed to rethink theological reflection in light of the natural sciences.

There is perhaps no better icon of someone committed to exploring the insights of the theory of evolution for our understanding of the human person within a theological context than Pierre Teilhard de Chardin. Born in 1881 into a wealthy French family, Teilhard lived at a time in the church when the compatibility of natural sciences with the manualist traditions of propositional theology was unthinkable.[28] This made him—and anybody else of his generation—an unlikely apologist for a Christian presentation of the human person within an evolutionary view of the world. For whereas the world of scientific inquiry was reckoning with shifts in biology and physics the likes of which the world had not seen since the axial shift of Copernicus, theological reflection consisted of repeating the standard iterations of reactive doctrine made concrete at the Council of Trent in the face of Reformation queries. The former fields represented the promise of modernity, while the latter fought as hard as possible against the shifting tides of human knowledge—ostensibly for the sake of the faith and the integrity of the church.

Teilhard de Chardin, however, found such a dichotomous worldview untenable. A faithful Jesuit priest and a notable paleontologist, Teilhard had a deep appreciation—both scientific and mystical—for the wholeness of being and the catholicity of all God's creation. In his posthumously published book (most of

---

[28] For an overview of Teilhard's life, see Ursula King, *Spirit of Fire: The Life and Vision of Teilhard de Chardin*, rev. ed. (Maryknoll, NY: Orbis Books, 2015).

his work in the area of spirituality and theology was published posthumously due to the church's antimodernist suspicion of his integral outlook on science and religion) *The Heart of Matter*, he offered a reflection of his bourgeoning attunement to a world shaped by the presence of God that did not know the bifurcated sacred and profane divide of his era. Recalling his time as a Jesuit scholastic in England, he writes:

> It was during the years when I was studying theology at Hastings (that is to say, immediately after I had experienced such sense of wonder in Egypt) that there gradually grew in me, as a *presence* much more than an abstract notion, the consciousness of a deep-running, ontological, total current which embraced the whole universe in which I moved; and this consciousness continued to grow until it filled the whole horizon of my inner being.[29]

This disposition, outlook, and burning curiosity grew in time and resulted in Teilhard's prodigious writing of essays and books on the relationship between Christianity and evolution.

Teilhard takes as his starting point the truth of evolution, recognizing from the outset of his reflections on the human person that, on one level, humanity is "a 'species,' no more than a twig, an offshoot from the branch of primates" and yet, "one that we find to be endowed with absolutely prodigious biological properties."[30] This is the tension of reality for Teilhard. On the one hand, humanity is indeed merely one species among others, created *ha-adamah* (to return to the scriptural description) and related in origin to other mammalian creatures and, on some level, to all creation. On the other hand, Teilhard is unapologetically anthropocentric in his outlook. Indeed, while

---

[29] Pierre Teilhard de Chardin, *The Heart of Matter*, trans. René Hague (New York: Harcourt Brace, 1978), 25.

[30] Pierre Teilhard de Chardin, *Man's Place in Nature: The Human Zoological Group*, trans. René Hague (New York: Harper and Row, 1966), 15.

Teilhard's cosmology resists any closed system as might be suggested in using a term like *anthropocentrism,* with its semantic allusion to a circle akin to the logic of *universalis* discussed in the Introduction, here it refers to his hermeneutical bias that presumes the human person and human attributes or characteristics to be the normative standard for evaluating nonhuman creatures. This approach stands in contrast with those who seek to decenter human-normative thinking about the cosmos, such as that based on the reflections of Jakob von Uexküll and others, as we will see in the next chapter. For Teilhard, humanity may be tied to the rest of creation by lineage and family tree, but it nevertheless rests atop a hierarchical ordering or serves as an arrowhead in the trajectory of evolution for all God's creatures toward the Omega Point. From this perspective we are the furthest ahead, the most evolved as creatures conscious of ourselves and beyond ourselves. And so, how do we make sense of this bipolar identity of similarity and difference within the broader community of creation?

To begin, Teilhard recognizes that we did not attain this current status as *Homo sapiens* in one fell swoop. The long and evolutionary process of becoming what we are in our current state of species is what is alternatively referred to as "anthropogenesis" or "hominization," that is, *becoming human.* This was, as Alice Vallé Knight recounts, the primary focus of Teilhard's research interest in the last decades of his life.[31] He was interested in exploring the emergence of the human person. His starting point was to look backward into the past, drawing on all of his resources and skills as a natural scientist. But this inquiry into human origins, arising as they did from the wider cosmic narrative of evolution, did not end in a retrospective appreciation for whence we came as a species. Instead, the recognition of what Teilhard would categorize in four evolutionary epochs of increasing complexity led to his querying about the *whither* of human existence and of the entire community of creation as a whole.

---

[31] Alice Vallé Knight, *The Meaning of Teilhard de Chardin: A Primer* (Greenwich, CT: Devin-Adair Company, 1974), 72.

Outlined in the detailed contents of *The Phenomenon of Man*, this process can be summarized as an evolutionary movement from "cosmogenesis" to "biogenesis" to "noogenesis." Teilhard uses "Christogenesis" to describe the divine recapitulation of cosmogenesis, offering an evolutionarily grounded theological perspective reminiscent of Irenaeus's theory of recapitulation.[32]

Cosmogenesis is the emergence and evolution of that which is contained within the cosmos, a movement from the greatest simplicity of matter toward life. *Biogenesis* is what Teilhard used to describe the ever-complexifying development of life that led to sentience or consciousness in creatures. *Noogenesis* describes the movement toward human self-consciousness that marks a noted shift in the history of creation. As a paleontologist or any other observer of cosmic history from a scientific perspective, this series of evolutionary development would be sufficient to recapitulate the cosmos as we know it and that can be, with ever-increasing specificity, empirically studied. However, for Teilhard, this led to a question about where a still-evolving universe—which included humanity—was going. Here, his theological insights align with his scientific inquiry in the form of his proposed *Christogenesis*. This future-oriented view of evolution and of humanity's place within it arises for Teilhard in reflection upon the directionality that the evolution of the cosmos, which remains ongoing, signals in its general thrust toward the future. This ultimate future, which Teilhard calls the "Omega Point," is an eschatological consummation of all creation in God. Humanity, by virtue of its reaching the evolutionary stage of noogenesis, is attuned to the Christocentricity of creation and therefore leads the way for all that has emerged over the course of cosmic history in this cosmic journey. Teilhard grounds his ideas in the scientific facticity of evolution and reads it through the scriptural insights of the New Testament. He explains:

---

[32] See Pierre Teilhard de Chardin, *The Phenomenon of Man*, trans. Bernard Wall (New York: HarperCollins, 2008). On this latter point, see Christopher F. Mooney, "Teilhard de Chardin and the Christological Problem," *Harvard Theological Review* 58 (1965): 91–126.

If the world is convergent and if Christ occupies its center, then the Christogenesis of St. Paul and St. John is nothing else and nothing less than the extension, both awaited and unhoped for, of that noogenesis in which cosmogenesis—as regards our experience—culminates. Christ invests himself organically with the very majesty of his creation. And it is in no way metaphorical to say that man finds himself capable of experiencing and discovering his God in the whole length, breadth, and depth of the world in movement. To be able to say literally to God that one loves him, not only with all one's body, all one's heart, and all one's soul, but with every fiber of the unifying universe—that is a prayer that can only be made in space-time.[33]

There are certainly echoes of not only the Pauline and Johannine texts of the New Testament in Teilhard's description of Christogenesis but resonances with the recapitulative vision of the single divine act of creation and salvation seen in the ancient writings of Irenaeus of Lyons.

Whereas a fuller account of Teilhard's many contributions to the fields of science and religion exceeds the scope of this chapter, it is worth mentioning that his early-twentieth-century synthesis of evolutionary theory and theological reflection, with all its strengths and weaknesses, paved the way for the generations of theologians that followed. Perhaps two of the most notable insights from Teilhard for our purposes are the place of humanity within the broader evolutionary history of the cosmos and the place of Christianity in understanding who we are and what the world is.[34]

Teilhard does not shy away from the unavoidable truth of our creatureliness, which emerged alongside all other creatures—sentient or otherwise—over several billions of years through a slow

---

[33] Teilhard de Chardin, *The Phenomenon of Man*, 297.

[34] On this latter point, see the essays collected in Pierre Teilhard de Chardin, *Christianity and Evolution*, trans. René Hague (New York: Harcourt Brace, 1969).

process of increasing complexity. Our elemental foundations, the shared origins of our historical emergence, the interrelatedness and interdependence we have with the broader community of creation—these are things that Teilhard presupposes and are necessary presuppositions for anyone who intends to engage seriously in theological reflection on the human person. While his creational outlook is admittedly more hierarchical and anthropocentric, his accounting for humanity's place within evolutionary history rightly acknowledges the principle that we are inextricably *ha-adamah*, and yet more than the sum of our material parts.

On this latter point, Teilhard's weaving together of Christianity with the pursuit of scientific knowledge provides a heuristic for his followers. Rather than viewing science and theology as antithetical or even as non-overlapping magisteria, as does Stephen Jay Gould,[35] Teilhard sees a complementarity between evolution and theology. His proposed Christogenesis with the creation's ultimate Omega Point, which he argues exists "strictly speaking, outside the scientifically observable process" of history,[36] builds upon the empirical observations of evolution, and provides for insights about who we are and what God intends for creation. Consequently, Teilhard's legacy is, in part, the resituating of humanity within both the broader community of creation and God's singular act of creation and salvation. Teilhard offers us a scientifically grounded unification of protology and eschatology, which is no small contribution to the church's effort at wholemaking.

Insights from Contemporary Theologians

Interest in the relationship between science and theology has dramatically increased over the last century, spurring innovative and constructive projects that explore previously unconsidered

---

[35] See Stephen Jay Gould, *Rocks of Ages: Science and Religion in the Fullness of Life* (New York: Vintage Books, 1999).

[36] Teilhard de Chardin, *Man's Place in Nature*, 116.

implications of the theory of evolution for theological reflection on the human person. Given the expanding breadth of scholarly literature at the intersection of science and theology and the limited space allotted here, we cannot examine much of the current insights emerging in the field. However, in order to explore at least the tip of the scholarly iceberg, we survey a few key themes that emerge from recent work by contemporary theologians. We look briefly at recent developments in the theological loci known as deep incarnation and resurrection; what the theory of evolution informs us about evil and suffering in the world; and the ongoing developments in the shifting meaning of human existence.

Deep Incarnation and Resurrection

The most central doctrinal claim of Christianity is that the eternal Word, the *Logos* or Second Person of the Trinity, became incarnate in the historical person Jesus of Nazareth. Without assent to this belief, you cannot have Christianity in its most fundamental form. Most people look at the celebration of Christmas and focus on the birth of an infant human (that is, if they can move beyond the increasing commercialization of the holiday). In general, there is nothing immediately wrong with this. In fact, Jesus of Nazareth was a human, which is something about which there was great contestation in the early centuries and during the first ecumenical councils of the church and is an essential theological claim finally made concrete in the Chalcedonian formula of 451 CE. Jesus Christ, we believe, had two natures: a human nature and a divine nature. And much of the christological consideration that has unfolded over the centuries since has been preoccupied with the relationship between the humanity and divinity of Jesus Christ.[37]

---

[37] For a classic essay on this, see Karl Rahner, "Current Problems in Christology," in *Theological Investigations*, vol. 1, trans. Cornelius Ernst (Baltimore: Helicon Press, 1961), 149–200.

In recent years there has been a notable development in the field of Christology that has taken the theory of evolution and the interrelatedness of all creation into account, which is certainly indebted to the prodigious work of Teilhard de Chardin, who helped pave the way for contemporary christological reflection on creation and the cosmos. This development has yielded insights about the significance of the incarnation of the Word for the whole of creation.[38] Delineated in terms of "strict" and "broader" senses, Celia Deane-Drummond describes two approaches to the incarnation:

> There are two meanings of incarnation worth clarifying. "Strict sense" incarnation refers to the incarnation of God in the physical body *(sarx)* of Jesus Christ as a single human being. "Broader sense" incarnation is inclusive of other beings in the sense that Christ also shares the social and geo-biological conditions of the whole cosmos.[39]

The "broader sense" of incarnation is often described today as "deep incarnation," a term coined by Danish theologian Niels Henrik Gregersen.[40] Gregersen develops this approach within the

---

[38] For a survey of scholarship on this theme, see the collected essays in *Incarnation: On the Scope and Depth of Christology*, ed. Niels Henrik Gregersen (Minneapolis: Fortress Press, 2015).

[39] Celia Deane-Drummond, *A Primer in Ecotheology: Theology for a Fragile Earth* (Eugene, OR: Cascade Books, 2017), 75.

[40] See Niels Henrik Gregersen, "The Cross of Christ in an Evolutionary World," *Dialog: A Journal of Theology* 40 (2001): 192–207. Subsequently, Gregersen has developed this concept in several places, including "Deep Incarnation: Why Evolutionary Continuity Matters in Christology," *Toronto Journal of Theology* 26 (2010): 173–88; "Christology," in *Systematic Theology and Climate Change: Ecumenical Perspectives*, ed. Michael S. Northcott and Peter M. Scott (London: Routledge, 2014), 33–50; Gregersen, *Incarnation: On the Scope and Depth of Christology*; "Deep Incarnation: From Deep History to Post-Axial Religion," *HTS Teologiese Studies/Theological Studies* 72 (2016): 1–12; and "The Emotional Christ: Bonaventure and Deep Incarnation," *Diaog: A Journal of Theology* 55 (2016): 247–61.

broader context of his exploration of the theology of the cross and theodicy in an evolutionary world (something we explore in the next section). He explains:

> In this context, the incarnation of God in Christ can be understood as a radical or "deep" incarnation, that is, an incarnation into the very tissue of biological existence, and system of nature. Understood this way, the death of Christ becomes an icon of God's redemptive co-suffering with all sentient life as well as with victims of social competition. God bears the costs of evolution, the price involved in the hardship of natural selection.[41]

From an evolutionary viewpoint, Gregersen is reading Darwin's "entangled bank" through the lens of Christology, asking, as Deane-Drummond puts it, "What happens, then, when God becomes physical material, enfleshed, taking on human 'nature' in the historical person of Jesus Christ?"[42] Gregersen and others have concluded that the relevance is not limited to human creatures alone but that the incarnation (and, by extension, the cross) bears theological significance for all God's creatures. Gregersen summarizes his understanding of deep incarnation:

> Deep incarnation: is the view that God's own Logos (Wisdom and Word) are made flesh in Jesus the Christ in such a comprehensive manner that God, by assuming the particular life story of Jesus the Jew from Nazareth, also conjoined the material conditions of creaturely existence ("all flesh"), shared and ennobled the fate of all biological life forms ("grass" and "lilies"), and experienced the pains of sensitive creatures ("sparrows" and "foxes") from within. Deep incarnation thus presupposes a radical embodiment that reaches into in the roots *(radices)* of material

---

[41] Gregersen, "The Cross of Christ in an Evolutionary World," 205.
[42] Deane-Drummond, *A Primer in Ecotheology*, 74.

and biological existence as well as into the darker sides of creation: the *tenebrae creationis*.[43]

This argument is rooted in the richly Pauline and Johannine worldview that foregrounds the incarnation of the Word *(Logos)* becoming "flesh" *(sarx)*, which is manifold in meaning. In this christological context the

> Greek term *sarx* thus means (1) the concrete body of Jesus, (2) the human world of sin, and (3) the whole warp and wharf of materiality—everything material, from cosmic dust to mud, to life-forms of grass and weed onwards to animal and human existence. Accordingly, the theological concept of incarnation has to be extended into the whole fabric of physical and biological creation.[44]

This understanding of the incarnation reflects the catholicity of an evolutionary world in which all humans are situated within a dynamic network of interrelated creatures that have and continue to evolve. God's decision to enter this evolutionary world is a decision to enter creation as such. It is through the particularity of the Word's incarnation in the *sarx* of a singular human person two millennia ago that is the very condition for the universality of its significance, for just as each of us is a part of the Darwinian "entangled bank" so too the Word, in Jesus of Nazareth, the Christ, became part of the same cosmic community of creation.

In this view God does not only tolerate material existence, but God becomes involved with the world, appears within it, shares creaturely experiences from within, and—if we follow the particular trajectory of the Jesus story—takes side with the victims of evolution and social injustice. Jesus the Immanuel ("the God

---

[43] Niels Henrik Gregersen, "The Extended Body of Christ: Three Dimensions of Deep Incarnation," in Gregersen, *Incarnation: On the Scope and Depth of Christology*, 225–26.

[44] Gregersen, "Deep Incarnation: From Deep History to Post-Axial Religion," 2.

with us") died the death of an animal, and he died as a social outcast, his death being the result of a miscarriage of justice by religious authorities as well as political powers, and in the end scorned even by ordinary people. If God's own being was present in the life story of Jesus, as Christians believe, then Christ is present from the bottom of the universe and up, emerging from within the realm of creation no less than descending from above. The proposal of deep incarnation is thus both "high" in Christology and "low" in materiality.[45]

This renewed approach to Christology avoids overt anthropocentrism, which focuses exclusively on the human implications arising from the incarnation. According to the deep incarnational view, one cannot talk about God becoming human apart from recognition that God also became material in Christ's corporeality, thereby extending divine solidarity to all God's creatures. God enters into the evolutionary world that God created.

But it is not just the divine entrance into creation that is significant. Building on Gregersen's proposal of deep incarnation, Elizabeth Johnson has argued for "deep resurrection."[46] This is the logical outcome of our profession of faith in a God who became part of the created, material world *(sarx)* just like us. When we profess belief in the resurrection of the body, when we celebrate the great solemnity of Easter, in which we bear witness again to Christ who is "the firstborn of the dead" and "the firstborn of all creation" (Col 1:15–20), we are saying something about how this salvific act of God matters for the whole cosmos and not just our own species. Johnson explains:

> The reasoning runs like this. This person, Jesus of Nazareth, was composed of earthly matter; his body existed in a network of relationships drawn from and extending to the whole physical world. If through death and resurrection

---

[45] Gregersen, "Deep Incarnation: From Deep History to Post-Axial Religion," 2.

[46] See Elizabeth A. Johnson, "Creation: Is God's Charity Broad Enough for Bears?" in *Abounding in Kindness: Writings for the People of God* (Maryknoll, NY: Orbis Books, 2015), 97–123.

this "piece of this world, real to the core," as Karl Rahner writes, is now forever with God in glory, then this signals the beginning of redemption not just for other human beings but for all flesh, all material beings, every creature that passes through death. The evolving world of life, all of matter in its endless permutations, will not be left behind but will likewise be transfigured by the resurrecting action of the Creator Spirit.[47]

To understand the significance of incarnation for our understanding of the human person, it is necessary to recall that we are always already part of a larger community of creation that God not only loved into existence but continues to relate to, support, and sustain *(creatio continua)*. Our profession in the resurrection of the body is not a belief reserved for our species alone, but a doctrine that makes sense only within the broader evolutionary view of the cosmos. A theological anthropology that reflects catholicity and embodies a spirit of wholemaking true to what we understand about evolution understands the implications of our christological promulgations as having universal creaturely significance. Therefore, as Johnson says so well, "the risen Christ embodies the ultimate hope of all creation."[48]

Evolutionary Theodicy and Suffering

Over the centuries the typical approach to questions of theodicy has focused on the evil or suffering experienced by human beings.[49] However, developments in theology that take seriously the challenge and promise of evolution have called theologians

---

[47] Johnson, "Creation," 113.

[48] Johnson, "Creation," 114.

[49] A modern classic is Marilyn McCord Adams, *Horrendous Evils and the Goodness of God* (Ithaca, NY: Cornell University Press, 2000). Also see Eleonore Stump, *Wandering in Darkness: Narrative and the Problem of Suffering* (New York: Oxford University Press, 2012); and Terrence W. Tilley, *Evils of Theodicy* (Washington, DC: Georgetown University Press, 2000).

to revisit the problem of evil and suffering in the broader community of creation, which includes human and nonhuman creatures alike. At the forefront of this reconsideration of theodicy is British theologian Christopher Southgate, who explores the problem of evil in relationship to the community of creation in *The Groaning of Creation: God, Evolution, and the Problem of Evil*.[50] As Southgate rightly notes, "The creation that science describes for us is one in which suffering is endemic, and intrinsic to its development, a creation moreover in which over 98 percent of all species ever to have evolved are now extinct."[51] He maintains that suffering and what is typically described as natural evil (that is, traditionally non-volitional catastrophes or events that lead to suffering) are indeed part of the natural evolutionary order and, at the same time, not incompatible with affirmation of a "God who is creative, redemptive, and all-loving."[52]

Southgate's argument presupposes the veracity of biological evolution and treats this means of creation as the result of God's will ("an evolving creation was the only way in which God could give rise to the sort of beauty, diversity, sentience, and sophistication of creatures that the biosphere now contains").[53] Furthermore, it's not simply that God is some distant actor who creates and then retires. Instead, Southgate follows in a longstanding theological tradition of asserting a divine solidarity with all creation in its suffering—not simply solidarity with the human species. God creates so as to utilize evolution as the primary means and concurrently accompanies all creatures in the process, a further development of the *creatio continua* tradition. Creation as a whole is understood in the Genesis sense to be "very good" (1:31) in its eschatological summation rather than

---

[50] Christopher Southgate, *The Groaning of Creation: God, Evolution, and the Problem of Evil* (Louisville, KY: Westminster John Knox Press, 2008).

[51] Southgate, *The Groaning of Creation*, 15.

[52] Southgate, *The Groaning of Creation*, 15.

[53] Southgate, *The Groaning of Creation*, 16.

as a static mode of perfection at its origin from which human and nonhuman creatures alike decline or fall.[54]

Concerning humanity's place within this vision of creation and the reality of evil and suffering, Southgate offers some interesting insights. He goes to great lengths to dismiss anthropomonism, which is the theological claim that God is only concerned with human beings within the economy of salvation. Instead, God is concerned with the salvation of all God's creatures. And yet, precisely as humans—as a particular species within the broader community of creation—we have a responsibility to recognize and address our role within the community. There is an inherent anthropocentrism to much of our theological and ethical discourse because we are naturally viewing creation and Creator from our perspective. It is appropriate for us to inquire about *our role* in creation, provided that this unavoidable form of anthropocentrism does not rise to an unmitigated anthropocentrism or anthropomonism at the expense of all nonhuman creatures.[55] What Southgate asserts follows from the work of those who have argued for deep incarnation and deep resurrection, suggesting that we refashion our own self-understanding as *Homo sapiens* to appreciate our role as divine co-creators in a manner conscious of our place within the broader community of creation. He explains:

> What God alone can do, has done, once and for all, was to suffer death for the transformation of the world, to bear in the Christ the pain of the creation and of human sin. But our lives can side with that sacrifice in ways both ingenious and costly. If we were to grow into the fullness of our life

[54] Southgate, *The Groaning of Creation*, 78–91.

[55] Here Southgate is inclined to allow a reconceived stewardship model of creation for ethical reasons. While his argument is understandable and has many advantageous dimensions, I explain elsewhere why I believe the terminology of stewardship is inescapably problematic for theological reflection (see Daniel P. Horan, *All God's Creatures: A Theology of Creation* [Lanham, MD: Lexington Books/Fortress Academic, 2018]).

under God we might be able to realize a further call—a call to participate more actively in the healing of a wild nature that may be seen both as "very good" *and* as (through the will of the same God who made it) "groaning in travail." In doing so we would be acting in the image of God that we see, in the life of the earthly Jesus, as always moved to compassion by the need for healing.[56]

Indeed, while God is concerned and in solidarity with the pain and suffering of all creation, God also provides human beings with a pattern for what it means to be human within creation through the witness of Jesus's life, death, and resurrection. We can simultaneously be more fully human and more fully members of creation when we follow the self-sacrificial model of Christ in our own lives. This classic call of Christian spirituality manifests itself in myriad ways, but Southgate's work suggests that our concern and care for our fellow creatures ought to be incorporated into our Christian theological outlook—and therefore ethical praxis—in this sense.[57] And while no theological account of theology and evolution, including Southgate's, ever offers a completely satisfying response to the challenges of evil and suffering in creation, insights about what it means to be human and how to rethink our Christian doctrinal claims and spiritual practices arise when we take seriously the reality of evolution and its compatibility with a contemporary theology of creation.

The Meaning of Human Being

Given that this book is focused on exploring the ways in which our understanding of the human person continues to shift, develop, and emerge, at times challenging our inherited philosophical and theological anthropologies, this section on insights

---

[56] Southgate, *The Groaning of Creation*, 114–15.
[57] See Southgate, *The Groaning of Creation*, 116–33; and Neil Messer, "Sin and Salvation," in Northcott and Scott, *Systematic Theology and Climate Change*, 124–40.

from contemporary theologians on the meaning of the human being will be brief. Additionally, because the next chapter takes up the theme of the doctrine of *imago Dei*, this section can serve as a bridge between consideration of the challenge and promise of evolution for theological anthropology and a reevaluation of *imago Dei*. What is of particular interest here concerns the meaning of human existence in light of the reality of evolutionary history and what it reveals about our creatureliness, interrelatedness, and animality.

Some theologians and philosophers have taken the conversation about reconsidering our place within creation in a direction known as *transhumanism*.[58] According to scholars Heidi Campbell and Mark Walker, "Transhumanism is the view that humans should be permitted to use technology in order to remake human nature, offered as the next stage in human evolution."[59] While Campbell and Walker describe transhumanism as an effort to "remake" human nature, other scholars understand transhumanism as a process of human "enhancement" rather than a kind of reconstruction and, as such, offer a cautious optimism about the plasticity of the meaning of human nature.

On the one hand, this approach that advances a trajectory of enhancement makes sense. It appears to follow the logic of evolution, which traces the development of ever-more-complex organisms emerging from simpler life forms. Furthermore, as a species, *Homo sapiens* has already utilized technology to bolster dimensions of human living—or some human lives as such—that were viewed as inadequate, undesirable, or disabilities. You can think of the computer I used to type this manuscript or the prescription eyeglasses I wore to see this screen or the myriad other

---

[58] For perspectives on this, see John C. Haughey and Ilia Delio, eds., *Humanity on the Threshold: Religious Perspectives on Transhumanism* (Washington, DC: The Council for Research in Values and Philosophy, 2014).

[59] Heidi Campbell and Mark Walker, "Religion and Transhumanism: Introducing a Conversation," *Journal of Evolution and Technology* 14 (2005): 1.

devices or supplemental technologies we use each day unthinkingly. In this sense, as Ilia Delio notes, "The term *transhumanism* refers to technologies that can improve mental and physical aspects of the human condition such as suffering, disease, aging, and death."[60] Thus, from this perspective, transhumanism is both a natural process of human becoming and something to be welcomed alongside developments in technology and science.[61]

On the other hand, some people have been deeply skeptical or directly critical of such lines of consideration. What is presented optimistically as enhancement of human nature nevertheless bears a sense of neo-Manichaeism that sees our corporeality as secondary to our mind, at best, or, at worst, to be despised and supplanted. Additionally, transhumanism strikes me as another possible anthropocentric pitfall that seeks a superior, nonmaterial path for human beings that transcends our present collective, interrelated, and shared creatureliness. Transhumanism, therefore, can be viewed as the desire of our species to evolve *out of creation* and therefore justify the self-ascribed perspective of human uniqueness or "human separatism."

Celia Deane-Drummond has also been critical of much of the theological discussions around transhumanism.[62] Deane-Drummond's theological answer to transhumanism is christological. She argues that "in order to understand humanity, we need to understand who Christ is, and that encounter with Christ need not separate us from either the Jesus of history or the community of creation."[63] In turning to Christ, the incarnate Word of faith, we are confronted by the radical claims of the Christian

---

[60] Ilia Delio, *The Unbearable Wholeness of Being: God, Evolution, and the Power of Love* (Maryknoll, NY: Orbis Books, 2013), 157.

[61] See Donna Haraway, *Simians, Cyborgs, and Women: The Reinvention of Nature* (London: Routledge, 1990).

[62] For example, see Celia Deane-Drummond, "Future Perfect? God, the Transhuman Future and the Quest for Immortality," in *Future Perfect? God, Medicine, and Human Identity*, ed. Celia Deane-Drummond and Peter Scott (New York: Continuum, 2006), 168–82; and Deane-Drummond, *Christ and Evolution*, 256–67.

[63] Deane-Drummond, *Christ and Evolution*, 269.

profession in the goodness of creation and the centrality of materiality and corporeality in the tradition. Transhumanism calls for a new *apologia* in the vein of Irenaeus against the Gnostics or Paul of Tarsus against the Hellenists of his age. In more recent works Deane-Drummond has encouraged a return to the community of creation alongside the study of Christ as illuminative for theological anthropology.[64] If we take seriously what evolutionary history has revealed to us about our being embedded within the broader community of creation—Darwin's "entangled bank"—we can learn something about who we are from how we are with other creatures.

By way of illustration Deane-Drummond presents three case studies about human interspecies relations with hyenas, elephants, and macaque monkeys. Archeologists and anthropologists have shown that there has been a symbiotic relationship between humans and hyenas in some parts of the world that spans millions of years during which time both species experienced coevolution. Over millennia of proximate habitation, behaviors exhibited by one species affect and shape social, personal, and even biological shifts and developments in the other. Some contemporary communities, such as those in Ethiopia mentioned by Deane-Drummond, have a robust sense of hyena agency that helps inform the humans' religious outlooks and that implies "that other animals in some sense are viewed as mediating agents with the divine."[65] Regarding elephants, Deane-Drummond points to the significant work of Piers Locke, whose research "puts emphasis on subjective agency in both humans and elephants, their coevolution, and a method of research that

---

[64] See Celia Deane-Drummond, *The Wisdom of the Liminal: Evolution and Other Animals in Human Becoming* (Grand Rapids, MI: Eerdmans, 2014). Also see idem, "Windows to the Divine Spirit: Between Species Encounters, Wild Justice, and Image Bearing in Ecological Perspective," in *The Nature of Things: Rediscovering the Spiritual in God's Creation*, ed. Graham Buxton and Norman Habel, 157–69 (Eugene, OR: Pickwick Publications, 2016).

[65] Deane-Drummond, *A Primer in Ecotheology*, 97.

interweaves the biological with the cultural."[66] The patterns of relationship between the human and nonhuman animals, in this case, transcend the limitations of the predator-prey binary to which anthropocentric worldviews so frequently reduce the natural world. Over time, the behavior, socialization, and even religious patterns of elephants have an impact on the coevolutionary process of their human neighbors—and vice versa. Finally, Deane-Drummond highlights the research of Agustin Fuentes, who has studied the symbiotic and communal relationship between humans and macaques in Bali. As with humans and elephants, the Balinese recognize a complex interrelatedness with the monkeys, who are viewed by their human neighbors as religious agents who participate in religious rituals and practices. To understand the development of both the biology and culture of the human community, one also has to explore the development of the macaque community.[67]

The key element here is that in examining the ongoing evolutionary development of human beings, it is less worthwhile from a theological perspective to focus on the theoretical eschewing or radical shifting of the material reality of human existence than it is to look at the fellow creatures with whom we live and move and share a multi-million-year evolutionary history. To understand the meaning of human beings, we cannot explore ourselves as a species in isolation. A theological anthropology that is not always aware of the facticity of evolutionary history and the intrinsic interrelatedness to all other creatures it implies will never tell us anything true about ourselves. Such misguided efforts only run the risk of reinscribing outmoded anthropocentric fairytales of human separatism.

---

[66] Deane-Drummond, *A Primer in Ecotheology*, 98. Also see Piers Locke, "Explorations in Ethnoelephantology: Social, Historical, and Ecological Intersections between Asian Elephants and Humans," *Environment and Society* 4 (2013): 79–97.

[67] See Agustin Fuentes, "Naturalcultural Encounters in Bali: Monkeys, Temples, Tourists, and Ethnoprimatogy," *Cultural Anthropology* 25 (2010): 600–624.

Chapter 3

Imago Dei and the Community of Creation

As we have already seen in the previous two chapters, much of the Christian theological tradition has presumed a degree of human uniqueness that separates ourselves from the broader community of creation not just in degree but categorically and naturally.[1] This presumption has led to an eisegetical reading of scripture and the theological tradition to justify human sovereignty, the destructive results of which we witness in the increased extinction of species, pollution, and global climate change. The general placeholder for this anthropocentric uniqueness is the longstanding Christian doctrine of *imago Dei*—the belief that human beings, and traditionally human beings *alone*, are created in the image and likeness of God. Given the exclusive application of the doctrine to the species *Homo sapiens,* scriptural exegetes and theologians alike have sought to identify what precisely constitutes this particular qualification that disqualifies humans from association with nonhuman animals and other creatures, while simultaneously raising us to a status of quasi-deities on earth. As we will see in this chapter, the scrip-

---

[1] See Joshua M. Moritz, "Evolutionary Biology and Theological Anthropology," in *The Ashgate Research Companion to Theological Anthropology,* ed. Joshua R. Farris and Charles Taliaferro (London: Routledge, 2015), 50–52; and Eric Daryl Meyer, *Inner Animalities: Theology and the End of the Human* (New York: Fordham University Press, 2018), 58–85.

tural sources for the doctrine of the *imago Dei* are extremely sparse and the literary, historical, anthropological, and semantic contexts are exceptionally ambiguous. Given the absence of any clear meaning that can be tied to the doctrine of the *imago Dei*, generations of biblical commentators and theologians have effectively projected meaning into the term, which has further made concrete the anthropocentric logic undergirding the Christian tradition's understanding of the human person as set apart from the rest of creation.[2]

In an effort to arrive at an understanding of *imago Dei* that is in keeping with the spirit of catholicity, this chapter begins by examining the current state of scholarship on the meaning of *imago Dei* to identify the best understanding of its original context. We then survey some modern approaches to the doctrine. And finally, we close with a constructive argument on behalf of an understanding of *imago Dei* that moves toward embodying both inclusivity and distinction, which best reflects a theological anthropology of wholemaking.

The Ambiguity of the Image of God

It is striking that an expression (image of God) that appears in the Hebrew Bible only three times, and each time only in the Book of Genesis (1:26–27; 5:1; 9:6), would serve such a definitive purpose in the course of theological reflection on the human person and that person's relationship to the rest of creation. However, scripture scholars and theologians have recently reconsidered the concept of *imago Dei*, particularly as it emerges in the canonical scriptures. J. Richard Middleton notes that the longstanding inattention to the literary and historical contexts of the Hebrew Bible, generally, and of the Book of Genesis, specifically, has led many interpreters of scripture to "turn to extrabiblical, usually philosophical, sources to interpret the image and end up

---

[2] See David Fergusson, *Creation* (Grand Rapids, MI: Eerdmans, 2014), 11–13.

reading contemporaneous conceptions of being human back into the Genesis text."[3] Middleton convincingly argues that "most patristic, medieval, and modern interpreters typically asked not an exegetical, but a speculative question: in what way are humans *like* God and *unlike* animals?"[4]

And yet, the terms *image (selem)* and *likeness (demut)*, which appear in Genesis 1:26–27 and serve as the foundation of the Christian doctrine, need not only be read speculatively. They can be read in light of the biblical text itself, which Middleton undertakes.[5] What is uncovered upon close examination of the historical and literary contexts of these words is the wide semantic range they present to interpreters. The word *selem* (image) primarily designates three-dimensional cult statues of various "false gods" (idols) but can also refer to three-dimensional statues that are not of deities. Middleton concludes that *selem* is best understood to mean a "carved or hewn statue or copy."[6] The word *demut* (likeness), particularly as it is used in reference to human beings, as in Genesis 5:3, where Seth's affinity with his father Adam is described, typically appears as a term of comparison between two things wherein one thing has the appearance or form of the other. Often, it is accompanied by phrases such as *like, as, something like, similar to*, and so on.[7] Modern exegetes have made distinctions between these two terms, suggesting that

---

[3] J. Richard Middleton, *The Liberating Image: The Imago Dei in Genesis 1* (Grand Rapids, MI: Brazos Press, 2005), 17.

[4] Middleton, *The Liberating Image*, 19. Also see Claus Westermann, *Genesis 1—11: A Commentary* (Minneapolis: Fortress Press, 1984).

[5] This is an effort to examine the text apart from deeply influential early speculative interpretations such as is found in the writings of Philo of Alexandria. For more on Philo of Alexandria's long-ranging influence on Christian interpretations of *selem* and *demut*, see Daniel P. Horan, *All God's Creatures: A Theology of Creation* (Lanham, MD: Lexington Books/Fortress Academic, 2018), 4–7. Also see David Fergusson, "Humans Created according to the *Imago Dei*: An Alternative Proposal," *Zygon* 48 (2013): 439–53.

[6] Middleton, *The Liberating Image*, 45.

[7] Middleton, *The Liberating Image*, 46–47.

selem is primarily a reference to some physical or concrete quality, whereas *demut* means something more abstract.[8]

Subsequently, Middleton posits two things that follow from these observations of the literary context itself. First, neither *selem* nor *demut* is univocal in meaning. They are both polysemous and therefore have a respective range of signification. Second, even if we accept the general trend to distinguish between the two terms by means of "concreteness" versus "abstraction," they still do not disclose exactly what the resemblance or likeness of humanity to God is.[9]

In an effort to resolve the ambiguity of these terms, thinkers such as Karl Barth have proposed that the line "male and female he created them" (Gen 1:27), which immediately follows the identification of creation in *selem* of God, offers an interpretive key. This is the root of Barth's claim that relationality is the distinctive characteristic of humanity and therefore what is meant by the references to *selem* and *demut*.[10] Middleton insists that this interpretation is incorrect, at least from a literary perspective, because the third line of this particular Hebrew poetic

---

[8] Middleton, *The Liberating Image*, 48.

[9] Middleton, *The Liberating Image*, 48.

[10] See Karl Barth, *Church Dogmatics* III.1, trans. J. W. Edwards, O. Bussey, and Harold Knight (London: T & T Clark, 2004), 194–97. Here Barth introduces his descriptor *analogia relationis* as the distinctive characteristic of human personhood denoted by the *imago Dei*. Relatedly, Phyllis Trible argues that *imago Dei* (*selem* and *demut* in this instance) means that both those things "stereotypically" understood as "male and female" equally reflect both the masculine and feminine "qualities of God" (*God and the Rhetoric of Sexuality* [Minneapolis: Fortress Press, 1984], 16–21). However, Middleton makes a compelling syntactical argument against this reading. He observes that "male" (*zakar*) and "female" (*neqeba*) are biological, not social, terms and thus cannot support either the notion of human relationality or culturally male/female characteristics. Whereas Genesis 2 uses social categories of *is* (man) and *issa* (woman, wife), the terms *zakar* and *neqeba* from Genesis 1:27 are used of the animals that Noah brought into the ark in the flood account (6:19, 7:9) specifically to designate that they were pairs capable of reproduction (Middleton, *The Liberating Image*, 50).

construction does not repeat earlier patterns but introduces a new idea.[11] Therefore, the text itself provides us with no specified meaning, especially regarding human uniqueness.

The most formidable proposal Middleton introduces into the discussion relies not on exegesis of the Hebrew Bible as such, but requires an inter-textual reading drawing on Ancient Near Eastern texts that provide parallels in usage. Middleton constructs his proposal in two steps.

First, while it is not immediately clear what the precise meaning of *imago Dei* is, Middleton asserts there is an intentional connection established between *selem* and *demut* with *rada* (rule) two verses later in Genesis 1:28 along with the verb *kabas* (to subdue). Though often used in a royal sense, *rada* is understood by Middleton to include the semantic category of "shepherding" (for example, Ezek 34:4). Further support is lent to this argument by the presence of the animals, including livestock, in Genesis 1. Middleton suggests that in Genesis 1:28, *kabas* refers, minimally, to the "right of humanity to spread over the earth and make it their home. Since the earth has already sprouted with vegetation in 1:12 and plants for human consumption are mentioned in 1:29, *kabas* may even anticipate human cultivation of the earth by agriculture."[12] To understand what "rule" *(rada)* means here, it might be helpful to look at the broader context of creation during the preceding days during which each aspect of the created order (the firmament, the sun/moon, and so on) were expressed along with their purpose. The firmament separates; that is what it does and how it is intended to function. In this way *rada* may be a purpose statement that suggests the *imago Dei* should be understood in terms of the "rule" that human beings exercise by virtue of being human.[13]

Second, Middleton takes what he sees as the close association and perhaps purpose statement of *rada* and compares and contrasts this term and usage with intra-biblical passages elsewhere

---

[11] Middleton, *The Liberating Image*, 49–50.
[12] Middleton, *The Liberating Image*, 52.
[13] Middleton, *The Liberating Image*, 52–54.

in the Hebrew Bible. He then compares and contrasts *rada* with those of other Ancient Near Eastern texts. Middleton claims that this type of study renders two results.

> On the one hand, careful exegesis of Genesis 1:26–28, in conjunction with an intertextual reading of the symbolic world of Genesis 1, does indeed suggest that the *imago Dei* refers to human rule, that is, the exercise of power on God's behalf in creation. This may be articulated in two different, but complementary, ways. Humans are like God in exercising royal power on earth [and] the divine ruler *delegated* to humans a share in his rule of the earth.[14]

The ruling style and quality of oversight implied by *rada* is seen as modeled after divine action and intention. The condition of the possibility for this particular kind of rule is therefore humanity's creation *imago Dei*. In contrast to other Mesopotamian narratives in which only the monarch was granted a kind of semi-divine standing by virtue of titles like *imago Dei*, the narrative of Israel appears to be a democratizing concept that subverts the exclusivity of contemporaneous monarchical traditions. Regarding the *imago Dei*, Middleton notes that "correlative with this mutuality of power and agency is the implicit claim of the *imago Dei* that all persons have equal access to God simply by being human."[15] When examined alongside comparable Ancient Near Eastern texts and usage, *selem* and *demut* are deployed in a more egalitarian way, applied to all humans rather than a select individual or particular sect. Therefore, the *imago Dei* can be seen as the fulfillment of a universal duty or purpose performed rather than some particularly inherent trait or characteristic that identifies human uniqueness as such.[16]

---

[14] Middleton, *The Liberating Image*, 88.

[15] Middleton, *The Liberating Image*, 207.

[16] For an allied reconsideration of the *imago Dei*, see William L. Power, "*Imago Dei—Imitatio Dei*," *International Journal for Philosophy of Religion* 42 (1997): 131–41.

As thorough and insightful as Middleton's study is, it never-theless leaves us with a persistent sense of *imago Dei*'s ambiguity. There is nothing absolutely clear or conclusive about its meaning in the Hebrew Bible/Old Testament, and therefore we remain in a similarly uncertain place to where we began. The persis-tent ambiguity has elicited further critique from contemporary theologians who have presented alternative interpretations that provide additional insights that can ultimately help us situate the doctrine of *imago Dei* within a paradigm of catholicity.

Modern Approaches to the Doctrine

David Clough has argued that restricting the notion of *imago Dei* to human beings alone reinscribes a "human-separatist view that posits a qualitative distinction between human beings and other species that is incompatible with the belief that human beings evolved from other animals."[17] Against J. Wentzel Van Huys-steen, who has argued that human beings, through biological and cultural evolution, have crossed an absolute divide that dis-tinguishes them from other creatures, Clough is convinced that the inextricability of interspecies relationship presupposed by the theory of evolution prohibits such an absolute demarcation.[18] Clough accuses such "separatist" views as "pre-Darwinian" in that they fail "to appreciate the full consequences of what the Darwinian revolution means for Christian theology," a view echoed in the previous chapter.[19] Likened to issues such as gender

---

[17] David Clough, "All God's Creatures: Reading Genesis on Hu-man and Nonhuman Animals," in *Reading Genesis after Darwin*, ed. Stephen C. Barton and David Wilkinson (New York: Oxford University Press, 2009), 156.

[18] See J. Wentzel Van Huyssteen, *Alone in the World? Human Uniqueness in Science and Theology* (Grand Rapids, MI: Eerdmans, 2012). For a collection of essays offering commentary and response to the text, see Christopher Lilley and Daniel J. Pedersen, eds., *Human Origins and the Image of God: Essays in Honor of J. Wentzel van Huys-steen* (Grand Rapids, MI: Eerdmans, 2017).

[19] Clough, "All God's Creatures," 156.

equality and the immorality of slavery, Clough insists that we must allow our theological reflection on the *imago Dei* and creation to be challenged and informed by our scientific and cultural knowledge.[20] That the tradition of Christian theological reflection has been so overtly anthropocentric does not preclude the possibility of its revision, which is especially timely given the continuity recognized between humanity and nonhuman creatures in both scripture and the natural sciences as outlined in the previous chapters. In this same spirit several theologians have attempted just such a reconsideration of a more capacious meaning of *imago Dei*. Here we will examine three such lines of exploration: rejection of *imago Dei*; redefinition of *imago Dei*; and expansion of *imago Dei*.

Rejection of Imago Dei

Like many other theologians, David Cunningham does not find any compelling evidence to suggest that—at least, theologically—one can assert a definitive distinction between humans and other animals. Rather, so presupposed is such an absolute distinction that few theologians ever argue for it and instead simply take it for granted. And yet, Cunningham likens such an apodictic demarcation to other classical distinctions made throughout history and "justified" by ostensible empirical and cultural influences. Here one might think of subordinating and discriminatory distinctions based on sex or gender, sexual orientation, race or ethnicity, and the like. While Cunningham does not believe that the human/nonhuman distinction is necessarily as egregious as the examples just cited, he does want to contest such axiomatic distinctions and believes that they are not theologically warranted.[21]

---

[20] Clough, "All God's Creatures," 157–58.

[21] David S. Cunningham, "The Way of All Flesh: Rethinking the *Imago Dei*," in *Creaturely Theology: On God, Humans, and Other Animals*, ed. Celia Deane-Drummond and David Clough (London: SCM Press, 2009), 103.

Concerning the distinction generally presupposed in the doctrine of the *imago Dei*, Cunningham notes that "if we wish to maintain this distinction, we must do so on *theological* grounds because the scientific distinction has long fallen out of favor and no longer sustains the evidential critiques of history and research."[22] Indeed, evolutionary biology, contemporary ethology, psychology, and other social sciences have all bolstered a more complex vision of the creaturely family within which the human species is found, rather than affirming an absolute distinction that has been long presumed.[23] Cunningham sees the ambiguity of "image" *(selem)* to be almost insurmountable and, given the paucity of scriptural support for its usage, proposes an alternative term to serve as the focal point for the doctrine that would be rooted in a more common scriptural concept and be capacious enough to overcome what Clough calls the "human separatist" tendency of our deeply anthropocentric vision of *imago Dei.*

Instead of *image,* Cunningham makes the bold proposal that we ought to focus more on the term *flesh (sarx)*. His claim is that flesh *(sarx)* is the primary way in which God relates to creation, as one finds in John 1:14, where we read that "the Word became flesh [*sarx*]." God's relational life *ad extra* is not only with human beings, but rather it extends to all flesh, all creatures.[24] Although he does not fully develop his proposal to shift attention from image *(selem)* to flesh *(sarx)*, he does argue that Christian theologians would be able to develop a theology "that could better account for the complex and nuanced relationship between human beings and other animals," if they were to focus as much attention to flesh as has been afforded the *imago*.[25] Furthermore, he offers five heuristic points to guide future consideration and bolster the case for *sarx* over *imago*.

---

[22] Cunningham, "The Way of All Flesh," 103.

[23] This is something also affirmed by Fergusson, "Humans Created according to the *Imago Dei*," 441.

[24] Cunningham, "The Way of All Flesh," 114.

[25] Cunningham, "The Way of All Flesh," 117.

- *The abundance of biblical reference:* The term *flesh* (Hebrew *basar* and Greek *sarx*) appears 321 times in the NRSV translation of the Bible, which lends greater support for focusing on this term over the infrequently appearing *imago Dei*. Additionally, it is used in many ways, including to describe the body of both humans and nonhuman animals. The idea of kinship also appears frequently within the broader context of "flesh," such as when the expression "all flesh" is used in reference to all living creatures, which appears thirty-six times.

- *The relationship between God and "all flesh":* In several cases, particularly in the books of Genesis, Job, and throughout the Psalms, God's relationship to creation is described in terms of "all flesh" rather than restricted to human beings alone. This is precisely what is illustrated by the so-called Noahide covenant after the flood when God enters into renewed relationship with "all flesh."

- *Commonality and differentiation:* Unlike the expression *imago Dei* which has often been used in an absolutist, binary way, *flesh (basar, sarx)* offers both a sense of commonality and differentiation. Every creature has flesh, but there are many different kinds. Even Saint Paul writes about the different types of flesh found among creatures as diverse as human beings, birds, and other animals (cf. 1 Cor 15:39). It is a concept that speaks both to what is shared and what is distinguishing among the community of creation, something we explore in greater detail at the end of this chapter.

- *Linking Christology and creation:* Whereas *imago Dei* in the New Testament most often distances Christ from the rest of humanity, referring to a notably high christological characteristic, *flesh* is that which the incarnate Word shares most intimately with both human beings and the entire creation. In the Gospels and in early Christian tradition it is Christ's *fleshiness* that is treated as primary, his humanity and its accidental qualities are secondarily.[26]

---

[26] Some theologians have opted to read into the Genesis accounts of *imago Dei* the christological meaning of the concept present in the

- *The need for redemption throughout the entire cosmos:* Looking to the Pauline letters, among other sources, we can say that all of creation is somehow affected by the finitude of what we have long referred to as "the fall," which leads all of creation to groan for that shared redemption (for example, Romans 8). Because the entire creation needs healing, this further bolsters the significance of the previous heuristic point in which we reconnect the incarnation to all of creation, and that it is not just for human beings alone.[27]

Each of these themes draws on the broader theological and scriptural tradition to encourage reconsideration of the long-standing presumption of human uniqueness associated with the doctrine of *imago Dei* and refocus attention toward the broader reality of the community of creation. The means to achieving this correction, for Cunningham, involves, in effect, the rejection of the terminology of *imago Dei* in order to adopt a *sarx*-based grounding for a theological anthropology that takes as its starting point the whole community of creation.

Redefinition of Imago Dei

While some scholars have argued for jettisoning the term *imago Dei* altogether, seeking an alternative concept or term as Cunningham has, others have suggested that we might overcome the doctrine's anthropocentrism by redefining the meaning of the concept itself. Among those who have offered compelling

---

New Testament texts. For example, see Marc Cortez, *Christological Anthropology in Historical Perspective: Ancient and Contemporary Approaches to Theological Anthropology* (Grand Rapids, MI: Zondervan Publishing, 2016); Marc Cortez, *ReSourcing Theological Anthropology: A Constructive Account of Humanity in the Light of Christ* (Grand Rapids, MI: Zondervan Publishing, 2017); and John F. Kilner, *Dignity and Destiny: Humanity in the Image of God* (Grand Rapids, MI: Eerdmans, 2015); among others.

[27] Cunningham, "The Way of All Flesh," 114–17. For more on the eschatological dimensions of a more-capacious interpretation of *imago Dei*, see Horan, *All God's Creatures*, 67–78.

arguments in this vein is Joshua Moritz, who has written exten-
sively about the problematic and restrictive concerns surrounding
theologies of the *imago Dei* that identify the doctrine with "some
characteristic or capacity which presumably makes humans
unique—*in a non-trivial way*—from other animals and from
the non-human hominids."[28] Moritz refers to this widespread
tendency as the defense of "*Homo singularis*," or that species
which is special, unique, singular and, ultimately, above the
rest of creation. Typically, various thinkers identify a particular
capacity or characteristic of their choosing to symbolize the
qualitative difference between humans and nonhuman animals.
Among the most common characteristics are freedom, lack
of innate instincts, self-consciousness, self-awareness, culture,
rationality, religious thought and practice, moral behavior, and
emotive affectivity. Drawing on scientific, philosophical, and
theological resources that demonstrate the fallacy of uncritically accepting human uniqueness over against all nonhuman
creatures, Moritz suggests that a better way to understand the
imago Dei is in terms of a theology of election. By this he means
that there is nothing intrinsically physical, psychological, or ontological about *Homo sapiens* as such that qualifies the species
to claim creation according to the *imago Dei* exclusively. Rather,
one can ultimately claim humanity's exclusive right to the *imago*
on purely theological grounds with reference to God's volitional
act of choice—essentially, this means that God picks humanity
(elects) or calls humanity to be *imago Dei*.

Moritz makes clear that when he talks about election he
does not mean election in the classical Calvinist sense of double

---

[28] Joshua M. Moritz, "Evolution, the End of Human Uniqueness,
and the Election of the *Imago Dei*," *Theology and Science* 9 (2011):
307. Also see idem, "Animals and the Image of God in the Bible and
Beyond," *Dialog: A Journal of Theology* 48 (2009): 134–46; idem, "Human Uniqueness, The Other Hominids, and 'Anthropocentrism of the
Gaps' in the Religion and Science Dialogue," *Zygon* 47 (2012): 65–96;
and idem, "Made as Mirrors: Biblical and Neuroscientific Reflections
on Imaging God," *Ex Auditu* 32 (2016): 94–120.

predestination. Instead of the individualistic and arbitrary selection of some to salvation and others to damnation, Moritz uses "election" in the "historical or biblical concept."[29] Here, he is referencing the longstanding tradition of understanding that the community of Israel is regarded as God's "chosen people." It is a concrete conceptualization that is not tied to any particular merit, capacity, skill, or character of the people, but instead is understood according to God's free choice to call this community to a particular place and purpose in salvation history.

> Election in the Biblical understanding relates to a people whom God has chosen in the midst of history for a special *purpose* within the wider context of God's design. This purpose of election is furthermore defined not in terms of privilege, but rather it is for the sake of *service*.[30]

It does not take much effort to see how Moritz ties this scriptural concept to the theological doctrine of *imago Dei*. Rather than referring to some special aspect of the human species in terms of capacity or character, the doctrine of *imago Dei* understood through the lens of election suggests that God has exercised divine freedom in choosing this particular species—*Homo sapiens*—for a particular purpose within salvation history. That purpose, Moritz argues in keeping with the Eastern Christian tradition's interpretation of the primeval history in Genesis, is to be a steward of and priest on behalf of nonhuman creation. "As Abraham and Sarah are elected by God to be a *nation* (ethnicity or race) of priests and a light to the other *nations* (ethnicities or races) so Adam and Eve, as the primal human pair, are chosen and called to be a species of priests to the non-Adamic humans (the other hominids) and to other non-human

---

[29] Moritz, "Evolution, the End of Human Uniqueness, and the Election of the *Imago Dei*," 320.

[30] Moritz, "Evolution, the End of Human Uniqueness, and the Election of the *Imago Dei*," 321.

animals."[31] As opposed to relying on something conceived physically or ontologically, the *imago Dei* is understood in this context as a distinctive vocation or calling that humanity—and, for Moritz, *only humanity*—receives from God. It is a status that humans are meant to live into, striving to become what Moritz calls *Homo sanctus*—"holy humans," which are creatures set apart by God for a distinctive purpose in the plan of salvation. Moritz summarizes his point: "Human specialness lies not in the content of our characteristics, but in the very fact that *Homo Sapiens* are the animal species who are both called and chosen as God's image."[32]

There is much that is appealing about Moritz's redefinition of *imago Dei*, not least its ostensible alignment with the scriptural witness. Anticipating the work of other theologians who have called for an expansion of the *imago* to other creatures (something we examine in the next section), he explains that such a move is unwarranted by the tradition of biblical exegetical interpretation and Christian theological consensus. On this latter point he is correct. It is true that Christian theologians have largely operated with a "human separatist" hermeneutic over the centuries, presuming uniqueness that divides *Homo sapiens* from other creatures. However, given what we have already seen regarding the semantic and contextual ambiguity of the scriptural sources, it is hardly justifiable to claim that the "Jewish and Christian traditions agree that the divine image and likeness applies to humans and *humans alone*."[33] In fact, while the text of Genesis 1 clearly makes reference to humans having been created *imago Dei*, the theological and biblical tradition simply does not *preclude* nonhuman creation from being recognized

---

[31] Moritz, "Evolution, the End of Human Uniqueness, and the Election of the *Imago Dei*," 324.

[32] Moritz, "Evolution, the End of Human Uniqueness, and the Election of the *Imago Dei*," 330.

[33] Moritz, "Evolution, the End of Human Uniqueness, and the Election of the *Imago Dei*," 318.

as also bearing the *imago*. While Moritz's work offers a novel approach to understanding the *imago Dei* that also maintains human uniqueness, other theologians do not necessarily see the value in protecting this extrinsic anthropocentrism.

Expansion of Imago Dei

Langdon Gilkey and Leslie Muray serve as representatives of theologians who do not regard the uncritically accepted tradition on exegetical and doctrinal anthropocentrism something to maintain in the manner of Moritz. Gilkey has argued that we should extend our understanding of what it means to represent the Divine according to the *imago Dei* and in doing so we will be able to include the entire natural world to some degree within this theological category.[34] Returning to something of a more traditional consideration of capacities or characteristics, Gilkey suggests that our consideration of the *imago* begin with an appreciation for those divine characteristics that have been unveiled through revelation. Among these characteristics he identifies power, order, and the dialectical relationship between life and death.[35] Gilkey makes the case that "nature manifests or reveals certain unmistakable signs of the divine" in an analogous way to the manner in which humanity has long been understood to manifest such signs.[36] The semantic framework Gilkey proposes is that of a vestigial approach, according to which we might "draw out, articulate, and so bring into clearer view those traces of the divine, of the activity and presence of God in nature, that are to be dimly discerned in our experience of nature."[37] He explains that anthropologists and other scholars have noted the longstanding presence of such recognition of the divine in nature

---

[34] See Langdon Gilkey, *Nature, Reality, and the Sacred: The Nexus of Science and Religion* (Minneapolis: Fortress Press, 1993), 175–92.

[35] Langdon Gilkey, "Nature as the Image of God: Signs of the Sacred," *Theology Today* 51 (1994): 127–41.

[36] Gilkey, "Nature as the Image of God," 127.

[37] Gilkey, "Nature as the Image of God," 128.

as a tenet of archaic religious traditions.[38] This appreciation for
the manifold ways the Divine is manifest in creation, beyond an
exclusively anthropocentric view, has been lost in recent history,
especially in the West. Nevertheless, the Christian tradition re-
tains often overlooked resources that can be retrieved in order
to renew such an awareness of the *imago Dei* in both human
and nonhuman creation.

Gilkey proposes three aspects of the divine image that are
borne not just by humans but also by the entire natural world.
The first is the *dynamic power* present within the order of
creation. Drawing on the notion that power's dynamic process
within creation can be equated with being as such, "to existing,
that is, to coming into being, remaining there, and projecting
into the future," he sees the presence of the divine image in the
collective community of creation's creating, sustaining, and moving into a future.[39] This would appear to align comfortably with
what we explored in the last chapter concerning the promise of
evolution.

The second aspect is the *order* present within the community
of creation. Gilkey asserts that order is present throughout the
whole of creation, though analogously existing within it according to whichever "level" of creation we are examining at a given
moment. Empirical science and technology have disclosed this
reality, mysterious as it nonetheless remains. Echoing Elizabeth
Johnson, who sees a pneumatological process under way in what
Gilkey describes as the paradox of order amid "radical spontane-
ity and openness," the assertion here is that the order established
by the Creator is both micro cosmically and macro cosmically
present throughout the natural world.[40] The principle of an

---

[38] For an excellent study of the complementarity of such indigenous
or archaic religions and the developments of phenomenology, see David
Abram, *The Spell of the Sensuous: Perception and Language in a More-
Than-Human World* (New York: Vintage Books, 1996).

[39] Gilkey, "Nature as the Image of God," 129.

[40] Gilkey, "Nature as the Image of God," 132–33. Also see Elizabeth
A. Johnson, "Does God Play Dice? Divine Providence and Chance,"

ordered creation is not present only within the human species but found within the whole community of creation.

The third aspect is what Gilkey describes as the *unity of death with life* in nature. Admittedly, this is perhaps the weakest characteristic of the three he proposes. He argues that this is, like power and order, a unifying principle of creation shared across species-delimited borders. "Everywhere we look life is interlocked with death, being seems intertwined with non-being: in nature, in historical experience, and in individual life."[41] Gilkey then examines the ways that the unity of life and death in nature connects to divine revelation:

> What is only dimly and obscurely seen in nature, and reflected in early human religion, becomes clear and explicit in revelation. Then we can, with hindsight, see or begin to see what these signs and traces in nature meant. Life is fulfilled only when it is willing to give itself for another, only when love directs and suffuses the affirmation of life. And such love incarnates the courage that makes the affirmation of life in the face of possible death a reality. Correspondingly, the God who creates life and death and who wills a world structured in terms of both is also the God who calls us to life and to face death for God's sake—and who promises an existence beyond life and death.[42]

Though perhaps more of a reach than power and order, the interplay between life and death at all levels of creation can be seen as reflecting what is concretely disclosed in the scriptural witness of divine revelation. The interdependence of each aspect of the whole community of creation bears an intuitive likeness,

---

Theological Studies 57 (1996): 3–18; and idem, *Ask the Beasts: Darwin and the God of Love* (New York: Bloomsbury, 2014), 154–80.

[41] Gilkey, "Nature as the Image of God," 137.

[42] Gilkey, "Nature as the Image of God," 141.

carries a distinguishable trace of the *agapic* love described as God's very being in the New Testament and modeled for us in the life, death, and resurrection of Jesus of Nazareth.[43]

Leslie Muray proposes a more expansive way to consider the doctrine of *imago Dei*. Unlike Cunningham, who proposed bracketing the terminology of "image" to focus on "flesh," Muray wants to rehabilitate the category alongside Gilkey to include nonhuman creatures with their human counterparts within the one community of creation. Setting up his proposal in contradistinction to J. Wentzel van Huyssteen's defense of human uniqueness, Muray argues that we cannot go beyond a claim of "human distinctiveness."[44] The simple argument for this terminology is this: "While *human uniqueness* has the connotation of a 'quantum leap' between the human and non-human, *human distinctiveness* suggests that while there is differentiation between the human and non-human, that difference is not *absolute*."[45] Furthermore, "while humans are different from non-humans and have a 'special' role to play (as do all species), we are firmly implanted in non-human nature. . . . Humans and non-humans alike are part of the natural world. The difference between humans and non-humans is a matter of degree and not of kind."[46]

Muray's contribution to this discussion of the *imago Dei* is found in his argument that the concept of *imago Dei* is best

---

[43] For more on an *agapic* ethic of creation, see Christopher J. Vena, "Beyond Stewardship: Toward an Agapeic Enviromental Ethic," PhD diss., Marquette University, 2009.

[44] Leslie A. Muray, "Human Uniqueness vs. Human Distinctiveness: The *Imago Dei* in the Kinship of All Creatures," *American Journal of Theology and Philosophy* 28 (2007): 306.

[45] Muray, "Human Uniqueness vs. Human Distinctiveness," 306.

[46] Muray, "Human Uniqueness vs. Human Distinctiveness," 306. Additionally, although she is not as uncomfortable with the emphasis on rationality as a dimension of humanity's expression of the *imago Dei* as others, Kathryn Tanner nevertheless also allows for a continuum or system of degree in assessing the whole of creation's ability to, in some way, bear the divine image. See *Christ the Key* (New York: Cambridge University Press, 2010), see esp. 9–17.

understood as an expression of "individual-in-community." Muray explains:

> Describing the individual, human and non-human, as an individual-in-community is to claim that the self is a relational self, internally related to its environment, human and non-human. The word "community" includes the whole of the environment, human and non-human, of any individual event. The individuated event is part of the whole of that community, and the community is a part of the individuated event.[47]

In other words, to understand the *imago Dei* as pertaining to a collective network of relations—or, as Muray suggests, "the all-inclusive matrix of relationality"[48]—is to incorporate the truth of the community of creation unveiled in scripture and confirmed by contemporary natural science, especially evolutionary biology, into Christian doctrine explicitly.

While the contributions of all those considered in this section shed valuable light on the discussion of how best to understand the doctrine of *imago Dei* in our contemporary setting, the intuition to expand the theological concept of *imago Dei* is more in keeping with a hermeneutic of catholicity than the rejection of the term, which will prove exceptionally difficult given its current instantiation in the tradition, or a redefinition of the term that continues to maintain a strict anthropocentrism, as appealing as Moritz's argument may be. Nevertheless, while illuminating, what Gilkey, Muray, and others have done so far falls short of accounting for both the inclusivity sought through doctrinal expansion (and which has been demonstrated reasonably well so far) *and* the distinctiveness of the human person within the broader community of creation. While the extensive work needed to develop this doctrine more fully exceeds the limits of this book, I propose now a tentative path forward.

---

[47] Muray, "Human Uniqueness vs. Human Distinctiveness," 308.
[48] Muray, "Human Uniqueness vs. Human Distinctiveness," 309.

Toward Inclusivity
and Distinction

So, why can't we talk about all God's creatures bearing the *imago Dei*? In light of the ambiguity of the originating concept in Genesis and the doctrine's history so far explored in this chapter, the approach most in keeping with a hermeneutic of catholicity is one that incudes expanding the *imago Dei* while also exploring the manifold ways this doctrine becomes manifested in the respective species and individual creatures God brings into existence and sustains in life. Neither the rejection of the doctrine of *imago Dei* nor its constitutive language is a tenable option; its place as a central theological concept in the Christian tradition seems reasonably secure. While others have suggested a significant reconceptualization of the concept that aligns more with the biological sciences yet maintains a noted anthropocentrism, I do not believe the latter point is necessary. Merely expanding the target population to whom the *imago Dei* applies in a universal sense, while seemingly offering an inclusive strategy, nevertheless risks flattening the creational landscape and does not adequately respect the individual integrity, dignity, and value of such a diverse community of creation.

Instead, I propose an approach to the doctrine of *imago Dei* that prioritizes both inclusivity and distinction. A paradigm governed by a concurrent commitment to inclusion and distinction can fit with the truths of evolutionary biology while also respecting the particularity of each creature as it reflects the Creator in its own way. And this approach to the *imago Dei*, drawing on the doctors of the church and the resources of the tradition, remains entirely orthodox.

First, the inclusive dimension of the *imago Dei*. Although David Cunningham ultimately concludes that the term *image* may be too problematic to sustain continued use in a theological anthropology that takes seriously the natural sciences, his points about the broader applicability of *flesh (sarx)* can also be read into *imago*. We can all agree that the account in Genesis 1 affirms humanity as created *imago Dei*; however, it does not provide any proviso about an exclusive claim to that right. Cunningham takes this lack of proscription as a constructive opportunity to offer one more expansive reading of the *imago*. He returns to the word *image* itself in order to illustrate that it necessarily resists being conscripted for demarcating purposes such as has historically been the case with human beings. Instead, the term better designates something roughly analogous to degree or a continuum of representation. His example of visual art is worth citing at length:

> The word "image" does not lend itself to a simple either/or test. Imagine a painting that you know well; it might be Van Gogh's *Vase with Fifteen Sunflowers* or Caravaggio's *Calling of St. Matthew* or Mary Cassatt's *The Child's Bath*. Now imagine a very fine reproduction of that painting, of the same size and shape, with every detail precisely in place, right down to the texture of the paint and the irregularly faded colors of the pigments. This reproduction—so accurate it borders on forgery—would certainly be an image of the original. Now imagine a slightly less accurate reproduction—smaller, perhaps, or without texture. It would seem odd to deny such a work the label "image," when a momentary glance would immediately identify it as a reproduction of the famous painting. Now make the image a bit less detailed—a very small reproduction, perhaps, printed from a home computer on a printer with fairly low resolution. Still an image? How about one of those modern digital mosaics, in which the various colors of the whole are duplicated by individual blocks that are themselves images of something else altogether? When we get up close, this will look very different from the original; but from a distance it is clearly recognizable as a reproduction. Now imagine a child's watercolor drawing of the painting, unrecognizable as such to anyone but the fondest parent. At what point (in this journey of increasing distance from the

original) does the attempted copy cease to be appropriately
described as an image?[49]

Though imperfect, his point about the analogous quality of
imago is well put. It is reasonable to consider that all creatures,
like individual artworks brought into existence by the divine
Artist, bear some likeness to their creator. This is not something
novel or merely contemporary. The medieval Franciscan theologian and doctor of the church Saint Bonaventure (d. 1274)
builds on the work of his Christian theological predecessors to
argue that *all creatures* are a vestige *(vestigium)* of the Creator.
Understood from its etymological roots, Bonaventure conceives
of each aspect of the created order as bearing something like a
"footprint" *(vestigium)* of the Divine, a particular imprint of
that which is the source of the thing's very existence. Because
all creatures have an intrinsic relationship to God as *principium
creativum*, every creature is therefore a vestige.[50] Every stone,
blade of grass, tree, squirrel, bat, dog, and person is, at least,
a vestige of the Creator and therefore (a) inherently capable of
revealing something about God to the rest of creation, and (b)
intrinsically related to all other aspects of creation according to
what Francis of Assisi recognized as a singular cosmic family and
what we might call the community of creation. Though Bonaventure certainly did not have the scientific resources we do today
to understand the multiple ways we human beings relate to one
another and the rest of creation, we can nonetheless look to his
intuition that God is reflected in all creation as further support
for a contemporary and inclusive rereading of the *imago Dei*.

---

[49] Cunningham, "The Way of All Flesh," 110.

[50] See Bonaventure, *Quaestiones disp. De scientia Christi*, q. 4, resp.,
ed. Zachary Hayes (St. Bonaventure, NY: Franciscan Institute Publications, 1992), 135–36 (*Opera Omnia*, V:24a); and Bonaventure, *Quaestiones disp. De mysterio SS. Trinitatis*, q. 1, art. 2, resp., ed. Zachary
Hayes (St. Bonaventure, NY: Franciscan Institute Publications, 1979),
128–29 (*Opera Omnia*, V:54). Also see J. A. Wayne Hellmann, *Divine
and Created Order in Bonaventure's Theology* (St. Bonaventure, NY:
Franciscan Institute Publications, 2001), 107.

The second dimension of the *imago Dei* is that of distinctiveness. There is a reasonable fear on the part of some that when theologians begin talking about a more inclusive understanding of *imago Dei* that we are in effect wiping out differences between creatures. The logical terminus of such thinking resembles something of the Jain religious tradition, which recognizes the universal sacredness of all life on a more or less equal footing. In other words, the fear is that to say all creatures bear the *imago Dei* is to suggest earthworms are equal to apes and squirrels are equal to humans in all respects. This line of thinking arises from centuries of our associating the doctrine of *imago Dei* with a rotating list of ostensibly unique human characteristics. Rather, a more catholic understanding of *imago Dei* is one that—as we have already argued in earlier chapters—does not uncritically begin with the human person alone but resituates us within the broader community of creation. Once we engage our theological imagination in such a way as to start inclusively, we can then state with confidence that indeed all creatures bear the image of God in some way, but each does so according to its species and in line with God's plan for creation. This is where the distinctiveness of creation comes in, including the distinctiveness of the human person with regard to other creatures.

Returning again to the Franciscan theological tradition, this diverse reflection of the divine *imago* is present in Francis of Assisi's famous *Canticle of the Creatures*, wherein this thirteenth-century patron saint of ecology offers a poetic reflection on the manifold ways the various aspects of creation give praise to God:

> [1]Most High, all-powerful, good Lord,
> Yours are the praises, the glory, and the honor,
> and all blessing,
> [2]To You alone, Most High, do they belong,
> and no human is worthy to mention Your
> name.
> [3]Praised be You, my Lord, with all Your
> creatures,
> especially Sir Brother Sun,

who is the day and through whom You give
us light.
[4]And he is beautiful and radiant with great
splendor;
and bears a likeness of You, Most High One.
[5]Praised be You, my Lord, through Sister
Moon and the stars,
in heaven You formed them clear and precious
and beautiful.
[6]Praised be You, my Lord, through Brother
Wind,
and through the air, cloudy and serene, and
every kind of weather,
through whom You give sustenance to Your
creatures.
[7]Praised be You, my Lord, through Sister
Water,
who is very useful and humble and precious
and chaste.
[8]Praised be You, my Lord, through Brother
Fire,
through whom You light up the night,
and he is beautiful and playful and robust and
strong.
[9]Praised be You, my Lord, through our Sister
Mother Earth,
who sustains and governs us,
and who produces various fruit with colored
flowers and herbs.
[10]Praised be You, my Lord, through those who
give pardon for Your love,
and bear infirmity and tribulation.
[11]Blessed are those who endure in peace
for by You, Most High, shall they be crowned.
[12]Praised be You, my Lord, through our Sister
Bodily Death,
from whom no one living can escape.

Woe to those who die in mortal sin.
¹³Blessed are those whom death will find in
     Your most holy will,
for the second dearth shall do them no harm.
¹⁴Praise and bless my Lord and give Him
     thanks
and serve Him with great humility.[51]

The canticle begins with an address to God as Creator and Lord of creation: "Most High, all-powerful, good Lord, Yours are the praises, the glory, and the honor, and all blessing, to You alone, Most High, do they belong, and no human is worthy to mention Your name."[52] The significance of this particular address to God and the immediate claim that human persons are not worthy to *speak* the name of God is often underappreciated. The significance of this proscription is that humanity, due to sin rooted in pride and hubris, has forgotten its intrinsic relationship with the rest of creation and rightful place within the created order, which is ostensibly reflected in the impediment of humanity from recognizing its right relationship to the Creator and offering, in a literal sense, *orthodoxy* or "right praise." Immediately, however, Francis recognizes that the rest of the created order, although similarly finite, is not impeded by sin from "praising" God and doing so in diverse ways.[53] What follows in verses three through

---

[51] Francis of Assisi, "The Canticle of the Creatures," in *Francis of Assisi: Early Documents*, ed. Regis A. Armstrong, J. A. Wayne Hellmann, and William Short, 3 vols. (New York: New City Press, 1999), 1:113–14. I have added numbers corresponding to the verses as they appear in the critical edition for ease of reference. The organization of the translation according to sense lines follows the format of the English translation editors of the text. This text is hereafter cited as *FAED*.

[52] Francis of Assisi, "The Canticle of the Creatures," in *FAED* 1:113.

[53] The moral context of this opening sequence is affirmed elsewhere in the authentic writings of Francis of Assisi. For example, see Francis of Assisi, "Admonition V," nos. 1–5, in *FAED* 1:131: "Consider, O human being, in what great excellence the Lord God has placed you, for He created and formed you to the image of His beloved Son according to the body and to His likeness according to the Spirit. *And all creatures*

nine is a series of joyful professions of gratitude for and recognition of the rest of creation's "rightly ordered praise." The sun, the moon, the earth, stars, wind, fire, and water are all acknowledged for the praise of God that is offered by and through them.[54] The nonhuman creatures have, according to Francis's cosmic and fraternal vision, no inhibition or problem praising God through the actions that most accurately reflects God's plan for a well-ordered creation. It is humanity—which Francis explicitly names in verse ten—that must be reminded of what it means to be truly human and therefore truly reflect the Creator.[55] Humanity does not stand apart from the rest of creation in Francis's eyes, but all men and women do need to be reminded that they give praise to God when they are in *right relationship* through the giving of pardon, the bearing of infirmity and tribulation, and endurance in peace.[56] For Francis of Assisi, nonhuman creatures actually reflect the Creator better than we typically do. Consequently, the nonhuman aspects of creation can actually serve as teachers

---

under heaven serve, know, and obey their Creator, each according to its own nature, better than you. And even the demons did not crucify Him, but you, together with them, have crucified Him and are still crucifying Him by delighting in vices and sins. In what, then, can you boast? Even if you were so skillful and wise that you possessed all knowledge, knew how to interpret every kind of language, and to scrutinize heavenly matters with skill: you could not boast in these things," emphasis added.

[54] There has long been a scholarly debate about the most authentic translation of Francis's use of the word *per* in the vernacular Umbrian-Italian dialect of his day as the preposition preceding each aspect of creation in the canticle. Most scholars today translate it as "through," with the generally recognized denotation that each aspect of the created order Francis names is, in fact, praising God by doing what it was created or intended to do (in contradistinction to humanity, for example, which sins and lives in discord with God's original intention, according to Francis). For more, see Susanna Peters Coy, "The Problem of 'Per' in the *Cantico di frate sole* of Saint Francis," *Modern Language Notes* 91 (1976): 1–11.

[55] See Francis of Assisi, "The Canticle of the Creatures," v. 10, in *FAED* 1:114 (122–23).

[56] Francis of Assisi, "The Canticle of the Creatures," v. 10, in *FAED* 1:114 (122–23).

and models, reflecting God and reminding human persons to live their vocations as creatures in relationship.

So much of our way of viewing the world around us is shaped by a kind of anthropological hubris grounded in a sense of human separatism presupposed in the traditional approaches to the *imago Dei*. More recently, various scholars have been following in Francis's footsteps, considering the ways that creaturely distinctiveness need not be demarcated only along the lines of human and nonhuman but might be broader and more relative. The work of Jakob von Uexküll (d. 1944), the founder of so-called semiotic biology, comes to mind as a useful analog in thinking about *imago Dei* in its myriad manifestations. Uexküll has gained some renewed attention in recent years, especially for his research into the social and physical *Umwelten* (roughly translated "environments" or "worldviews") of various species and inquiry into the unity of nature.[57] During his graduate studies he was strongly influenced by two biological schools of thought that represented two poles on the spectrum of the then-contemporary biological frontier: First, the relatively new theories of Charles Darwin (1809–82); and second, the contemporaneous thought of Karl Ernst von Baer (1792–1876).[58] He was convinced (perhaps mistakenly) that Darwin's approach bordered too closely on complete randomness without accounting for the principles of scientific law according to which nature conformed. Uexküll didn't discount the reality of evolution; in fact, he affirmed at least the validity of Darwin's (and his predecessors') claims.[59] Additionally, he had a problem with Baer's overly teleological view,

---

[57] Most of his work remains untranslated, but in recent years several key texts have been translated into English, including Jakob von Uexküll, *A Foray into the Worlds of Animals and Humans with a Theory of Meaning*, trans. Joseph O'Neil (Minneapolis: University of Minnesota Press, 2010).

[58] See Brett Buchanan, *Onto-Ethologies: The Animal Environments of Uexküll, Heidegger, Merleau-Ponty, and Deleuze* (Albany: SUNY Press, 2008), 9.

[59] Kalevi Kull, "Jakob von Uexküll: An Introduction," *Semiotica* 134 (2001): 7–8.

holding that the teleological view has a "deceptive tendency to anthropomorphize nature; that is, to see nature as guided toward ends that only we humans can objectively perceive."[60] Uexküll sought to develop something of a middle ground, articulating what he called the "conformity with a plan" (*Planmäßigkeit* in German) approach to biology. As Brett Buchanan explains:

> Uexküll's "conformity with plan" attempts to steer a path between the mechanical laws of chemistry and physics and the apparently random variations in nature suggested by Darwinism. For Uexküll, nature is neither entirely causal, nor is it just random; it is neither simply physical, nor is it spiritual. Rather, nature accords with an overarching plan that has set parameters in which life forms can interact (thus not entirely random) as well as inclusive of agents and forces other than the parental genes as developmentally constitutive for the organism (thus not exclusively materialistic or organic).[61]

In addition to his formation in the biological sciences, Uexküll's outlook was deeply shaped by the philosophy of Immanuel Kant (1724–1804). In fact, Uexküll opens his 1926 masterwork *Theoretical Biology* with neither Baer nor Darwin but with Kant. He writes that the task of biology consists in expanding the results of Kant's investigations, which he summarizes succinctly, stating that "all reality is subjective appearance."[62] Uexküll's interpretation of Kant's philosophy serves as the foundation for his guiding thesis: "The reality we know and experience is ultimately what we subjectively perceive in the world. There is no objective reality in the form of objects, things, or the world; there is nothing outside of the individually subjective experiences that create a world as mean-

---

[60] Buchanan, *Onto-Ethologies*, 20.
[61] Buchanan, *Onto-Ethologies*, 19.
[62] Jakob von Uexküll, *Theoretical Biology*, trans. D. L. McKinnon (New York: Harcourt Brace, 1927), xv.

ingful." In other words, "Reality is created through the experiences of each and every subject, and this, as we shall see, holds for all animals just as much as it does for humans."[63] Because we have for so long constructed a worldview in which human beings are the only subjects, we have neglected to consider that all creatures—human and nonhuman—do not perceive the world the same. Just because we do not perceive the world as other animals do and, conversely, they do not perceive the world as we do, does not mean that nonhuman animals do not have subjective experiences of the world and, we might add, of the Creator.

Uexküll boldly and insightfully argues that *all* creatures are meaning makers, but we are blinded by a pervasive anthropocentrism. Uexküll writes in his 1934 book, *A Foray into the Worlds of Animals and Humans*:

> We comfort ourselves all too easily with the illusion that the relations of another kind of subject to the things of its environment play out in the same space and time as the relations that link us to the things of our human environment. This illusion is fed by the belief in the existence of one and only one world, in which all living beings are encased. From this arises the widely held conviction that there must be one and only one space and time for all living beings. Only recently [*again, this was written in the 1930s*] have physicists raised doubts as to the existence of one universe with one space valid for all beings.[64]

In terms of the contention of many philosophers and theologians that nonhuman animals do not have access to "world," Uexküll would concur insofar as what was meant by "world" was *this particular human person's* "world" or *Umwelt*. However, Uexküll strongly argues against the hegemony of human experience as determinative or absolute for all creation. Instead,

---

[63] In Buchanan, *Onto-Ethologies*, 13.
[64] Uexküll, *A Foray into the Worlds of Animals and Humans*, 54.

Uexküll reacts to the then (and even now) pervasive physiological presupposition that denies any kind of subjectivity to nonhuman animals. This inherited way of thinking, so prominently displayed in the influential twentieth-century philosopher Martin Heidegger's work and in the uncritically accepted foundations of many theologians and ethicists today, posits "one objective environment for all life forms and, subsequently, proceeds to analyze animals from the outside in."[65]

This way of viewing the world around us, of making judgments about nonhuman aspects of creation from our vantage point alone, reflects a fundamental anthropological hubris and is borne out in the traditional approaches to the *imago Dei*. In his 1940 text *A Theory of Meaning* Uexküll likens this present analysis of nonhuman creation to studying a house. He writes:

> If we compare an animal's body with a house, then the anatomists have studied closely the way it is built and the physiologists have studied closely the mechanical appliances located in the house. Ecologists, too, have demarcated and investigated the garden in which the house is located. But the garden has always been depicted as it offers itself to our human eye, and it has therefore been neglected to take into account how the garden changes when looked at by the subject who lives in the house.[66]

We cannot be content to presume that because a squirrel is not a human it therefore does not experience meaning or even the world building that Heidegger and others withhold for humans alone. Nonhuman creatures are just as much subjects as human creatures are, and they also have worlds of their own, integrated

---

[65] Geoffrey Winthrop-Young, "Afterword—Bubbles and Webs: A Backdoor Stroll through the Readings of Uexküll," in Uexküll, *A Foray into the Worlds of Animals and Humans*, 231.

[66] Jakob von Uexküll, *A Theory of Meaning*, trans. Joseph D. O'Neil (Minneapolis: University of Minneapolis Press, 2010), 200.

and complex worlds in which meaning is made and in which they themselves are constructed just as we are in our own world.

Using human language and experience, Uexküll judges what we might call the relative complexity of each creature's world. "All animal subjects," he writes, "from the simplest to the most complex, are inserted into their environments to the same degree of perfection. The simple animal has a simple environment; the multiform animal has an environment just as richly articulated as it is."[67] What we know with more or less certainty is the experience of our *human world*, our *Umwelt*. What Uexküll likewise affirms is that all creatures similarly have their own *world*, their *Umwelt*. We cannot know apodictically what that world of another creature is like, for it is ultimately a view reserved for the resident of the "house" Uexküll described earlier. However, we can, through our observation and imagination, consider what the experience of the other might be like. At the very least we can gain an appreciation for the fact that other creatures indeed *have* a subjective experience of meaning making. "Organisms, according to Uexküll, actively interpret their surroundings as replete with meaningful signs. They are not merely passive instruments or message bearers, but actively engaged in the creation of a significant environment."[68]

Creatures, human and nonhuman alike, have a priori perceptive capacities for objects within our respective *Umwelten*. There are things that human beings perceive and interpret that have, as it were, no meaning for a squirrel. The converse is also true. Some of Uexküll's most famous theoretical contributions center on intellectual case studies involving different types of creatures and extrapolating their possible *Umwelten* based on observation and biological study. Some of the classic examples include amoebas, sea urchins, fish, dogs, snails, birds, spiders, flies, bears, ants, and the tick. Due to the limitations of space here, I will prescind

---

[67] Uexküll, *A Foray into the Worlds of Animals and Humans*, 50.
[68] Buchanan, *Onto-Ethologies*, 32.

from the details of these respective *Umwelten* and draw instead on the philosopher John Deely's keen summarization:

> What Uexküll uniquely realized was that the physical environment, in whatever sense it may be said to be the "same" for all organisms, is not the world in which any given species as such actually lives out its life. No. Each biological life-form, by reason of its distinctively bodily constitution (its "biological heritage," as we may say), is suited only to certain parts and aspects of the vast physical universe. And when this "suitedness to" takes the bodily form of cognitive organs, such as are our own senses, or the often quite different sensory modalities discovered in other lifeforms [such as in a bacterium or tick], then those aspects and only those aspects of the physical environment which are proportioned to those modalities become "objectified," that is to say, made present not merely physically but cognitively as well.[69]

It is not simply a matter of what this or that creature, human or otherwise, can "sense" with the sensory receptors with which each species is endowed. Rather, it is a matter of *how* those things that are perceived in the "world" are networked together to constitute "objects of experience."[70]

Perhaps Uexküll's greatest gift to theologians is the articulation that all creatures experience a world and make meaning according to their respective *Umwelt*. Nonhuman creatures are not simply "objects" or biological "machines," as the traditional anthropocentric readings of *imago Dei* have contended; rather, all creatures are makers of meaning within their environments—as limited or capacious as each is (and how to judge that should not be limited to the human person through human experience alone). This sense of distinctive *Umwelten* for each creature offers a scientific and phenomenological analog to the theological

---

[69] John Deely, "Umwelt," *Semiotica* 134 (2001): 126.
[70] Deely, "Umwelt," 127.

doctrine of *imago Dei* more broadly conceived. Indeed, humans reflect the divine image when, as Francis noted, we live in such a way and pattern our choices after God's plan for us. So, too, our nonhuman creaturely neighbors reflect the divine image when they live and move and have their being in accord with God's plan for them.

This renewed approach to the *imago Dei,* one that prioritizes inclusivity and distinctiveness, serves as a foundation or starting point for reconsidering this central Christian doctrine in light of a hermeneutic of catholicity. In the spirit of this theological project of wholemaking, we now shift our focus from our place within and interrelatedness to the broader community of creation to look at the human family more specifically, always taking for granted what we have laid out already in these first three chapters.

Part II

Exploring
the Human Person

Chapter 4

Individually Loved into Existence

Having explored the foundations for a contemporary theological anthropology grounded in a renewed sense of creation and humanity's place within it in the first part of this book, we now turn our attention to the human person. While we cannot claim human uniqueness, separatism, or exceptionalism in terms of an absolute break from the rest of creation, as previously discussed, we may rightly talk about the human person—or, more broadly, the species *Homo sapiens*—in distinctive terms. Humans are of a kind, a distinctive collection of creatures that can be recognized, classified, and studied as a group. Over the centuries Western Christian thinkers that have been shaped by Hellenistic philosophical culture and worldviews have approached the human person with an interest in what is shared in common. These characteristics, which are thought to be timeless truths, make humans the unique and superior beings that they are. Essentially, it is often simply called human nature. This nature is traditionally viewed as universal and atemporal, the same for every person at every era.

Chances are that this initially seems correct to many Christians, and the reason for the perceived sensibility of this description of human nature is that we have been socialized to think this way and our theological reflection has likewise presumed this to be universally true. However, the emphasis on an unchanging human nature places a nearly exclusive focus on what is universal to the exclusion of what is particular. Instead of an understanding of humanity that is wholemaking, which would account for both what is shared in common as well as what is distinct about each creature in general and human person in particular, the tradition of disproportionate to nearly exclusive attention to the universal has resulted in a distorted sense of essentialism. But this does not have to be the case. If we allow ourselves to look back into the Christian tradition, we may retrieve resources that help us rethink our understanding of the human person so as to avoid some of the pitfalls and challenges that persist in contemporary theological anthropology.

Medieval Franciscan philosopher and theologian Blessed John Duns Scotus (d. 1308) offers us an often overlooked resource for theological anthropology in his unique theory of the principle of individuation, popularly known as *haecceitas*.[1] For several reasons identified below, Scotus's approach offers rich possibilities for contemporary retrieval and critical engagement. His concerns were not those of contemporary theologians. It is therefore not my aim to suggest that this medieval Franciscan anticipated what we have come to recognize as problematic about essentialism and other implications that have arisen from

---

[1] Due to the dearth of instances in which Scotus explicitly uses the term "principle of individuation," some scholars, such as Jorge J. E. Gracia, prefer to use the term "individuating entity" or some other moniker. However, as Allan Wolter has argued, the term that Scotus's disciples came to adopt (*haecceitas*) best reflects the Scotist tradition in this regard. For this reason I will use *haecceitas* when referring to Scotus's "principle of individuation" or "individuating entity." See Jorge J. E. Gracia, "Individuality and the Individuating Entity in Scotus's *Ordinatio*: An Ontological Characterization," in *John Duns Scotus: Metaphysics and Ethics*, ed. Ludger Honnefelder, Rega Wood, and Mechthild Dreyer (Leiden: E. J. Brill Publishers, 1996), 229–49; and Allan Wolter, "Introduction," in *Early Oxford Lecture on Individuation*, ed. Allan Wolter (St. Bonaventure, NY: Franciscan Institute Publications, 2005), xi–xii. For an in-depth study of the emergence, history, and usage of the term *haecceitas*, see Robert Andrews, "Haecceity in the Metaphysics of John Duns Scotus," in *Johannes Duns Scotus 1308–2008: Die Philosophischen Perspektiven seines Werkes*, ed. Ludger Honnefelder et al. (Münster: Aschendorff, 2010), 151–62.

the standard assumptions associated with a general approach to human nature. Nevertheless, the unique theory posited by Scotus (known even in his time as the Subtle Doctor) for understanding the particularity and individuation of "singulars" in his time might provide us with a foundational principle and model from which to develop a theological anthropology in our time that moves beyond many of the problems that have perennially arisen in previous theological projects and lead us toward a more catholic approach.

To move our discussion forward, let's consider briefly the complications surrounding the meaning of human *nature* followed by a call for theologians to reconsider human nature according to the hermeneutic of catholicity. Then we will briefly examine the concept of *haecceitas* as developed by John Duns Scotus and explore its implications for theological anthropology. Finally, this chapter closes with a short consideration of the implications of reimagining the human person with *haecceitas* as the ground and starting point of theological anthropology.

Rethinking Human Nature

So drastic have the developments of science been over the last few centuries and so unscientific are the outlooks of the ancient and medieval theologians that form the core of classic Christian anthropology that it can be difficult to reconcile these two threads of insight. The famous socio-biologist Edward Wilson commented along these lines some decades back when he hypothesized that, because of this incompatibility between disciplines, "theology is not likely to survive as an independent intellectual discipline."[2] On one level that strikes me as an overstatement. It seems extreme to suggest that theology is destined to disappear in the wake of scientific advancement. And yet, Wilson also makes a compelling point—echoing one of the overarching themes of this book—that

---

[2] E. O. Wilson, *On Human Nature* (Cambridge, MA: Harvard University Press, 1978), 192.

a classicist, static, and narrowly conceived understanding of the world cannot adequately describe the fullness of the world around us and the creatures we are. Certainly, there is truth in what many medieval thinkers have said, for as Christians we confess faith in the Holy Spirit's continued presence acting in the world and aiding us in our quest to make sense of our faith *(fides quaerens intellectum)* in every age. But, as we have discussed in earlier chapters, the underlying truth—manifested in principles such as the existence of a loving, personal God; the reality of the incarnation; the commandment to love; and so on—should not be confused with the incomplete and partial facts presented as unchanging and complete answers at any given point in history. We can, and must, continue to affirm the truths of faith while deepening our understanding of human and nonhuman creation with the aid of multiple disciplines.

As moral theologian Jean Porter keenly reminds us, there is no such thing as (or at least no real access to) any absolute or pure sense of "nature."[3] So much of our theological imagination and many of our ethical norms have been shaped by reliance upon and reference to a human nature conceived in absolute and static terms. This is problematic for it displays our epistemological hubris at its worst. Too often we assume we know with certitude what it means to talk about human nature as if it corresponded to a static reality outside our own hypothesizing. We must recall always that we are social creatures that construct meaning and systems of symbolic reference. History has all too tragically borne witness to the dehumanizing effects of social groups claiming determinative agency over what constitutes authentic human nature and what, or *whom*, does not comport with such a view.

This is seen most prominently in the theological work of Thomas Aquinas (d. 1274). Ever since Pope Leo XIII's 1879 encyclical letter *Aeterni Patris*, the Roman Catholic Church has presupposed the philosophical and theological anthropology of Thomas Aquinas as normative, elevating the Angelic Doctor to the status of the "Common Doctor." Thomas appropriated an

---

[3] Jean Porter, *Nature as Reason: A Thomistic Theory of Natural Law* (Grand Rapids, MI: Eerdmans, 2005), 117.

Aristotelian framework within which he developed his understanding of human nature, emphasizing both the hylomorphic
and teleological features of Aristotle's worldview. *Hylomorphism*
is the metaphysical construct that understands all things that
exist in reality as a composite of matter and form, which in the
case of humans is determined by an immortal soul. Regarding
teleology, I am referring to an understanding of nature that is
generally described in terms of a particular existent's goal or
purpose, which is singular. Teleological ethics is governed by
an understanding that an action ought to correspond with its
"natural" end or aim. For example, according to sexual ethics informed by Thomism, the natural end or aim of the human sexual
act is procreation or reproduction of the species. Despite the
more recent acknowledgment of the secondary good of spousal
intimacy and affection, the church has persisted in interpreting
this teleological moral logic in such a way as to assert that any
sexual activity that does not explicitly seek this primary "natural
end" of procreation is, by definition, "objectively disordered,"
for it is in practice an action not ordered to the end intended by
God.[4] This is, of course, simply a brief summation that does not
do full justice to the complexity of hylomorphic or teleological
metaphysics in general or the varieties of historical and contemporary Thomism specifically. My aim, here, is not to rehearse
Thomist metaphysics but to propose the foundations of another
way to consider the human person.[5]

---

[4] For one discussion of this teleological logic in Thomistic sexual
ethics, see Jack A. Bonsor, "Homosexual Orientation and Anthropology: Reflections on the Category 'Objective Disorder,'" *Theological
Studies* 59 (1998): 60–83. For an alternate proposal that attempts to
move away from ontological discussions in general and toward virtue
ethics specifically, see Margaret A. Farley, *Just Love: A Framework for
Christian Sexual Ethics* (New York: Continuum Publishing, 2006).

[5] For more on Thomas's metaphysical approach, see, among others,
Etienne Gilson, *Thomism: The Philosophy of Thomas Aquinas*, trans.
Laurence K. Shook and Armand Maurer (Toronto: Pontifical Institute of
Medieval Studies, 2002); W. Norris Clarke, *Explorations in Metaphysics:
Being, God, Person* (Notre Dame, IN: University of Notre Dame Press,
1994); and Brian Davies, *The Thought of Thomas Aquinas* (New York:
Oxford University Press, 1992).

Theologically, one of the often overlooked problems with Thomas's philosophical worldview is his reliance on a participatory metaphysics that maintains a distinction between essence and existence. As philosopher Norris Clarke explains, "This undoubtedly is at once the most central and the most original doctrine of St. Thomas's metaphysics, put forward by him as his response to what metaphysicians generally agree is *the* central problem of all metaphysics, the problem of the one and the many."[6] Drawn from Aristotelian philosophy, the distinction between essence and existence suggests that one can consider the *what* of something independently from the fact *that* something exists. Existence, as it were, gets subordinated to the essence ("what") of something because all existence or *being* depends entirely on the absolute or highest being (that is, God) for existence, which is known as participatory metaphysics.[7]

The primary focus of interest and inquiry for Thomas is the "what" *(quiddity)* that a thing is rather than the particular thing in itself. Consequently, the starting point for consideration of the human person specifically, and all creatures in general, has centered on the essence or nature of a given thing. The unchanging, static, and timeless nature of this metaphysical foundation is apparent when we consider that, for Thomas and the tradition that follows him, the existence of a thing comes totally from and is absolutely dependent on God as pure Being *(Esse)*, and the essence or nature of a person or thing is universal. This has set up a distorted outlook that abstracts from the particular existent—that individual person or thing—something perceived as essential, static, and atemporal. The uniqueness or particularity of the singular is overshadowed by interest in what constitutes the metaphysical nature of a being, and therefore an "anthropology from above" is developed, which serves as the standard by

---

[6] Clarke, *Explorations in Metaphysics*, 13. Also see John F. Wippel, "Thomas Aquinas and Participation," in *Studies in Medieval Philosophy*, ed. John F. Wippel (Washington, DC: Catholic University of America Press, 1987), 117–58.

[7] See Gilson, *Thomism*, 204–18.

and against which all individuals are evaluated. This top-down approach to anthropology builds, perhaps unwittingly, an understanding of humanity on a socially constructed notion of a universal essence or nature. Matched with a teleological view of the world mentioned earlier, this approach lays a problematic foundation for a strict vision of metaphysical necessity and claims about the human person understood as perennial and absolute (for example, the complementarity of gender, the identification of gender with biological sex, and so on). And this sort of essentialist worldview has governed so much of our thinking about humanity and Christianity.

The Concept of *Haecceitas*

Articulated in a philosophical key the tension between an essentialist approach to human nature and a particular, contextual, or experiential approach to theological anthropology can be identified as a problem of universals and singulars. On the one hand, there is the desire of scholars to consider the ways in which human persons share or participate in some universal dimension of human "nature." Put colloquially, we might ask: What makes all of us *human*? On the other hand, recent critical theory and contextual theology have challenged the tradition to account for the particular experiences of individuals in theological reflection on the human person.[8] To bridge the seeming divide between these two approaches, we explore the possibility that Scotus's principle of individuation, what is popularly known as *haecceitas*, might serve theological reflection on the human person in our contemporary context.

The late Scotist scholar Allan Wolter has noted that the philosophical question of what precisely individuates something— what makes something an individual, particular thing—has

---

[8] For a fuller discussion, see Daniel P. Horan, "Beyond Essentialism and Complementarity: Toward a Theological Anthropology Rooted in *Haecceitas*," *Theological Studies* 75 (2014): 94–117, esp. 97–108.

theological implications: "The problem of individuation in the latter portion of the thirteenth century became one of the more controversial and hotly discussed issues in university circles, especially at Paris and Oxford."[9] Although the philosophical and theological milieu out of which Scotus's approach arises helps contextualize how radical his thought is when compared to many of his predecessors and contemporaries, the various other theories of individuation that Scotus considers prior to advancing his own original argument is beyond the focus of this chapter.[10] Instead, we examine the assertive response of the Subtle Doctor to the question: "Is a material substance individual through something positive determining the nature to be just this individual substance?[11] with the claim that the "material substance is determined to this singularity by some positive entity and to other diverse singularities by other diverse positive entities."[12]

---

[9] Allan Wolter, "Scotus's Individuation Theory," in *The Philosophical Theology of John Duns Scotus*, ed. Marilyn McCord Adams (Ithaca, NY: Cornell University Press, 1990), 68. See also Timothy Noone, "Individuation in Scotus," *American Catholic Philosophical Quarterly* 69 (1995): 527–42.

[10] The primary text for the five theories Scotus engages prior to advancing his own is *Lectura* II, d. 3, pars 1, q. 1–5 (Vatican XVIII: 229–73). The critical edition of Scotus's work is *Opera Omnia: Studio et Cura Commissionis Scotisticae ad fidem codicum edita*, ed. Carlo Balíc et al., 21 vols. (Vatican City: Typis Polyglottis Vaticanis, 1950–). Subsequent references to this edition will be noted by the Latin text with this edition's internal notation, followed by the volume and page number in parenthesis. Unless otherwise noted, English translations of this section of the *Lectura* are from John Duns Scotus, *Early Oxford Lecture on Individuation*, trans. Allan Wolter (St. Bonaventure, NY: Franciscan Institute, 2005). It should be noted that Wolter's paragraph numbering in his translation varies with the Vatican Latin text, although he cites the Vatican critical edition. The numbers cited here follow the Vatican demarcation. Additionally, Scotus's slightly later reflections on the principle of individuation can be found in the *Ordinatio*. For selections, see Giovanni Duns Scoto, *Filosofo Della Libertà*, ed. Orlando Todisco (Padova: Edizioni Messaggero Padova, 1996), 164–85.

[11] *Lectura* II, dist. 3, pars 1, q. 6, n.139 (Vatican XVIII: 273).

[12] *Lectura* II, dist. 3, pars 1, q. 6, n. 164 (Vatican XVIII: 280). For a translation of this argument as it appears in Scotus's later *Ordinatio*,

Like his medieval contemporaries, Scotus's reflection arose from the ongoing conversation about the individuation of angels and other nonmaterial substances.[13] Angels were often invoked in the Middle Ages as something like test cases or thought experiments, especially when reflecting on the question of the relationship between universals and particulars. Since angels are understood to be incorporeal, not having accidental or physical qualities, the issue was to explain metaphysically how you could tell individual angels apart. Nevertheless, Scotus's ultimate concern was rooted in what Wolter describes as "a more fundamental and psychological question."[14] Scotus was interested in the objective nature of intellectual knowledge. In this sense Scotus can be understood as something of a realist, a thinker grounded in the experience of the human person's ability to generalize or abstract something universal from a variety of material objects. At the same time Scotus recognized that there was something unique, something that is *individual*, about those things that the intellect perceives in this common group. Contrary to more recent critiques of Scotus that label him a "nominalist,"[15] he rejected a "purely logical or conceptual division."[16] He believes that there is such a thing as "common nature" *(natura communis)* following his reading of the medieval Arabic philosopher

---

see Paul Vincent Spade, ed., *Five Texts on The Medieval Problem of Universals* (Indianapolis: Hackett Publishing, 1994), 57–113.

[13] See *Lectura* II, dist. 3, pars 1, q. 1, n. 2 (Vatican XVIII: 229–30), and following.

[14] Wolter, "Scotus's Individuation Theory," 71. Also see Mary Beth Ingham and Mechthild Dreyer, *The Philosophical Vision of John Duns Scotus: An Introduction* (Washington, DC: CUA Press, 2004), 102–3.

[15] The best examples of such accusations are perhaps those associated with the Radical Orthodoxy movement, especially the work of John Milbank, *Theology and Social Theory*, 2nd ed. (Oxford: Blackwell Publishers, 2006) and Catherine Pickstock, *After Writing: On the Liturgical Consummation of Philosophy* (Oxford: Blackwell Publishers, 1998). For an analysis and corrective, see my *Postmodernity and Univocity: A Critical Account of Radical Orthodoxy and John Duns Scotus* (Minneapolis: Fortress Press, 2014).

[16] Wolter, "Scotus's Individuation Theory," 73.

Avicenna, and that this "common nature" is a way of maintaining a real sense of the universal that differs from the alternative theory advanced by Thomas Aquinas.[17] Scotus agrees with Avicenna that a "nature" cannot exist outside of some concrete thing, either intellectually in the mind or in extra-mental reality.[18] Both thinkers were concerned with explaining how something universal can be predicated of multiple individuals. However, for Scotus, that which is shared implies a "community." Scotus believed that "common nature" is only universal if there are individuals to which such a nature could be applied. In other words, the universality of this common nature presupposes particularity. For example, one could not have a sense of a common nature called "horseness" without a prior collection of individual horses. Thus, Scotus asserts, a nature cannot exist as such on its own.[19] While Scotus follows Aristotle in maintaining the category "substance" (from *sub-stare*, meaning "that which stands beneath") as the "bearer of qualities," in his usage a substance does not exist apart from the individual "singulars" that, in fact, actually exist in the world. In other words, while Scotus will conceive of a substance that could be called "human" or "stone" or "cat," such substances (a) do not exist apart from or prior to a singular, individual existing thing, and (b) such universals, albeit certainly "real" in some sense, only follow from the existence of particulars and not the other way around.[20]

---

[17] See Allan Wolter, "The Realism of Scotus," in McCord Adams, *The Philosophical Theology of John Duns Scotus*, 42–53.

[18] It should be noted, though, that Scotus does distance himself from what Avicenna calls the "neutral nature" and posits the "common nature" as the universal dimension. Wolter keenly notes the ways in which Scotus's "realism" might better be described as "moderate realism" in contrast to more platonic approaches associated with a certain positive realism. See Wolter, "Scotus's Individuation Theory," 94–95, and "The Realism of Scotus," 42–53.

[19] See Ingham and Dreyer, *The Philosophical Vision of John Duns Scotus*, 102–5.

[20] Because we are not here concerned with Scotus's position on universals, as such, this overview is necessarily simplistic and offered only to establish a preliminary foundation for understanding the context

Scotus moves to make his argument in question six of this distinction of his text known as the *Lectura*. Philosophers Mary Beth Ingham and Mechthild Dreyer summarize this position well: "[According to Scotus], the material substance becomes individual through a principle that contracts the common nature *(natura communis)* to singularity. Scotus calls this principle the individuating entity *(entitas individualis)*. In the literature on Scotus, this is as a rule described as thisness or *haecceitas*, a term that Scotus uses in his *Questions on Aristotle's Metaphysics*."[21] The justification for Scotus's advancing such a claim comes in the form of two presuppositions; these arise from his earlier argumentation in this particular section within the *Lectura*.

First, Scotus has shown that any "common nature" must bear a unity that is less than that of the individual.[22] As Wolter explains, "This positive entity to which we attribute singularity [*haecceitas*] must be formally other than the entity constituting the specific nature. Though formally distinct, this individuating difference must form with that nature a *per se* unity; hence, its proper 'haecceity' is not accidental to any individual."[23] This argument is significant for the absolute maintenance of the intrinsic constitution of this principle. It is, in other words, bound up *really* with that singular iteration of the "common nature" such that Scotus can argue that "being" (the existence of the thing) and the unity of the particular instantiation of the "common nature" can be understood as "interchangeable or convertible."[24]

---

that Scotus provides in responding to the question of individuation. For more on the relationship between Scotus's understanding of universals and singulars, see Timothy Noone, "Universals and Individuation," in *The Cambridge Companion to Duns Scotus*, ed. Thomas Williams (New York: Cambridge University Press, 2003), 100–128.

[21] Ingham and Dreyer, *The Philosophical Vision of John Duns Scotus*, 113.

[22] *Lectura* II, dist. 3, pars 1, q 6, n. 166 (Vatican XVIII: 280–81). Also see Ingham and Dreyer, *The Philosophical Vision of John Duns Scotus*, 115.

[23] Wolter, "Scotus's Individuation Theory," 90.

[24] Ingham and Dreyer, *The Philosophical Vision of John Duns Scotus*, 113.

Second, Scotus's thesis is rooted in the affirmation that, following Aristotle's notion of "[the difference among] other-same things" *(diversa aliquid idem entia)*,[25] there is an intuitive and logical distinction among different natures (for example, dogs and cats). Yet, there must be something that differentiates things of the same nature (for example, Plato and Socrates). This distinguishing characteristic cannot be the common nature as such, Scotus argues, because

> the nature in the one and the other is not primarily the cause of their difference, but their agreement. Though the nature in one is not the nature in the other, nature [of "Plato"] and nature [of "Socrates"] are not that whereby the two differ primarily, but that whereby they agree . . . hence there must be something else whereby they differ. But this is not quantity, nor existence, nor a negation, as was established in the preceding questions; therefore, it must be something positive in the category of substance, contracting the specific nature.[26]

By means of a number of comparisons, Scotus demonstrates the ways in which these two foundational principles of his thesis demand that the principle of individuation is, in fact, "one" with the *natura communis*, albeit "formally distinct" from it.[27] Ingham and Dreyer summarize this point:

---

[25] Wolter's translation in *Early Oxford Lecture on Individuation*, 81.

[26] *Lectura* II, dist. 3, pars 1, q 6, n. 167 (Vatican XVIII: 281).

[27] Following in the tradition of Bonaventure's *distinctio rationis* and Henry of Ghent's "intentional distinction," Scotus develops the notion of the "Formal Distinction," which is a *via media* of sorts between something that is only conceptually (and, therefore, non-extramentally) distinct and something distinct in reality (like an apple and an orange). For a more extended treatment of this philosophical theory, see Allan Wolter, "The Formal Distinction," in *The Philosophical Vision of John Duns Scotus*, 27–41; Richard Cross, *Duns Scotus* (New York: Oxford University Press, 1999), 149; Ingham and Dreyer, *The Philosophical*

This distinction of the common nature [*natura communis*] from the principle of individuation [*entitas individualis* or *haecceitas*] is a formal one; the two are merely formally distinct *(formaliter distinctae)* in the individual. While two individuals are in themselves really distinct, two formally distinct entities are not in themselves distinct in reality; instead, they only become distinct through the intellect, i.e., they can be conceived independently of one another. Nevertheless, they are not mere concepts because the intellect does not produce them.[28]

What makes an individual an individual according to Scotus's principle of individuation *(entitas individualis* or *haecceitas)* is identical with a thing's very existence or being. It is not an external, accidental, or material modification of an eternal idea or of a universal *substantia* but a real, positive, unique, unalienable, and unrepeatable principle, as is the case for someone like Thomas. This principle Scotus proposes, *haecceitas*, is absolutely intrinsic to that which it individuates within creation—including both material and nonmaterial things[29]—and *really* identical with such an individual thing's very *being*.

Vision of John Duns Scotus, 33–38; Marilyn McCord Adams, "Universals in the Fourteenth Century, in *The Cambridge History of Later Medieval Philosophy*, ed. Anthony Kenny et al. (New York: Cambridge University Press, 1982), 411–39; and Stephen Dumont, "Henry of Ghent and Duns Scotus," in *Medieval Philosophy*, ed. John Marenbon (London: Routledge, 1998), 291–328. Antonie Vos also presents an accessible presentation of Scotus's "Formal Distinction" among the various competing forms of philosophical distinction in *The Philosophy of John Duns Scotus* (Edinburgh: Edinburgh University Press, 2006), 253–63.

[28] Ingham and Dreyer, *The Philosophical Vision of John Duns Scotus*, 116.

[29] Including angels (nonmaterial individuals), which is why this question of the possibility of a material individuating principle in Aristotelian terms frequently became the source for medieval debate in terms of the ontological constitution of differing angelologies.

The Significance of *Haecceitas*
for Theological Anthropology

John Duns Scotus's seemingly esoteric response to the question of what makes a particular thing *particular* might at first seem removed from the theological concerns of those who are trying to understand the meaning of the human person within the Christian tradition. However, Scotus's unique approach to the question of individuation provides a surprisingly valuable contribution to our contemporary efforts. The way he used the tradition, reason, and the philosophical tools at his disposal to imagine an alternative approach to disputed questions on individuation in his time gestures us toward a way of engaging theological anthropology today and points us toward a new framework by which to move beyond current anthropological impasses.

Scotus's notion of *haecceitas* resituates the focus of human value and dignity from an essential and universal "essence" or "nature" to a location of radical particularity. Primacy is placed on the individual, while concurrently recognizing the inherent relationality and community among creation by virtue of the common nature *(natura communis)*, on the one hand, and by the more expansive presupposition of *being* on the other hand. For Scotus, as Dutch theologian Antonie Vos explains, "the basic category is not *universality*, but individuality—the individual has their own identity, something essential which cannot be shared with anything else. They [their respective *haecceities*] are unique, not something negative."[30] This notion of a negative principle (in contradistinction to Scotus's positive principle) could be found

---

[30] Antonie Vos, "John Duns Scotus: An Anthropology of Dignity and Love," in *Words Made Flesh: Essays Honoring Kenan B. Osborne, OFM*, ed. Joseph Chinnici (St. Bonaventure, NY: Franciscan Institute Publications, 2011), 163. For additional treatments of Scotus's contribution to the theological concept of person, see Isidoro Manzano, "Ontología de la persona humana según Escoto," *Antonianum* LXXVIII (2003), 321–56; and Carmela Bianco, *Ultima solitude: la nascita del concetto modern di persona in Duns Scoto* (Milan: Franco Angeli, 2017).

in other medieval iterations of hylomorphic philosophical anthropology, such as in the theology of Thomas Aquinas. Mary Beth Ingham summarizes Scotus in contrast with other thinkers by emphasizing that his individuating principle is "a *this* rather than a *not-that*," referencing, of course, the *quiddity* (whatness) or nature of a given thing, as Thomas and others do.[31] While Scotus maintains a logical place for a common nature that might at first glance risk being confused for another form of essentialism, he actually subordinates this as secondary to the more primary and intrinsic transcendental reality of *haecceitas*.[32] Recognizing *haecceitas* as a necessarily constitutive dimension of human (and other creaturely) existence, Vos explains that to talk about the need for an individuating principle almost seems unnecessary from a Scotist viewpoint "since *individuality* is an essential property of everything that is" by means of *haecceitas's* ontological status.[33] Scotus might not push this anti-essentialist approach quite as far, nor is there textual evidence for such a claim, but there is a sense in which Vos's somewhat hyperbolic statement captures the revolutionary changes of Scotus's philosophical anthropology: "The ontological tables have been turned upside down: universals are not the pillars of being, individuals are."[34]

Scotus's overturning of the ontological priority of substance or nature through the subordination (yet realistic acknowledgment)

---

[31] Mary Beth Ingham, "The Tradition and the Third Millennium: The Earth Charter," in Chinnici, *Words Made Flesh*, 183. Also see Jorge J. E. Gracia, ed., *Individuation in Scholasticism: The Later Middle Ages and the Counter-Reformation 1150–1650* (Albany, NY: SUNY Press, 1994).

[32] Scotus's views on universals and singulars, particularly as those philosophical considerations relate to individuation, are more nuanced than the space and scope of this chapter would allow for full elucidation. A sampling of the comprehensive treatments of this subject by specialists include Noone, "Universals and Individuation," 100–129; Wolter, "Scotus's Individuation Theory," 68–97; Woosuk Park, "*Haecceitas* and the Bare Particular," *The Review of Metaphysics* 44 (1990), 375–97; and Woosuk Park, "Common Nature and *Haecceitas*," *Franziskanische Studien* 71 (1989): 188–92.

[33] Vos, "John Duns Scotus," 164.

[34] Vos, "John Duns Scotus," 164.

of something he calls common nature can be read as decentering the theological focus of the inherited tradition's concern with establishing clarity of a universal human nature or seeking to uncover an absolute and timeless essence of the human person. While Scotus remains a thinker of his time and maintains a reserved type of essentialism in terms of a collection of similar kinds *(natura communis)*, what is promising for our purposes here is his capacity to imagine another starting point in our theological reflection without ignoring the importance of commonality, community, or genus. One can see how Scotus's thought fits with the constructive understanding of the *imago Dei* proposed at the end of the last chapter.

It is easy to recognize how Scotus's *haecceitas* approach to individuation likewise responds to another common critique of essentialism, namely, the depersonalization of humanity. The uniqueness, unrepeatability, and inalienable inherency of one's *haecceitas* can be interpreted as an elevation of the particular and personal over the universal or the common. This resituating of human personhood within a theological framework where the individual is understood as primary and the universal is seen as concurrently present and real (yet secondary) unveils the intrinsic relationality, dignity, and value of *each* person over against the depersonalizing elevation of *humanity* in a general and essentialist sense. Ingham reiterates this point: "Each being within the created order already possesses an immanent dignity whose foundation is relational; it is already gifted by the loving Creator with a sanctity beyond our ability to understand."[35]

One's value as a human being is not predicated on the ability (or lack thereof) of a particular person to exhibit a certain universal human nature.[36] Such a theological requirement would necessarily exclude whole populations of people who do not

---

[35] Ingham, "The Tradition and the Third Millennium," 184.

[36] On a related theme the prominent Scotist Richard Cross engages the thought of Scotus, among others, as a resource for contemporary disability studies and theologies of personhood in "Disability, Impairment, and Some Medieval Accounts of the Incarnation: Suggestions for a Theology of Personhood," *Modern Theology* 27 (2011): 639–58.

emulate the (arbitrary and external) qualities of "authentic human personhood." Rather, Scotus's *haecceity* locates human value and dignity as a constitutive element of a person's very being or existence from the outset. This inherent relationality and intrinsic dignity of the human person precisely as an individual is not limited solely to humanity. Rather, Scotus predicated *haecceitas* among all of the created order, such that every blade of grass, each stone, and every living creature is unrepeatably unique and inherently valued according to the divine act of creation.[37] One can see the manifold applicability of Scotus's approach to the further development of a community of creation paradigm, one that sustains the interrelational dimension of created existence and simultaneously affirms the value and dignity of the nonhuman aspects of the created order without the determination of nonhuman creaturely worth by human beings.

As we note in the next chapter, Scotus's *haecceitas* avoids clear binary distinctions between genders and biological sexes. The value of human personhood is located within the context of the principle of individuation, which is really identical with (yet formally distinct from) a person's actual existence or being. As such, Scotus rejects the Aristotelian distinction between essence and existence as found in Thomas's metaphysics.[38] Value and dignity, then, are not located within a given person's status as "male" or "female," just as it does not reside within the generalized strictures of "human" conceived as a nature or essence. Individuals are what God primarily intends, not the biological

---

[37] As if to make his point about the extension of *haecceity* to all of creation abundantly clear, Scotus uses the example of a stone in his argumentation in distinction to the preferred example of a horse in Avicenna. Adopting this Scotist line of thought the twentieth-century writer Thomas Merton uses the example of a tree in *New Seeds of Contemplation*. For more on this expression in Merton, see Daniel P. Horan, "Thomas Merton the 'Dunce': Identity, Incarnation, and the Not So Subtle Influence of John Duns Scotus," *Cistercian Studies Quarterly* 47 (2012): 149–75.

[38] Mary Beth Ingham, *Understanding John Duns Scotus: 'Of Realty the Rarest-Veined Unraveller'* (St. Bonaventure, NY: Franciscan Institute Publications, 2017), 29.

sex or the socialized and constructed gender that is presumed within a given society. Fundamentally, all people share, on some level, their status as contingently existent and, on another level, they share a common nature as something we might call human, but any further demarcation is a material distinction made after the fact that reflects social or cultural norms rather than that which is metaphysical or ontological.

"Before I Formed You in the Womb I Knew You"

What Scotus fleshes out in terms of a robust metaphysical argument about the primacy of particularity can also be seen in less esoteric ways throughout the Christian tradition. Such is the case with the way certain passages in scripture allude to God's creative act. For example, while the dialogue between God and the soon-to-be prophet in the opening verses of the Book of Jeremiah have been a reassuring source of comfort for those who seek a loving, personal God, they also anticipate a sense of *haecceitas*:

> Now the word of the Lord came to me saying,
> "Before I formed you in the womb I knew you,
> and before you were born I consecrated you;
> I appointed you a prophet to the nations."
> (Jer 1:4–5)

Furthemore, they echo, in a profoundly pastoral sense, the significance of Scotus's medieval philosophical theology of *haecceitas*. There is in this poetic call of the prophet a reminder that God has loved us each into existence, not merely as an afterthought or some variation on a general theme ("humanity," as such). When God decides to create, God creates you and me and this particular stone and that specific bird. Our very existence bears witness to this truth, for Scotus rejects the metaphysical distinction between who we are and that we exist. For him, these are intertwined; they are one in the same.

One other aspect of Scotus's thought that has not yet been emphasized in this chapter is his strong commitment to the absolute contingency of God's creative action and therefore the contingency of all that exists. In other words, while other thinkers have adhered to in greater or lesser degrees to Aristotle's understanding of the necessity of the world and a sense of determinism that arises from a philosophical system that is inherently teleological and focused on causes/effects, Scotus always errs on the side of divine freedom, which resonates throughout the created world. There is an openness and creativity to the universe that reflects God's own loving freedom. Although Scotus maintains the importance of what is called logical necessity (for example, mathematical truths, the law of noncontradiction, among others), there is no room for fatalism or determinism in our understanding of creation according to belief in the God of Jesus Christ.[39]

Notable about this aspect of Scotus's thought are the implications that arise from it for our understanding of creation in general and humanity in particular. Essentially, anything that exists could be otherwise—there is no force, requirement, obligation, influence, pressure, guidance, or other outside factor that affects God's free choice to create. Given this truth, we can open our hearts and minds to see that all that exists in this evolving universe is here precisely because of God's creative freedom. This includes each and every human person. Indeed, just as we are creatures that are situated within an intrinsic network of relationships as members of the community of creation, we are also members of the human family, *Homo sapiens*. But what God desires first, from all eternity, is not the creation of this species or that species *in general,* but a community of diverse and inexhaustibly unique individuals that bear inherent dignity and value by virtue of their existence and nothing more. When God looks out at the "entangled bank," as Darwin put it, the Creator does not merely enjoy the abstract goodness of humanity and

---

[39] See Ingham, *Understanding John Duns Scotus,* 18–19.

sea lions and sandstone, and so on in some distant, anonymous, and general way but rejoices in the fact that each and every particular creature that has existed, does exist, or will exist is "very good" (Gen 1:31). What constitutes creation is not the result of some necessity but is contingent, the result of a divine desire to bring each individual into existence, and reflects the freedom of divine love.

The combination of the absolute contingency of creation and the uniqueness of each creature's *haecceity* as the source for individuation provides us with a renewed foundation for thinking about the human person. The opening words of Jeremiah are no longer just romantic poetry but now bear witness to a profound truth about our very existence. This naturally raises questions that need to be examined. What would it look like to start with the particular, the individual, the person, rather than pursue a quest to find a universal, unchanging, static "essence" when describing the human person? How does this emphasis on the uniqueness and irrepeatability of each and every person affect our understanding of identity and relationship within the human family specifically and the community of creation more broadly? In the next chapter we explore some of these and other questions regarding our understanding of gender, race, and identity.

Chapter 5

Gender, Identity, and Race

Most of the theological research on issues relating to the human person and gender, race, and identity have come from the field of theological ethics or moral theology. The result has generally been an acts-based focus, which is understandable given the ubiquity of Thomistic metaphysics and teleology governing Catholic discussions of the human person. In recent years several ethicists have offered creative and insightful studies that propose ways of understanding the complexity of human persons in light of the natural and social sciences, as well as contemporary realities, while at the same time adhering to the received metaphysical and anthropological foundation that has been largely in place since the thirteenth century.[1] While ethicists have accomplished significant advances in addressing some important subjects pertaining to the human person, what they all share in common is a later-order consideration that

---

[1] Although this chapter is dedicated to considering some of the more contentious issues that arise within Christian theological reflections on the human person, I am not interested in rehearsing all of the many fine ethical arguments that have already been made. For example, on issues related to human sexuality, see, for example, Todd A. Salzman and Michael G. Lawler, *The Sexual Person: Toward a Renewed Catholic Anthropology* (Washington, DC: Georgetown University Press, 2008); Margaret A. Farley, *Just Love: A Framework for Christian Sexual Ethics* (New York: Continuum, 2006); and James F. Keenan, "Prophylactics, Toleration, and Cooperation: Contemporary Problems and Traditional Principles," *International Philosophical Quarterly* 29 (1989): 205–20.

does not propose alternative sources for a renewed theological anthropology. This way of approaching the human person does little to move our understanding of the faith toward development and wholeness. A deeper engagement with the tradition and the foundational principles of our theological reflection is necessary. Therefore, rather than focus on the ethical standing of an issue—is this or that act morally right or wrong—let us consider a more foundational perspective rooted in the theological anthropology that undergirds moral and ethical consideration.[2]

In this chapter, we examine three illustrative subjects—a set of investigations or case studies—wherein the classical view of the human person grounded in a Thomistic worldview has led to problematics and impasses. The cases include the sexism of gender complementarity, the reality of transgender persons, and the dehumanization of racism. We consider them with the tentativeness appropriate for a constructive enterprise that does not presuppose apodictic certainty or the last word. Hopefully, this will make a small contribution to corresponding efforts to better understand the human person in various fields within and outside of theology. Building on the previous chapter's discussion of the promise of a theological anthropology rooted in *haeccietas*, we discover alternative ways to understand what it means to be human from a Christian perspective. But, admittedly, this is the beginning of a much larger project that fully fleshes out all the nuances of and implications arising from a theological anthropology developed with a hermeneutic of catholicity. What follows here is nevertheless a start; a prolegomenon to a theological anthropology of catholicity that invites renewed ethics and pastoral praxis.

---

[2] Even when I address an ethical discussion, such as I do at the opening of the second section of this chapter, it is with the aim of showing how even ethicists acknowledge the unavoidable limitations of their secondary reflection on theological anthropology in debating the establishment and application of moral norms.

It is also important to restate here my own social location as a white-identified, cisgender male who is a Franciscan friar and an ordained Roman Catholic presbyter. I do so not only to acknowledge and own my particular social location in an admittedly racist and patriarchal society and faith community but also because I wish to state unequivocally that I in no way intend to speak on behalf of or for any other person or community, especially one that is historically disenfranchised, subjugated, or silenced. This last point speaks to why I, in part, feel compelled to address these three investigations or case studies if only in a preliminary way, namely, because I occupy a location in my society and church that affords me unearned and unsought power and privilege—gender, racial, and clerical, among others—I recognize my responsibility to deploy that power and privilege to deconstruct unjust systems that unfairly advantage some while disadvantaging others. While a small effort, it is my hope that what follows makes some positive contribution to that cause.

This chapter is organized into three sections, each of which opens by naming a contemporary problem in our theological reflection on the human person and then considers how our Christian understanding of the human person might appear grounded in a theology informed first by the dynamic particular rather than the abstract essence, in other words, a foundational theological anthropology according to Scotus rather than Thomas.

The Sexism
of "Gender Complementarity"

Some theological aphorisms, like some well-known civil laws, may sound good to some people in theory but in practice nevertheless prove to be disastrous. Such is the case with the oft-repeated theological anthropological trope about gender complementarity, just as it was with the shameful history of racial segregation in the United States. In both cases the infamous phrase "separate but equal" cuts right to the point.[3] As with the doctrine of *imago Dei* examined in Chapter 3, the disproportionate emphasis on the importance of two "separate" but "equal" genders intended by God at creation relies heavily on a brief passage from Genesis 1:27 that reads:

> So God created humankind in his image,
>   in the image of God he created them;
>   male and female he created them.

Similar to the history of interpreting *imago Dei*, the history of "male and female he created them" reflects the ambiguity of the phrase within the biblical text itself as well as centuries of eisegetical readings that have provided tautological results. Simply put, God created two distinct genders; men and women are different but complementary, and God intended them to be separate but equal.

This way of viewing gender presupposes an essentialist metaphysical worldview.[4] Not only is human nature understood to be immutable and universal, but the two *kinds* of humanity—male

---

[3] In the civil sphere this phrase was used in the United States to describe the ostensible conditions of equality within the social and juridical context of racial segregation, which was made concrete in the late-nineteenth-century Supreme Court case *Homer A. Plessy v. John H. Ferguson*, 163 U.S. 537 (1896). It took more than a half-century for this unjust law to be overturned in the case *Oliver Brown, et al., v. Board of Education of Topeka*, 347 U.S. 483 (1954).

[4] For more on this, see Daniel P. Horan, "Beyond Essentialism and Complementarity: Toward a Theological Anthropology Rooted in *Haecceitas*," *Theological Studies* 75 (2014): 97–102; and Susan Frank Parsons, "To Be or Not to Be: Gender and Ontology," *Heythrop Journal* 45 (2004): 327–43. Regarding definitions of *gender* and *biological sex*, both of which will be used in this chapter, I borrow Michelle A. Gonzalez's succinct and clarifying explanation: "When I speak of *biological sex* I am referring to the biological embodied distinction between men and women. The word *gender* refers to the social construction of masculine and feminine identity or socially acquired roles of men and women. Often these two have become confused in the Christian tradition, when biology is interpreted as destiny and is used to justify socially constructed gender roles" (*Created*

and female—are further instances of a static common nature understood to be represented by timeless characteristics.[5] These characteristics, which in many Christian contexts have been articulated in terms of Western social norms, have been used to justify the separation of gendered spheres wherein only men or only women are allowed or expected to operate.[6] The home or domestic sphere has long been associated in Western European and North American societies as the domain of women. Conversely, places of business or industry were presumed the natural domain of men. Furthermore, this dynamic has played out over the centuries *within* the Christian community as well, with the sphere of religious leadership—think in Catholicism and Orthodoxy of the all-male clergy—designated a domain of men. These social norms have been theologized by religious leaders and (again, mostly all male) theologians as divinely intended, tied to the Genesis 1:27 account and reflective not of a greater or lesser inherent dignity or worth but a "natural" separation supported by appeals to differentiation in gender and, at times, with recourse to biological sexual difference. Perhaps the most popular Christian systematization of this defense of gender complementarity as constitutive of God's intention for humanity is found in the personal and catechetical writings of John Paul II, best known as "the theology of the body."[7] Theologian Mary Aquin O'Neill summarizes what this gender complementarity looks like in practice:

---

in God's Image: An Introduction to Feminist Theological Anthropology [Maryknoll, NY: Orbis Books, 2007], xx).

[5] See Pamela R. Lightsey, *Our Lives Matter: A Womanist Queer Theology* (Eugene, OR: Pickwick Publications, 2015), esp. 51–66.

[6] This is not to suggest that hierarchical dualism is present *only* in Western social norms to the exclusion of other contexts, because such dynamics are also present across various cultures.

[7] See John Paul II, *Man and Woman He Created Them: A Theology of the Body* (Boston: Pauline Books and Media, 2006). Variations on this theme also appear in John Paul II's 1988 Apostolic Letter *Mulieris Dignitatem*. See also Russell Hittinger, "Human Nature and States of Nature in John Paul II's Theological Anthropology," in *Human Nature in Its Wholeness: A Roman Catholic Perspective*, ed. Daniel Robinson,

Such thinking and teaching leads to a two-nature anthropology, a vision of human being as divided into two distinct kinds, each with identifiable differences that become normative for the sex. This anthropology of complementarity, as it came to be known, posits a theology in which the sexes complete one another, not only on the level of reproduction, but in the full range of human existence: social, intellectual, psychological, spiritual. There is a male way of being and a female way, and these can be known from an examination of the bodies of the two and given a fair degree of specificity. Thus men are supposed to be, by nature, active, rational, willful, autonomous beings whose direction goes outward into the world; women are to be passive, intuitive, emotional, connected beings whose natural inclination is inward. This bipolar vision of the sexes leads to an equally bipolar understanding of their respective places, namely, the world and the home.[8]

There are a number of problems that arise as a result of this way of thinking and the ubiquity of this worldview within Catholic Christianity. Among the most striking concerns is that the construction of these "complementary" characteristics presumed to be immutable, universal, and natural, are in fact, male projections onto the identity and experience of women (understood, more specifically, as "woman" in the universal singular). As theologian Michelle Gonzalez notes, "Gender complementarity denies the fullness of the individual human and his or her nature by characterizing certain attributes based on biological sex. Too often, the dualisms found within the complementarity model are grounded in an outdated, essentialist biology."[9]

Gladys Sweeney, and Richard Gill (Washington, DC: Catholic University of America, 2006), 9–33.

[8] Mary Aquin O'Neill, "The Mystery of Being Human Together: Anthropology," in *Freeing Theology: The Essentials of Theology in Feminist Perspective*, ed. Catherine Mowry LaCugna (San Francisco: HarperOne, 1993), 149.

[9] Gonzalez, *Created in God's Image*, 113.

Indeed, Gonzalez's latter point about the dualism inherent in a complementary view of anthropology has often been grounded in the essentialism of Thomistic metaphysics masquerading as thirteenth-century biology. "This incorrect Aristotelian biology, canonized in Aquinas's theology, remains the norm of Roman Catholic anthropologies even today."[10]

We see the explicit sexism of this theological anthropological presupposition of gender complementarity when we revisit the writings of Thomas Aquinas. Although Thomas first demarcates the human person from nonhuman creation in his reflection on the *imago Dei* such that it appears to be predicated of *all humans*, male and female, in the same universal and immutable way, at least primarily, he goes on to argue that "in a secondary sense the image of God is found in man, and not in woman, for man is the beginning and end of woman, just as God is the beginning and end of every creature."[11] This qualification has implications for understanding human dignity and value, particularly in Thomas's unequal application of ostensibly universal dignity and value to women. Returning to this section's opening analogy, at first glance it appears that Thomas's insistence that male and female is a divinely intended separation within the human species, but that these distinct genders share equally human nature, signified best for Thomas by the gift of human rationality. Only we discover that, for Thomas, women bear human nature to a lesser degree than men do—they are in fact *not* equal. Here, Thomas's anthropology draws on both Aristotle's metaphysics and a skewed reading of Genesis 2, wherein he interprets the creation of woman as primarily utilitarian: men were created human as such, whereas women were essentially an afterthought to assist men in procreation. Thomas writes: "It was necessary for woman to be made, as scripture says, as a helper of man;

---

[10] Gonzalez, *Created in God's Image*, 113–14.

[11] Thomas Aquinas, *Summa Theologica*, bk. I, q. 93, art. 4, reply to objection 1, trans. Fathers of the English Dominican Province, 5 vols. (Notre Dame, IN: Ave Maria Press, 1948), 1:472. Additional citations from this translation are included parenthetically after the respective *Summa* reference.

not, indeed, as a helpmate in other works, as some say, since man can be more efficiently helped by another man in other works; but as a helper in the work of generation."[12] In this same section of his *Summa Theologica* Thomas argues that men are superior to women because of the former's superior ability to reason. But why is this the case? Why does Thomas, who holds an essentialist view of human nature, believe that women are inferior? He explains:

> As regards the individual nature, woman is defective and misbegotten, for the active force in the male seed tends to the production of a perfect likeness in the masculine sex; while the production of woman comes from defect in the active force or from some material indisposition, or even from some external influence; such as that of a south wind, which is moist, as the philosopher [Aristotle] observes (*De Gener. Animal.* iv. 2). On the other hand, as regards human nature in general, woman is not misbegotten, but is included in nature's intention as directed to the work of generation. Now the general intention of nature depends on God, who is the universal author of nature. Therefore, in producing nature, God formed not only the male but also the female.[13]

Therefore, Thomas is making several claims and stating them as matter of fact in light of Aristotelian "science."[14] First, when it

---

[12] Thomas Aquinas, *Summa Theologica*, bk. I, q. 92, art. 1, resp. (1:446).

[13] Thomas Aquinas, *Summa Theologica*, bk. I, q. 92, art. 1, reply to objection 1 (1:446).

[14] It should be noted that in recent years several scholars have mounted defenses or deployed rereadings of Thomas in an effort to make his anthropology more palatable. For example, see Michael Nolan, "The Aristotelian Background to Aquinas's Denial That 'Woman Is a Defective Male,'" *The Thomist* 64 (2000): 21–69; Eric Johnston, "The Biology of Woman in Thomas Aquinas," *The Thomist* 77 (2013): 577–616; and Francisco Carrasquillo and Hilaire De Romero, "Aquinas on the Inferiority of Woman," *American Catholic Philosophical Quarterly* 87 (2013): 685–710.

comes to a universal human nature, it is imagined to be exclusively male, which is why Thomas, following Aristotle, asserts that women are "defective and misbegotten" because they are, well, *not men*. Second, he relies on what for us is an extremely antiquated "scientific" theory of human procreation and development that reads today as superstitious and bizarre. The presupposition is that all that is necessary for human conception is found in the male semen; the woman's contribution or role in procreation is to serve as a fertile ground for gestation. Furthermore, all things remaining equal, every child conceived would be male. The only explanation Thomas can surmise as to how a child becomes female is that something effectively goes wrong in the process, that there is some error in the process or some external acting force, such as a "moist south wind," as is suggested. Third, Thomas basically concedes the point about this essentialist anthropology being a case of equality of nature in theory but unequal and hierarchical in practice when he says that when it comes to "human nature in general" women are not defective, but rather serve an intended pragmatic function in their necessary role of reproduction. Finally, this passage concludes with Thomas ascribing this situation of human nature male and female as God's plan and desire. Commenting on this particular passage, Gonzalez highlights the "unbiblical notion of humanity" that is present throughout Thomas's arguments about human nature, noting that he relies almost exclusively on the presuppositions of "Aristotelian biology" to ground his case. "Here one finds a clear moment when it is non-Christian philosophy, and not the biblical witness, that leads to a profoundly offensive and sexist moment in Christian understandings of the human."[15]

Admittedly, this is but one brief illustration of the frequently unchecked deficiencies that form the foundation of the church's understanding of the human person. While most contemporary theologians and church leaders would never so overtly state that "women are misbegotten men," modern defenses of a "separate but equal" anthropology of gender complementarity is built

---

[15] Gonzalez, *Created in God's Image*, 45.

on the presuppositions of Thomistic essentialism. The result, as feminist theologians have highlighted over many decades, is an inescapable cycle of hierarchical dualism that subordinates women to men on account of "nature."[16] The inherent sexism of hierarchical dualism arises from the broader context of a patriarchal worldview. Drawing on the work of Joan Chittister, Eleazar Fernandez notes that there are four interlocking principles that characterize the social reality of this patriarchal context: dualism, hierarchy, domination, and essential inequality. Fernandez, further bolstering the critical analysis of the social norms arising from an essentialist anthropology, explains:

> It is a worldview or way of thinking and perceiving that is hierarchical and dualistic—mind over body, reason over passion—with women identified on the lower side of the

---

[16] The list of excellent feminist works on theological anthropology far exceeds what can be included in a single footnote. For a sampling, see Mary Aquin O'Neill, "Toward a Renewed Anthropology," *Theological Studies* 36 (1975): 725–36; Elizabeth A. Johnson, "Jesus, the Wisdom of God: A Biblical Basis for a Non-Androcentric Christology," *Ephemerides Theologicae Lovanienses* 61 (1985): 261–94; Rebecca Chopp, "Feminism's Theological Pragmatics: A Social Naturalism of Women's Experience," *Journal of Religion* 67 (1987): 239–56; Anne E. Carr and Elisabeth Schüssler Fiorenza, *The Special Nature of Women? Concilium* 1991/6 (London: SCM Press, 1991); Ann O'Hara Graff, ed., *In the Embrace of God: Feminist Approaches to Theological Anthropology* (Maryknoll, NY: Orbis Books, 1995); Rebecca S. Chopp, "Feminist Queries and Metaphysical Musings," *Modern Theology* 11 (1995): 47–63; Anne Carr, *Transforming Grace: Women's Experience and Christian Tradition* (New York: Continuum, 1996); Gonzalez, *Created in God's Image*; and Susan A. Ross, *Anthropology: Seeking Light and Beauty* (Collegeville, MN: Liturgical Press, 2012). It should also be noted that some scholars—including some self-identified feminists—continue to defend or seek to rehabilitate gender complementarity. For example, see Lisa Sowle Cahill, *Between the Sexes: Foundations for a Christian Ethics of Sexuality* (Minneapolis: Fortress Press, 1985); and Prudence Allen, "Integral Sex Complementarity and the Theology of Communion," *Communio* 17 (1990): 523–44.

dualism. As mind rules over body and reason over passion, so man rules over woman (domination). Men exercising power over women is thus derived from the nature of things. Hence, to change this arrangement, the argument goes, is to violate the nature of things or "the way things are" (essential inequality). This patriarchal worldview is buttressed by pseudo-science, justifying the putative biological inferiority of women.[17]

Far too often this socially constructed and patriarchal system is taken for granted and presumed as natural and immutable as the essentialist vision of human nature. Because these norms are human creations that have developed over time, they can in fact be changed and our understanding of the human person developed further as with all Christian doctrine.

As noted earlier, the aim of this chapter is not to provide an exhaustive accounting or study of Thomistic theological anthropology or wade into the debates about whether or not such an essentialist foundation could be resourced or refashioned in a more holistic and constructive way. Instead, we seek to challenge the systematic theological foundations of our Christian anthropology, suggesting that we not simply default to Thomas as the only orthodox answer. Let's consider, rather, what a theological anthropology that does not presuppose an essentialist view of human nature but instead begins with the Scotus's *haecceitas* might look like and how some of these perennially contentious issues in the church and academy might be reimagined or addressed anew according to this hermeneutic of catholicity.

A contemporary retrieval of Scotus's *haecceitas* avoids binary distinctions between genders and biological sexes and, therefore, circumvents the intra-human hierarchical dualism found in essentialist anthropologies such as found in that of Thomas Aquinas.

---

[17] Eleazar S. Fernandez, *Reimagining the Human: Theological Anthropology in Response to Systemic Evil* (St. Louis: Chalice Press, 2004), 106–7.

The value of human personhood is located within the context of the principle of individuation, which is really identical with, yet formally distinct from, a person's actual existence or being. Value and dignity, then, is not located within a given person's status as male or female, just as it does not reside within the strictures of what is considered the human. Individuals are what God primarily intends, not necessarily the biological sex or the socialized and constructed gender that is shared among a certain population of humanity. Fundamentally, all people share on some level their status as contingently existent and, on another level, their common nature *(natura communis)* as something we call human, but any further demarcation is an *a posteriori* material distinction that falls outside the traditionally essentialist and *a priori* ontological foundation that is the ground for theological anthropologies that engender complementarity.

While to most people the seemingly esoteric debates between approaches respectively presented by Thomas or Scotus might appear trivial or unimportant, the potential significance of *haecceitas* as a starting point for understanding the human person is extraordinary in practice. The theological shift, following the philosophical arguments, is toward a holistic understanding of the universe that unveils something of how and, more important, why God creates. The how is by means of prioritizing the particular. In other words, God does not first think of some abstract, timeless, immutable "essence" such as humanity in a generic sense and only secondarily create individual iterations of that universal human nature, some male and some female, some at this time and some at another time, some in this place and some somewhere else. Instead, the vast and expansive diversity of particular individuals—human and nonhuman creatures alike—that exists in the world is the result of God's desire to bring *this particular* creature into existence when absolutely nothing outside of the divine will can compel or persuade God to do or not do so. This brings us to the *why* God creates. For Scotus, given his philosophical emphasis on the primacy of the will over the intellect, the answer to why God creates anything at all is *love*.[18] God wills the existence of creatures in order to express the divine love *ad extra* and comes to know what was first loved into existence.

Returning to the issue of gender complementarity, a central implication of that metaphysical outlook is the claim that one gender is completed or *complemented* by the other, its opposite. And that the difference between the two genders is signified by the respective biological sex traditionally associated with the genders masculine or feminine. It does not take much reflection to arrive at a problem inherent in this anthropological perspective, namely, it suggests that individual human beings are intrinsically inadequate in themselves. Indeed, no individual is ever totally complete, self-sustaining, immune to the need for relationship and community. But, as ethicist Margaret Farley keenly notes, "to say that we are incomplete in ourselves does not mean that we are 'halves' of persons who will be 'whole' only when we find our gendered complement."[19] To reconsider Christian theological anthropology with *haecceitas* as our starting point is to put forward a perspective of the person that is fundamentally more catholic or wholemaking. It is a theological perspective rooted in a philosophical framework that bears an anthropological integrity not dependent on external social norms for establishing dignity or value. This person has inherent dignity and value by virtue of unrepeatable, intrinsic, and ineffable *haecceitas* as

---

[18] See Daniel P. Horan, "Light and Love: A Franciscan Look at the 'How' and 'Why' of Creation," in *Francis of Assisi and the Future of Faith: Exploring Franciscan Spirituality and Theology in the Modern World* (Phoenix: Tau Publishing, 2012), 145–57.

[19] Farley, *Just Love*, 157. In the lines immediately following this quotation, Farley references a beautiful passage from the poet Rainer Marie Rilke, who once wrote about moving "toward a time when 'there will be girls and women whose name will no longer signify merely an opposite of the masculine, but something in itself, something that makes one think not of any complement and limit, but only of life and existence'" (Rainer Maria Rilke, *Letters to a Young Poet*, trans. M. D. H. Norton [New York: W. W. Norton, 1993], 59). It strikes me that Rilke is describing a vision we might aptly call *haecceitas*.

created by God. A person's dignity and value is not conditioned by biological sex or gender identity, or by conformity to generalizations of sex and gender (more on this in the next section), but conditioned only by the fact of the person's existence, which was made possible by God's decision to create *this* particular person as *this* unique individual in a world of unique individuals.

The equality of human dignity, therefore, does not depend on which set of gendered characteristics an individual identifies with or presents to others. Equality is not grounded in correspondence to or association with one's gender; rather, equality is grounded in the shared existential reality of our utter particularity and individual identity. And all women and men rightly claim that theological status. Reframing the metaphysics and foundational systematic theology that undergirds our theological anthropology in this way, changing our starting point from an essentialist worldview that leads to complementarity to an anthropology grounded in *haecceitas*, could have dramatically positive implications for the roles of women and men in society, church, and the home. It would also invite a renewal in theological ethics as well as in other theological disciplines. Then, perhaps, we may begin to have a better understanding of the human person that does not rest upon a false need for separateness to claim equality. Instead, we could embark on developing a sense of equality rooted in our radical particularity.

The Reality of Transgender Persons

During 2016, the bioethics journal *Heath Care Ethics USA*, a joint publication of the Catholic Health Association and the Center for Health Care Ethics at St. Louis University, published a series of seven articles on the subject of transgender persons and Catholic healthcare systems.[20] This series of essays captured

---

[20] See Carol Bayley, "Transgender Persons and Catholic Healthcare," *Health Care Ethics USA* 24, no. 1 (Winter 2016): 1–5; Becket Gremmels, "Sex Reassignment Surgery and the Catholic Moral Tradition:

a robust and engaging discussion about the relationship between the increasingly visible phenomenon of transgender persons coming out into the public square and the potential conflicts regarding the medical, psychological, and other therapeutic treatment of such individuals at healthcare institutions that bear a Catholic mission identity. Immediately noticeable about this discussion is that it is dominated by ethical questions centering on normative practices and traditional Catholic bioethical categories, which is not at all surprising given the genre of the journal in which these essays were published. These respective scholars attempt to clarify what the best medical and pastoral approaches are for health professionals at Catholic institutions according to the usual moral norms and tools at the disposal of theological ethicists. The focus on moral norms and applied ethics at times oversimplifies and instrumentalizes the lived experience of transgender persons. Depending on the particular claims an ethicist wishes to make, this approach can lead to the erasure and dismissal of transgender experiences.

Before considering what ethicists have been arguing with regard to transgender persons, it may be helpful to examine briefly some key terminology. While transgender persons have been around as long as any other human beings have—despite attempts by those who deploy philosophical, theological, or social efforts to erase this population—the technical and scholarly language surrounding the diverse experiences of transgender

---

Insights from Pope Pius XII on the Principle of Totality," *Health Care Ethics USA* 24, no. 1 (Winter 2016): 6–10; Kevin FitzGerald, "Viewing the Transgender Issue from the Catholic and Personalized Health Care Perspectives," *Health Care Ethics USA* 24, no. 2 (Spring 2016): 7–10; E. Christian Brugger, "Response to Bayley and Gremmels on Transgender Ethics," *Health Care Ethics USA* 24, no. 3 (Summer 2016): 12–17; Elliott Louis Bedford and Jason T. Eberl, "Is the Soul Sexed? Anthropology, Transgenderism, and Disorders of Sex Development," *Health Care Ethics USA* 24, no. 3 (Summer 2016): 18–33; John F. Brehany, "Pope Pius XII and Justifications for Sex Reassignment Surgery," *Health Care Ethics USA* 24, no. 4 (Fall 2016): 18–21; and Becket Gremmels, "More Insights from Pius XII, a Reply to Brugger and Brehany, and a Clarification," *Health Care Ethics USA* 24, no. 4 (Fall 2016): 7–17.

persons is relatively new and developing. At present, it is generally accepted that the term *transgender* is something of an umbrella term "for those people whose gender identity and/or gender expression differs from what is typically associated with the sex they were assigned at birth."[21] Additionally, there is an array of other terms used to signal specific contexts or experiences of those who might identify as transgender.[22] Given the predominance of the term *transsexual* alongside *transgender* in the current theological and ethical discussion, it is worth also noting that *transsexual*—while viewed by some as an antiquated term—is nevertheless still widely used and appropriated in a non-pejorative sense. Nicholas Teich explains:

> By and large, *transsexual* refers to a person who identifies as the opposite sex of that which he or she was assigned at birth. Transgender, on the other hand, includes transsexual people, but the term also encompasses many more identities. . . . Many people use the terms transgender and transsexual interchangeably, but on a technical level this is incorrect. All transsexual people are transgender, but not all transgender people are transsexual.[23]

According to Teich, the term *transsexual* most closely approximates the context we are generally considering in this section of the chapter: individuals who identify with the gender not typically associated with the biological sex they were assigned at birth. By biological sex I am referring to the categories male and female usually tied to the possession of particular reproductive

---

[21] GLAAD, "GLAAD Media Reference Guide—Transgender," https://www.glaad.org/reference/transgender. For a fuller historical overview of the terminological development and usage of *transgender*, see Susan Stryker, *Transgender History: The Roots of Today's Revolution*, rev. ed. (New York: Seal Press, 2017), esp. 1–44.

[22] *Gender queer, gender variant, gender nonconforming*, and *transsexual*, among others.

[23] Nicholas Teich, *Transgender 101: A Simply Guide to a Complex Issue* (New York: Columbia University Press, 2012), 3.

organs, exhibited secondary sex characteristics, and other culturally identified morphology, or even chromosomal demarcation
(for example, XX, XY). By *gender*, I am referring to the identities
man and woman, which are usually performed both consciously
and tacitly in terms of gender expressions *masculine* and *feminine*, respectively.[24]

My particular aim in this investigation or case study is to
demonstrate that the problematic of erasure or denial of transgender persons found in theological and ethical arguments that
rely on an Aristotelian-Thomistic worldview and essentialist
anthropology may be avoided with the adoption of an alternative theological anthropology as a starting point—one rooted in
haecceitas, for instance. The preliminary outlines of what such a
project might look like sketched out below apply in a broad way
to the reality of transgender persons in general, but given that
most theologians and especially most ethicists are concerned with
transsexual persons (largely due to questions around psychological and surgical intervention), much of what follows focuses
on those transgender persons who might otherwise identify as
transsexual—even when my interlocutors use the more general
terminology of transgender. Having clarified these basic terms,
let us turn to the current Catholic theological discussion about
transgender persons.

As witnessed in the 2016 *Health Care Ethics USA* discussion,
some ethicists apply the principles of double effect and totality
in an effort to open a space within the received moral tradition
to accommodate surgical interventions to treat those transgender
persons suffering with what the medical community calls gender

---

[24] I want to acknowledge the limitations of what follows in terms of
a gender binary. Given the current state of the theological and ethical
discussion and the limitations of this chapter's scope, I do not explore
the small but growing collection of literature that reexamines the gender binary. As Teich rightly notes, "The gender binary exists for easy
categorization and labeling purposes" (Teich, *Transgender 101*, 5), and
readers should note that this is the primary reason for my prescinding
from further problematizing of the gender binary in this book.

dysphoria.[25] Those ethicists considering the principle of double effect, such as Carol Bayley, argue that surgical intervention resulting in unavoidable sterilization could be understood as morally permissible when the sterility is foreseen but not intended to achieve the good end, namely, relief from the effects of gender dysphoria.[26] Others, like Becket Gremmels, propose considering the principle of totality and draw on the prudential admonitions of Pope Pius XII as a resource in considering the moral justification for surgical intervention. The primary issue under review in this case is not so much the concern of sterility but the violation of bodily integrity resulting from the performance of surgery on an otherwise healthy body. Gremmels is admittedly tentative in his argumentation, suggesting in conclusion that Pius XII's approach to the moral principle of totality does not immediately clarify the moral status of such surgery as a just treatment for persons suffering gender dysphoria, but that it does not immediately preclude such treatment.[27]

What is interesting about the engagement of ethicists who are at least open to consideration of surgical treatment for gender dysphoria is that it remains always at the level of received Catholic *moral reasoning*. Curiously, those ethicists in the *Health Care Ethics USA* discussion who are unwilling to even consider the possibility—E. Christain Brugger, Elliott Louis Bedford, and Jason T. Eberl—do so with recourse to what they variously identify as traditional Catholic *theological anthropology*.[28] Accordingly,

---

[25] Gender dysphoria is the technical medical classification listed in the fifth edition of *the Diagnostic and Statistical Manual of Mental Disorders (DSM-V)* given by the American Psychiatric Association to those individuals for whom there is a serious and persistent discontent with the gender assigned to them at birth (see *DSM-V*, 302.6 and 302.85).

[26] Bayley, "Transgender Persons and Catholic Healthcare," 3–4.

[27] Gremmels, "Sex Reassignment Surgery and the Catholic Moral Tradition," 6–10; and idem, "More Insights from Pius XII, a Reply to Brugger and Brehany, and a Clarification," 7–17.

[28] Brugger, "Response to Bayley and Gremmels on Transgender Ethics," 12–17; and Bedford and Eberl, "Is the Soul Sexed? Anthropology, Transgenderism, and Disorders of Sex Develoment," 18–33. I should add

thinkers in this latter camp hold that no further conversation is necessary because the classic line of Aristotelian-Thomistic anthropology that forms the ground of most Catholic sexual and biomedical ethical teaching as they interpret it is unassailable or at least not subject to reconsideration. This resistance to exploring the etiology or substance of transgender realities is perhaps most starkly exhibited in the recent statement on transgenderism by staff members of the partisan think tank National Catholic Bioethics Center in Philadelphia. The authors refer to the phenomenon of increased visibility of transgender persons in conspiratorial terms, claiming that "the boldness of the gender ideology movement has now brought it to the forefront" of social discourse.[29] The authors ground their claims in a general reference to "a proper understanding of the nature of the human person," which through their argumentation—without referencing any primary theological or magisterial sources—gestures toward certain Aristotelian-Thomistic presuppositions contained within essentialist anthropologies.[30] Summarizing their perspective, they write: "In short, a person's sex is manifested in the body in accordance with how the person has been created, and so it cannot be in conflict with any truer or deeper sexual identity contrary to the bodily sex. This is a foundational anthropological point that no medical association or political ideology can overturn."[31] They not only dismiss the possibility of alternative considerations regarding the ethical implications that the medical and psychological treatment of transgender persons presents to healthcare workers and pastoral ministers, but they also effectively reject the reality of both gender dysphoria as a condition and transgender

---

that John Brehany could also be included among those unconvinced by the arguments of Bayley and Gremmels, but he focuses his rejoinder on providing alternative readings of Pius XII to those of Gremmels.

[29] The National Catholic Bioethics Center (NCBC), "Brief Statement on Transgenderism," *National Catholic Bioethics Quarterly* 16 (Winter 2016): 599.

[30] NCBC, "Brief Statement on Transgenderism," 600.

[31] NCBC, "Brief Statement on Transgenderism," 600

persons as such.[32] As long as ethicists operate with an essentialist gender anthropology as its basis for these ethical debates, these moral disputations will undermine the existence of transpersons.

It is clear that these ethicists do not agree with their Georgetown University colleague, Kevin FitzGerald, who writes:

In light of the research and our commitment to provide the best health care to all, *we need to update our understanding of sexual characteristics and gender identification and the various ways in which both can be experienced and expressed in human beings*. This recognition of the need to *update our understanding of human nature* is not new within our Catholic tradition. The Catholic Church has a long history of integrating scientific advances into its understanding of creation and human nature.[33]

And yet, in a sense, this is also where the conversation in *Health Care Ethics USA* ended, as seen in Gremmels's second essay, in which he concludes: "Finally, and hopefully the above conversation has made this clear, *my aim is to push the conversation towards metaphysics and anthropology*. This is where applicable

---

[32] This perspective is also argued with greater or lesser nuance by other scholars, including Michelle M. Schumacher, "Gender Ideology and the 'Artistic' Fabrication of Human Sex: Nature as Norm or the Remaking of the Human?" *The Thomist* 80 (2016): 363–423; and John A. DiCamillo, "Gender Transitioning and Catholic Health Care," *National Catholic Bioethics Quarterly* 17 (Summer 2017): 213–23, as well as by social commentators, such as Katherine Kersten, "Transgender Conformity," *First Things* (December 2016): 25–31; and Richard Corradi, "Transgender Delusion," *First Things* (October 2015): 17–19, who reveals his rigorist Aristotelian-Thomistic outlook in the stark opening line of his opinion piece: "Human nature does not change. . . . Our nature is immutable."

[33] FitzGerald, "Viewing the Transgender Issue from the Catholic and Personalized Health Care Perspectives," 8, emphasis added. As an aside, it is worth noting that Pope Francis named FitzGerald to serve on the Pontifical Council for Culture in 2014.

theological insights remain to be had."[34] Even though there is relatively little theological research on the question of transgender persons to date, Gremmels recognizes that until systematic theologians address the underlying theological anthropology upon which Catholic moral teaching is based, there will be little more that can be done from within the field of theological ethics in addressing this subject.[35] This is echoed in a recent article by British ethicist David Albert Jones, who is incredulous about the licit moral application of traditional ethical tools like double effect or the principle of totality to justify surgical intervention to treat gender dysphoria in transgender persons. Despite his resistance at present, he nevertheless signals the need for further systematic theological work before conclusive ethical norms can be established. Jones writes:

> Furthermore, it is only in the last decade or so that Catholic theologians have given serious consideration to the relationship between gender dysphoria and theological anthropology. It would be rash to suppose that the philosophical and conceptual tools needed to understand these phenomena already exist. There is a clear need in this area for further philosophical and theological thought.[36]

And this brings us back to the principle aim of this book: theological reflection on the human person through the lens of catholicity. Despite those who comfortably reassert an Aristotelian-Thomistic framework viewed as immutable and effectively

---

[34] Gremmels, "More Insights from Pius XII, a Reply to Brugger and Brehany, and a Clarification," 14, emphasis added.

[35] Perhaps one recent exception to this is found in an essay by Craig A. Ford, Jr., who takes seriously the metaphysical foundations of natural law theory while exploring the treatment of transgender persons in Catholic schools. See "Transgender Bodies, Catholic Schools, and a Queer Natural Law Theology of Exploration," *The Journal of Moral Theology* 7 (2018): 70–98.

[36] David Albert Jones, "Gender Reassignment Surgery: A Catholic Bioethical Analysis," *Theological Studies* 79 (2018): 335.

inerrant to justify the erasure of the reality of transgender persons, Jones is correct in stating that

> there is no explicit authoritative Catholic teaching on GRS [gender reassignment surgery]. . . . The topic has not been addressed directly by any pope or the Second Vatican Council. It is not addressed overtly by any public teaching document issued by the Congregation of the Doctrine of the Faith (CDF), nor is it covered in the extensive ethical section of the *Catechism of the Catholic Church* (CCC).[37]

I surmise that one of the primary reasons there is no clear magisterial teaching on the ethics of treating transgender persons is that the current Aristotelian-Thomistic essentialist anthropology that generally informs Catholic theological ethics cannot adequately accommodate such a reality. Essentially, this received essentialist anthropological tradition represents an incomplete and insufficiently nuanced vision of the human person and therefore an alternative approach, one that reflects greater wholemaking, is necessary.

Consider if, instead of an essentialist anthropology, we were to begin our theological reflection on the human person with the particularity of the individual. We have already seen how the principle of *haecceitas* accounts for each person's inherent dignity and value and that each person's particular *this*-ness is unrepeatable, intrinsic, and ineffable. We have also seen that such a starting point circumvents the essentialist impasse of gender complementarity regarding a renewed appreciation for the ontological wholeness of the individual loved into existence by the Creator. It is also the case that *haecceitas* might help us affirm the reality of transgender persons in our theological anthropology by means of shifting focus from the participation or instantiation of a singular iteration in a common nature *(quiddity)*—such as "humanity" in abstraction—and toward recognition of an infinite plurality of ontologically whole persons.

---

[37] Jones, "Gender Reassignment Surgery," 315.

Given the metaphysical importance of accidental attributes as the individuating principle in Thomas's Aristotelian anthropology, it is no wonder that those who presuppose this hylomorphic framework as correct and immutable argue for a strict congruence between one's biological sex assigned at birth (as identified morphologically, hormonally, genetically, or by some other culturally determined factor) and one's authentic gender.[38] Frequently, those who oppose the reality of transgender persons claim that such a phenomenon is rooted in a problematic body-soul dualism. Grasping at limited language and metaphor to express the experiences of gender dysmorphia, some transgender persons unintentionally speak in ways that sound as if they are "trapped" (either in terms of a soul or some cognitive sense) in the body that exhibits cultural signals of a biological sex incongruent with their true perceived gender. On the surface this sounds dualistic in that it appears to contradict longstanding theological doctrine about the integrity of creation and the material world going back to at least Irenaeus of Lyons in the second century of the Christian era. However, these individuals are not consciously engaging in philosophical or theological categories or debate, and therefore such interpretations of phenomenological experience, however phrased, should not be used to dismiss their experience or existence. Hearing such expression leads those who defend an Aristotelian-Thomistic anthropology to argue that the human soul is an "inseparable accident" that is in part responsible for individuation.[39] Ethicists such as Bedford and Eberl then argue that not only are our material bodies "sexed" (with apparent reference to assigned biological sex and, therefore, gendered in their telling), but also our immaterial soul bears some biological sex and/or gender as a result of its role in the particular human composite. "While strictly speaking the soul, which is immaterial,

---

[38] It is worth noting here that the discernment of one's sex at birth according to these characteristics or factors is itself deeply contested and an unsettled area of scientific, medical, and social debate.

[39] See John Finley, "The Metaphysics of Gender: A Thomistic Approach," *The Thomist* 79 (2015): 585–614.

is not sexed, each soul is created by God as the vivifying principle of sexed bodies and is thereby individuated and sexed as an inseparable accidental quality of the human being. In short, as the vivifying principle of actually existing human beings, the human soul is properly characterized as sexed."[40] The argument here is one of presumptive causation that is demonstrated by the effect, namely, if the assigned natal biological sex of the individual is female, then it is because the particular divinely created soul, which is an inseparable accident of this particular human being, was intended to be female by God and therefore the "true gender" of this individual is irrefutably girl or woman regardless of this same person's contestation or experience to the contrary. Because the human person is an integrated composite of body and soul, any recourse to a sense or description of incongruent gender identification as a kind of entrapment is metaphysically impossible from the Aristotelian-Thomistic perspective and therefore this person's reality is erased.[41]

There are at least three aspects of Scotus's notion of *haecceitas* that can help us reconsider the impasse presented by an Aristotelian-Thomistic essentialist anthropology. These are (a) the radical particularity of the individual creature; (b) the primacy of intuitive knowledge over abstractive knowledge; and (c) the final ineffability of an individual's "ultimate reality."[42]

---

[40] Bedford and Eberl, "Is the Soul Sexed?" 21.

[41] For an insightful discussion about overcoming the dualistic and binary worldview of much theological reflection in light of modern developments of science and mathematics, particularly as it pertains to the relationship between the Christian categories of body and soul or material and spiritual in theological anthropology, see Heidi Ann Russell, "Quantum Anthropology: Reimagining the Human Person as Body/Spirit," *Theological Studies* 74 (2013): 934–59; and idem, *Quantum Shift: Theological and Pastoral Implications of Contemporary Developments in Science* (Collegeville, MN: Liturgical Press, 2015).

[42] "Ultimate reality" is the phrase Scotus uses to refer to that principle of individuation—typically called *haecceitas*—in his work *Ordinatio* II, 3, q. 6, n. 188 (Vatican VII:483). For an English translation, see Paul V. Spade, *Five Texts on the Medieval Problem of Universals* (Indianapolis: Hackett Publishing, 1994), 107.

At the heart of the metaphysics undergirding Scotus's anthropological insights is the conviction that when God creates, God does so with each and every *particular* creature or individual in mind. God does not merely intend grass or horses or humans in general and then, by means of accidental attributes such as the soul, individuate a series of particular iterations of this or that *quiddity*. Instead, Scotus maintains that God desires a plurality of radically distinct individuals into existence, individuals that can, of course, be categorized according to what might be recognized as common, but it is their particularity that God primarily intends. It is "*this* blade of grass" and "Seabiscuit" and "Clare" that God loves into existence. "Scotus's emphasis upon the importance of individuality appears clearly in his notion of *haecceitas* (thisness) which makes each person as well as each object an irreplaceable piece of the glorious whole which is creation."[43] One of the major hurdles to recognizing the reality of transgender persons in Christian theological reflections on the human person is the apparent inapplicability of traditionally conceived cultural and even theological norms about gender and biological sex. A transgender person does not conform to what are often presented as the universal, static, and immutable norms of anthropological classification and valuation. When one's metaphysical priority is tied to an essentialist worldview, it is easy to see the problems the reality of transgender persons present to that person's way of perceiving and thinking. However, if one adopts a Scotist metaphysical foundation that prioritizes the radical particularity of each existing individual, those standard categories of evaluation no longer hold firm. Mary Beth Ingham fleshes out the significance of this shift in thinking.

> The thisness *(haecceitas)* which differentiates one person from another can only be known by a direct acquaintance, and not from any consideration of any common nature.

---

[43] Mary Beth Ingham, *The Harmony of Goodness: Mutuality and Moral Living according to John Duns Scotus*, 2nd ed. (St. Bonaventure, NY: Franciscan Institute Publications, 2012), 33.

> Thus, *haecceitas* makes a singular thing what it is and dif-
> ferentiates it from all other things (of a common nature) to
> which it may be compared (because of the commonality).
> . . . *Haecceitas* refers to that positive dimension of every
> concrete and contingent being which identifies it and makes
> it worthy of attention. At the turn of the fourteenth cen-
> tury, Scotus continues to shift the Franciscan metaphysical
> focus from the necessary and universal to the contingent
> and particular.[44]

Everybody is radically particular, not a more-or-less accurate
reflection of some abstraction or universal but the actual instantiation of himself or herself. One's true identity—one's *true self*
as Thomas Merton would later describe this aspect of Scotus's
thought[45]—is absolutely unique, positive, and unrepeatable. Because one's true self or real identity does not rely on its proximity
to an abstracted ideal or universal essence, the claim that transgender persons' identity could not possibly be what they testify
it is because it does not appear to conform to the preconceptions
of gender essentialism or typical congruence between their assigned biological sex and gender expression no longer holds. An
anthropology that begins with the *haecceitas* of each and every
person—cisgender or transgender—requires consideration of that
absolutely singular subject.

This brings us to the second of at least three significant anthropological insights from Scotus's thought: the primacy of
intuitive knowledge over abstractive knowledge. While many
medieval epistemological debates strike the majority of modern
Christians and nonbelievers alike as esoteric and generally ir-
relevant, Scotus's reflections on if and how we can know the
proper *haecceitas* of any given creature is illuminating and offers

---

[44] Ingham, *The Harmony of Goodness*, 34–35.

[45] See Thomas Merton, *New Seeds of Contemplation* (New York:
New Directions, 1961); and Daniel P. Horan, *The Franciscan Heart of
Thomas Merton: A New Look at the Spiritual Influence of His Life,
Thought, and Writing* (Notre Dame, IN: Ave Maria Press, 2014), esp.
95–116.

an important guide for pastoral praxis. In short, Scotus—following at least this aspect of Aristotle's thought closely—holds that empirical sense knowledge is prior to abstractive intellection. When it comes to an individual, it is what Scotus calls "intuitive intellection," something akin to empirical knowledge of a given person or thing, that is operative.[46] It is a kind of immediate knowledge, a familiar or experiential knowledge, something that is known at the deepest level. This is contrasted with what Scotus will call abstractive intellection. This is a kind of knowing that is removed from direct experience and therefore can apply to things that exist in reality or theoretically, whereas intuitive knowledge can only take place vis-à-vis an existing thing.[47] In his treatise *De Primo Principio*, Scotus contrasts these two ways of knowing:

> Knowledge through what is similar is merely knowledge under a universal aspect, to the extent that the things are alike. Through such a universal what properly distinguishes each would remain unknown. Furthermore, such a knowledge through a universal is not intuitive but abstractive, and intuitive knowledge is the more perfect of the two.[48]

Put in the colloquial of modern Spanish, the difference between intuitive intellection and abstractive intellection is like the difference between the verbs *conocer* and *saber*—both are literally translated as "to know" in English, but the former denotes a kind of deep, personal, and empirical knowledge whereas the latter

---

[46] See Scotus, *Quodlibet* 14, no. 10, in John Duns Scotus, *God and Creatures: The Quodlibetal Questions*, trans. Frank Alluntis and Allan Wolter (Princeton, NJ: Princeton University Press, 1975), 325: "Any such intellection, namely, that which is per se, proper, and immediate, requires the presence of the object in all its proper intelligibility as object [*propria ratio objecti*]. If the intellection is intuitive, this means in its own existence it is present as object. If the intellection is abstractive, it is present in something which represents it in all its proper and essential meaning as a knowable object."

[47] See Scotus, *Quodlibet* 7, no. 8 (*God and Creatures*, 167).

[48] Scotus, *De Primo Principio* 4.89, trans. Allan B. Wolter (Chicago: Franciscan Herald Press, 1966), 149.

refers to a general, intellectual, or abstract knowledge. It is also like the difference we note between saying, "I *know* this person" and "I know *about* this person."

Knowledge of some common nature is only possible in abstraction and therefore does not give us privileged insight into the identity of a real, existing, particular thing. Scotus's privileging of intuitive knowledge over abstractive knowledge says something about the significance of proximity in establishing verity. This is notable for us in two ways. First, it suggests that we ought to privilege the *experiential, intuitive knowledge* of transgender persons about their own gender identity over contestations by other parties with reference to abstractive knowledge. Second, it subordinates any claims to knowledge of universal essence to the particularity of a given individual's *haecceitas*. This second point raises challenging questions about our longstanding reliance on Aristotelian-Thomistic anthropological frameworks and the deployment of them to silence, dismiss, or deny the reality of transgender persons. Practically, cisgender persons such as myself have to ask ourselves: Who are we to claim to know better than the particular individual his or her true identity with recourse only to our less-intuitive or merely abstractive knowledge of who the individual is? This question signals the need for epistemological humility when facing matters of identity, being, and gender, which brings us to our last insight from Scotus.

Third, Scotus believes that we cannot actually know our (or, as it were, *anyone else's*) *haecceitas,* as such, in its entirety. He does not believe that our intellect in this life is capable of such knowledge and argues that only God knows us in our particularity—our *haecceity*—with absolute comprehension. Therefore, we can say with Ingham that "*haecceitas* enabled Scotus to emphasize the ineffable value of each contingent being," as well as gesture toward the special relationship each creature enjoys directly with the Creator who alone fully and intuitively knows each individual.[49] It is this insight that allows Thomas Merton

---

[49] Ingham, *The Harmony of Goodness*, 35.

to proclaim: "The secret of my identity is hidden in the love and mercy of God. . . . Therefore I cannot hope to find myself anywhere except in Him [*sic*]."[50] This sense of our truest identity's ineffability should inspire in all Christians both awe and humility. In truth, all persons, regardless of their gender identity, spend a lifetime of discovery, learning along the way—slowly but, God willing, surely—a little more about who they are and who God is. And these seemingly separate quests are in fact two sides of the one coin of human life.

Given these three insights arising from *haecceitas*, we can now approach the question of the reality of transgender persons anew. God loves into existence and creates a diversity of individuals, each of which has an ineffable identity known in completeness only by the Creator. Because we cannot rely on abstractions or universal essences when reflecting on human nature in the particular experience of this or that individual, we cannot say that we know with certitude the relationship between the morphological features, hormonal composition, or chromosomal status—what we typically call biological sex—and the ultimate reality of an individual's gender identity. The plurality of unique creatures loved into existence by God forms the wholeness of creation. It is not conformity to an abstract idea or type that brings joy to God, but rather the harmony that exists when we recognize it is our very difference that is the condition for the possibility of relationship. We still have a lot of work to do to understand better the complexity of this world in general and the theology of transgender persons in particular, but it is my conviction that Scotus's insights about our existence and identity can help us do just that.

The Dehumanization of Racism

An essentialist approach to human nature has not only harmed cisgender women and transgender women and men over the

---

[50] Merton, *New Seeds of Contemplation*, 35.

centuries, but it has also been deployed in such a way by Christians as to subjugate, dehumanize, enslave, and even destroy persons of African descent and indigenous peoples around the world. Within a distinctively Christian context one can recall the now-classic theological debates (with real pragmatic consequences) within the church of Spain between the Dominican theologian and missionary Bartolomé de las Casas (d. 1566) and Juan Ginés de Sepúlveda (d. 1573) on the anthropological and moral status of the newly encountered indigenous populations of the Americas.[51] The colonial logic of the time, informed by an Aristotelian-Thomistic anthropology advanced by Sepúlveda and likeminded thinkers, argued for the veracity of Aristotle's hypothesis that certain peoples are natural slaves. In *Politics* Aristotle had written:

> Therefore those people who are as different from others as body is from soul or beast from human, and people whose task, that is to say, the best thing to come from them, is to use their bodies are in this condition—those people are

[51] The most concentrated instance of this debate took place between 1550 and 1551 at the Colegio de San Gregorio in Valladolid, Spain (often referred to simply as the Valladolid Debate). For more on this, see Daniel P. Brunstetter, "Sepúveda, Las Casas, and the Other: Exploring the Tension between Moral Universalism and Alterity," *The Review of Politics* 72 (2010): 409–35; Lewis Hanke, *All Mankind Is One: A Study of the Disputation between Bartolomé de Las Casas and Juan Gines De Sepúveda in 1550 on the Religious and Intellectual Capacity of the American Indians* (DeKalb: Northern Illinois University Press, 1994); and Lewis Hanke, *Aristotle and the American Indians: A Study in Race Prejudice in the Modern World* (Indianapolis: Indiana University Press, 1970). For an analysis of Sepúlveda's misappropriation of Aristotle and other ancient resources in his defense of "natural slavery," see Camille Reynolds, "The Misapplication of Theoretical Doctrine in the Valladolid Debate," MA thesis, University of Michigan, 2010. For a recent theological engagement with this historical debate in the contemporary context of anti-black racism, see Santiago Slabodsky, "It's the Theology, Stupid! Coloniality, Anti-Blackness, and the Bounds of 'Humanity,'" in *Anti-Blackness and Christian Ethics*, ed. Vincent W. Lloyd and Andrew Prevot (Maryknoll, NY: Orbis Books, 2017), 19–40.

natural salves. . . . It is evident, then, that there are some people, some of whom are naturally free, others naturally slaves, from whom slavery is both just and beneficial.[52]

Along with proof texting passages from scripture, Sepúlveda defended the mass enslavement and genocide of native peoples, those of non-European (that is, non-white) descent, by invoking a version of the Aristotelian claim that some people were naturally inferior and even better off enslaved. By extension, Sepúlveda made a missiological argument that it was in the native peoples' "best interest" to be enslaved so as to be converted to Catholic Christianity, which he parlayed into a "just war" claim about the need to subdue those he described as "barbarian," presumably meaning those who would resist this enslavement.

Las Casas, who was the only one of these two thinkers to have lived in the so-called New World and therefore able to draw from not only abstractive but also intuitive knowledge, attempted to refute Sepúlveda's recourse to Aristotle, arguing that Aristotle's notion of natural slave did not apply to the indigenous peoples of the Americas.[53] It is notable that scholars have long stated that, despite Las Casas's firsthand account of and relationship with the indigenous peoples of the Americas, the debate about the humanity and agency of the indigenous peoples stayed within a theoretical realm.[54] The policies of both the Spanish Crown and the Catholic Church were grounded in arguments over interpretations of philosophical and theological anthropology of the sixteenth century. And many thousands of individuals were abused and murdered as a result, both in the name of the Crown and of Christ.

Centuries later the theoretical tactics deployed in the sixteenth century to justify the dehumanization of native peoples in the

---

[52] Aristotle, *Politics*, I.6, trans. C. D. C. Reeve (Indianapolis: Hackett Publishing, 1998), 8–9.

[53] See Bartolomé de Las Casas, *A Short Account of the Destruction of the Indies*, trans. Nigel Griffin (New York: Penguin Classics, 1999).

[54] See Hanke, *All Mankind Is One*.

Western Hemisphere continues to inform theological anthropologies, and to deleterious effect. In limiting this section of the
chapter to the realities of anti-black racism in the United States
context—though very aware that the implications of what follows
shapes the lived reality of other populations and individuals—we
explore the ways in which racism continues to lurk in the shadows of our Christian theological anthropologies and suggest that
another approach, one shaped by a hermeneutic of catholicity, is
possible. Black and womanist theologians have been drawing attention to these philosophical and theological deficiencies for some
time. Two recent works, one by Dwight Hopkins and the other
by M. Shawn Copeland, highlight the problems of essentialism
in terms of race found in the Western Enlightenment philosophical anthropology that undergirds so much of our contemporary
theological reflection on the human person.[55]

Hopkins notes that "contemporary paradigms of theological
anthropology, inherently and inevitably, drip with presuppositions about race."[56] As many feminist theologians have also
observed over the years, universal claims about what it means
to be human and the construction of the anthropological subject
unwittingly or deliberately shaped in the likeness of the white
male European necessarily carries problematic presuppositions
about what exactly it means to be human.[57] Hopkins explains:

> Elite white men (who claim objective, rational, calm, and
> detached reason) provided the intellectual justification for

---

[55] Dwight N. Hopkins, *Being Human: Race, Culture, and Religion*
(Minneapolis: Fortress Press, 2005); and M. Shawn Copeland, *Enfleshing Freedom: Body, Race, and Being* (Minneapolis: Fortress Press, 2010).

[56] Hopkins, *Being Human*, 119. Also, see Simon S. Maimela, "Man in
'White' Theology," *Journal of Theology for Southern Africa* 36 (1981):
27–42.

[57] For a succinct overview of the history of philosophical (and concurrently theological) anthropology's development in this pattern, see
Hopkins, *Being Human*, 138–60. Also see J. Kameron Carter, *Race: A
Theological Account* (New York: Oxford University Press, 2008), esp.
39–156.

the terrorist removal of dark indigenous people's lands, human bodies, water, cultural artifacts, ancestral bones, inventions, and natural treasures. More specifically, *philosophy*, *anthropology*, and *missiology* (that is, intellectual, scientific, and Christian grounds) are three conditions for the possibility of modern racism: the conscious and consistent belief in and ritualization of the subordination of darker-skinned people to demarcate permanent differentiation between the polar extremes of white and black. Dark skin color now inherently reveals mental, genetic, and moral deficiencies.[58]

As with gender, race was constructed as a marker and locus of "othering," by which the dominant group (male and white) developed an understanding of normative humanity in contradistinction to "the other" (typically female and black).[59] This is another iteration of a hierarchical dualism that forms identity by means of making concrete categories of the subordinated and the superior. The notion of race is itself an idea with a history that develops from ancient recognition of differences with varying significance to the "more refined white supremacist writings of white male intellectuals from later Europe and their elite offspring in the United States" in the seventeenth century through today.[60] The establishment of a phenotypically determined normative human inherently *dehumanizes* those who do

---

[58] Hopkins, *Being Human*, 137–38.

[59] While I am limiting my comments here to the white male in the philosophical and theological history of determining the human—for both personal reasons (my own social location) and historical ones (the traditional locus of unearned power and privilege)—the dynamic of othering according to a hierarchical dualism plays out in other modalities of relative power and privilege. Such is the case with white feminist theorists as deftly deconstructed by Ellen T. Armour in *Deconstruction, Feminist Theory, and the Problem of Difference: Subverting the Race/Gender Divide* (Chicago: University of Chicago Press, 1999). "White-feminism [*sic*] has erected itself in and through the exclusion of its raced others and its own race, and yet race leaves its (in)visible mark or trace on whitefeminism's woman and every turn" (166).

[60] Hopkins, *Being Human*, 131.

not conform to such conceptualizations of what it means to be a subject.

It is this erasure of full humanity and subjectivity of black persons and the history of their dehumanization that is the starting point for Copeland's theological reflections on the human person.[61] Rather than privileging the often unnamed but perennially present and determinative white male body as the locus for human subjectivity, Copeland begins her theological anthropology with the bodies of black women. She explains: "For centuries, black female bodies have been defiled, used, and discarded, quite literally, as refuse—simply because they are female and black, black and female."[62] In the response to the erasure of the suffering bodies of subjugated, despised, and enslaved persons of history, Copeland makes visible that which the powerful wish to ignore and makes present the mystery of the cross as lived reality for those with whom Jesus Christ continues to be present in solidarity, if not yet in terms of liberation. What has been treated in a theoretical frame, governed as it has been by presumptions of white superiority and normativity, has real, pragmatic, and detrimental effects for persons of color. "In a white, racially bias-induced horizon, blackness is aberration and defilement, a source of dread and intimidation; thus, the black body must be hidden, concealed, spatially segregated."[63]

In addition to the erasure of black bodies in our philosophical and theological anthropologies, there is also the homogenization that simultaneously occurs and is what makes such erasure of black bodies possible. This homogenization renders black bodies anonymous and therefore dismissible. Whiteness as a category

---

[61] Copeland describes the phenomenan as a "dangerous memory" of our Christian history. For more on "dangerous memory," see Johann Baptist Metz, *Faith in History and Society: Toward a Practical Fundamental Theology*, trans. J. Matthew Ashley (New York: Herder and Herder, 2007), esp. 60–84.

[62] Copeland, *Enfleshing Freedom*, 1.

[63] Copeland, *Enfleshing Freedom*, 16.

within the classic Western canon of philosophical and theological reflection is the unspoken and unacknowledged condition of the possibility of particularity and identity, that which allows for personhood to be named and the homogenization of so-called whites to be largely avoided by those in power.[64] The subordinated counterbalance to whiteness—that is, blackness; the racialized "other"—is distinguished by the effects of racial essentialism, which renders individual persons of color anonymous and ontologically bound to a group deemed inferior to the normative type. Whole communities and groups of people are lumped together and dismissed, treated as part and parcel of a racially determined cohort instead of treated with the respect, value, and dignity otherwise afforded to the individual white person.

This dynamic is what Victor Anderson describes as categorical racism.[65] Anderson explains:

> Categorical racism appropriates a species logic in which every individual member of a species shares essential traits that identify the member within the species. No accidental or particular instances of individuation (historical, economic, manners, or customs) can disconnect the individual member from the species, because the individual necessarily

---

[64] The category of whiteness has not received the attention it ought to have, in no small part due to the dynamics described here. The field of white studies as a subset of critical race theory has emerged to address precisely the sorts of questions implied in our discussion of the dehumanization of racism. For example, see George Yancy, *Look, A White! Philosophical Essays on Whiteness* (Philadelphia: Temple University Press, 2012); George Yancy, ed., *White Self-Criticality beyond Anti-Racism: How Does It Feel to Be a White Problem?* (Lanham, MD: Lexington Books, 2015); Linda Martín Alcoff, *The Future of Whiteness* (Cambridge, UK: Polity Press, 2015); and Robin DiAngelo, *What Does It Mean to Be White? Developing White Racial Literacy*, rev. ed. (New York: Peter Lang, 2016).

[65] Victor Anderson, *Beyond Ontological Blackness: An Essay on African American Religious and Cultural Criticism* (New York: Bloomsbury, 1995), 51–85.

or categorically belongs in the species if it shares all the essential traits identifying the species.[66]

Anderson explains that white anti-black racist logic during the Western Enlightenment era created the category of race as we understand it today and did so in an essentializing manner. This process was governed by and contributed to white racial ideology that largely shapes presuppositions about race, subjectivity, and the human person in the Euro-American context. This is witnessed not only in the now-classic treatises of modern philosophy but also in the political and social discourse from the seventeenth century through our present day. One of the key loci of reflection during this time was aesthetics, and the persistent influence of white racial ideology shaped what was considered beautiful and what was considered grotesque. Needless to say, the beautiful according to white racial ideology precluded black individuals (and other persons of color).[67]

In response, there has been a historical move on the part of black intellectuals and activists to recover a sense of black aesthetics and pride that aims at countering the subjugating discourse about dignity, value, and worth as determined by white racial ideology. Anderson refers to this movement and its discourse as "racial apologetics": "As a counter-discourse to categorical racism, black racial apologetics reinscribed black presence in American culture as aesthetically heroic and creative and morally masculine and self-determined."[68] Anderson points to the works of Howard Thurman and Martin Luther King, Jr., as illustrative of this response to categorical racism in the public square. The good intention and positive message notwithstanding, Anderson raises some serious concerns about the efficacious nature of black racial apologetics. The key issue is that this effort to recover and celebrate the dignity and value of black

---

[66] Anderson, *Beyond Ontological Blackness*, 51.

[67] A classic exploration of this dynamic is Frantz Fanon, *Black Skin, White Masks*, trans. Richard Philcox (New York: Grove Press, 2008).

[68] Anderson, *Beyond Ontological Blackness*, 79.

women and men is *entirely dependent* on the same categorical racism that governs white racial ideology. It reflects the same dynamics according to the same essentialist and anthropological terms. Whereas white racial ideology demeans, dehumanizes, and subjugates non-whites by means of pejorative attributes and characteristics, black racial apologetics seeks to celebrate and take pride in blackness by replacing the pejorative attributes and characteristics with positive and affirming ones. Ironically, according to Anderson, both white racial ideology and black racial apologetics serve as two sides of the same coin; this is a coin determined by the dynamic of categorical racism, on the one hand, and what Anderson calls ontological blackness, on the other. He states:

> In its apologetic form, ontological blackness mirrors categorical racism. It represents categorical ways of transferring negative qualities associated with the group onto others within the group. It creates essential criteria for defining insiders and outsiders within the group. It subjugates the creative, expressive activities of blacks (whether in performance arts or literature) under the symbolism of black heroic genius. In this case, black subjectivity has internal meaning insofar as it represents the genius of the group. It makes race identity a totality that subordinates and orders internal differences among blacks, so that gender, social standing, and sexual orientations are secondary to racial identity.[69]

Unwittingly, in an attempt to counter white racial ideology, those who engage in black racial apologetics espouse a system of ontological blackness that reinscribes the same problematics upon which categorical racism is constructed. Taking black liberation theology as also frequently subject to this dynamic, Anderson notes that much of black Christian theology privileges "the black

---

[69] Anderson, *Beyond Ontological Blackness*, 85.

community over black subjectivity."[70] In other words, Anderson is making the point that black liberation theology has prioritized the essential category of blackness over individual actualization of black subjectivity. He explains that while not always the case, many Womanist theologians offer theological reflection that draws more attention to the black subject, at least when compared to the work of many black male liberation theologians.[71] Nevertheless, for Anderson, the issue remains: "Where there exists no possibility of transcending the blackness that whiteness created, African American theologies of liberation must be seen not only as crisis theologies; they remain theologies in a crisis of legitimation."[72]

Recognizing the limitations Anderson describes, theologian Andrew Prevot has nevertheless argued that theology as a discipline may remain the one discourse able to maintain enough distance from "society's immanent frame of power/knowledge" to provide a critical space beneficial for "the struggle for black selfhood."[73] Within the context of a critical engagement with philosopher Charles Taylor's work on sources of self and formation of identity, Prevot offers a dialogical presentation between Taylor's reflections on the "capacity to be true to oneself in relationship with others" and Fanon's struggle for black selfhood in a society deeply marred by predominant white anti-blackness.[74] In part, the way forward relies on the return to the particular and individual. This is illustrated in Fanon's firsthand accounting of "his intuition of his own essence" and experience of his "quotidian body in motion" in his book *Black Skin, White Masks*.[75] This experience of the self is thrown into

---

[70] Anderson, *Beyond Ontological Blackness*, 104.

[71] See Anderson, *Beyond Ontological Blackness*, 104–16.

[72] Anderson, *Beyond Ontological Blackness*, 117.

[73] Andrew Prevot, "Sources of a Black Self? Ethics of Authenticity in an Era of Anti-Blackness," in Lloyd and Prevot, *Anti-Blackness and Christian Ethics*, 81.

[74] Prevot, "Sources of a Black Self?" 82–90.

[75] Prevot, "Sources of a Black Self?" 86–87. In addition to Fanon as interlocutor, for another phenomenological approach, see Linda Martín

crisis by the mechanism of anti-black racist constructs—what Copeland calls "white, racially bias-induced horizon"—which objectify, homogenize, essentialize, categorize, and distorts Fanon's sense of self. Forced into an alternative and, ultimately, unauthentic perspective of Fanon's own reality and existence by the racist "othering" inherent in the society around him, he powerfully recounts the effect of this white essentialist gaze: "My body is returned to me spread-eagled, disjointed, redone, draped in mourning on this white winter's day. The Negro is an animal, the Negro is bad, the Negro is wicked, the Negro is ugly."[76] Fanon names the overdetermination of his body and the erasure of his sense of self. Summarizing this ongoing dynamic, Prevot writes: "We live in a troubling age in which selfhood has been conflated with whiteness and in which blackness has been constructed in limiting and negative terms that threaten the freedom of black bodies."[77]

While in no way diminishing the destructive social constructions, problematic sources for philosophical and theological anthropologies, or the particularity of each person's struggle for authentic selfhood, Prevot offers a qualified hope illustrated by the personal narrative of Sojourner Truth, which gestures toward the possibility of divine victory over anti-blackness. "Black selfhood is possible because God loves black people in their bodies and wants them to be free. . . . Beyond racial conformity and racial antagonism, there is the hope of variously colored bodies living freely in relationships with one another."[78] The question this assertion elicits is what manner of theology can offer a way forward? This is particularly challenging when one takes seriously Anderson's critique of not only white theologies but also many black theologies as being unable to overcome the impasse of essentialism understood as ontological blackness. Anderson

---

Alcoff, *Visible Identities: Race, Gender, and the Self* (New York: Oxford University Press, 2006), 179–94.

[76] Fanon, *Black Skin, White Masks*, 93.

[77] Prevot, "Sources of a Black Self?" 95.

[78] Prevot, "Sources of a Black Self?" 95.

states at the end of his study: "When black identities are justified primarily in terms of ontological blackness, too many of the differences that genuinely signify black life and culture recede into the background."[79] What is named is a return to particularity; a call for wholemaking that does not homogenize or erase identity; a way of theologizing that attends to, as Copeland names, the "specificity and particularity [which] insists that we *all* are subjects."[80]

Turning again to Scotus's insights as a starting point for a more catholic theological anthropology, a theological view of the human person that is committed to wholemaking, there are at least two areas worth consideration for constructive engagement. The first is his emphasis on the particularity of *haecceitas* that resists the dehumanizing logic of racial essentialism, and the second is an exploration of Scotus's views on the universal injustice of slavery.

Returning to the previous chapter, in which we saw how Scotus's metaphysical starting point centers on the inherent dignity of the individual creature in God's plan for creation, his philosophical anthropology prioritizes the particularity of each person's respective *haecceitas* over anything that is secondarily shared in terms of a common nature. As already discussed, this starting point resists the depersonalization of humanity typically found in more essentialist approaches such as those governed by a hierarchical dualism in the cases of gender essentialism and what Anderson calls "ontological blackness." There is, of course, a chronologically concurrent, albeit logically secondary, sense of shared community, whether marked by gender, race, or some other identified characteristic. But what is important about theological reflection on the human person that begins with a radical commitment to particularity is that we are better able to avoid the racial homogenization that comes with essentialist understandings of human personhood.

---

[79] Anderson, *Beyond Ontological Blackness*, 162.
[80] Copeland, *Enfleshing Freedom*, 2.

Philosopher Timothy Noone has noted that among the various characteristics that define individuation (impredicability, identity, distinction, and so on), Scotus asserted that the most important was indivisibility, understood technically as noninstantiability or, put more simply, unrepeatability.[81] This is linked to Scotus's view that the principle of individuation had to be an ontologically positive entity independent of material or accidental attributes. Already, one can see the appeal in the case of an anthropological foundation that avoids the essentializing of race, phenotype, or other socially constructed marker. Other medieval theories of individuation, such as seen in the work of Henry of Ghent, who was one of Scotus's key intellectual interlocutors, argued for a negative principle of individuation. Put simply, Scotus argued that so-called negative principles merely *describe* individuation—Amanda is *not* divisible into species; Amanda is *not* Colleen—rather than *explain* what makes the individual *this particular* individual. As we have noted, Scotus argues that there is something absolutely unique that holds its own integrity and unrepeatability and that cannot be reduced to some material or perceptible difference. Scotus explains in his *Ordinatio*: "Again, every difference among the differing is reduced ultimately to some items that are diverse primarily."[82] Scotus affirms that there is something we might, for the sake of simplicity, call human nature present in each person, but that principle which individuates is co-extensive with that nature and not merely found within it. These multiple principles of individuation—*haecceitas*—"that are diverse primarily," are logically prior to and more fundamental than the human nature. Scotus summarizes his point:

Therefore, besides the nature [humanity, that is the same] in this individual and in that one, there are some primarily

[81] Timothy B. Noone, "Universals and Individuation," in *The Cambridge Companion to Duns Scotus*, ed. Thomas Williams (New York: Cambridge University Press, 2003), 113.

[82] *Ordinatio* II, dist. 3, pars 1, q. 6, n. 170 (Vatican VII: 475).

diverse items by which this and that individual differ, this one in this respect and that one in that. They are not negations. . . . Neither are they accidents. . . . Therefore, there are certain positive entities [*haecceity*] that *per se* determine the nature.[83]

This emphasis on the priority of a positive entity, some existential characteristic that is unrepeatable and absolutely unique, bypasses the pitfall that arises when a determined common nature or essence is made the foundational principle of value, dignity, meaning, and worth. A theological anthropology that begins with *haecceitas* avoids the essentialism of the white, racially bias-induced horizon and, therefore, the dehumanization of persons of color because such an understanding of individuation precedes any attempt toward homogenization and hierarchical dualism. What it means to be human arises from what it means to be authentically one's *self,* which, theologically, is prior to any common nature, let alone unjust socialization, because it was determined by the Creator from all eternity.

What this proposed starting point for theological anthropology in the key of catholicity calls for is a return to the subjectivity erased by the racial essentialism that is occasioned by most Aristotelian-Thomistic anthropologies. To begin with *haecceitas* is to recognize the inherent dignity, value, worth, subjectivity, belovedness, and particular identity that is inalienable and unrepeatable while leaving room for the secondary recognizing and celebrating of that which is shared in common. Therefore, we can still affirm that "black is beautiful" in a collective sense, as the Black Power movement rightly proclaimed, while still affirming the primacy of the individual and unique persons that embody this blackness. It is precisely our distinctiveness that occasions the possibility of relationship and community.

The second aspect of Scotus's thought that is particularly relevant here is his distinctive view on human slavery. It is distinctive

---

[83] *Ordinatio* II, dist. 3, pars 1, q. 6, n. 170 (Vatican VII: 475).

because, unlike most other late-medieval thinkers, Scotus rejected the validity of Aristotle's argument for natural slaves. Recalling the theological debates between Sepúlveda and Las Casas with which this section of the chapter opened, it is striking to think that a thirteenth-century philosopher and theologian saw the social and political consequences of how one's theological anthropology is formed. As Cynthia Nielsen explains, it was Scotus's robust understanding of the human person and his view of the natural law as they shape a sense of metaphysical freedom that "serves as the condition for the possibility of moral and political freedom."[84] For Scotus, there is a direct relationship between the foundational or metaphysical freedom God endowed all persons with and the striving toward justice in order to exercise that freedom in practice. Nielsen explains:

> On Scotus's account, metaphysical freedom is essential to what it is to *be* a human; consequently, human beings, as one would expect, naturally resist when their freedom is threatened. Historically speaking, resistance to oppressive regimes and dominating relations is a fairly constant, empirical, and transcultural phenomenon. Such a regular and consistent pattern across cultures and historical epochs suggests that human freedom has a goal. . . . That is, proper human freedom seeks a "place" in which it can flourish and express itself concretely in social and political life with others.[85]

Seeing freedom and the ability to exercise it agentially as constitutive of what it means to be a human person, as manifestly diverse as humanity actually is, Scotus rejects slavery as either

---

[84] Cynthia R. Nielsen, *Foucault, Douglass, Fanon, and Scotus in Dialogue: On Social Construction and Freedom* (New York: Palgrave Macmillan, 2013), 103–4.

[85] Nielsen, *Foucault, Douglass, Fanon, and Scotus in Dialogue*, 104–5.

natural or divinely intended. Enslavement violates freedom in several forms, from the metaphysical to the moral and political, and therefore actually stands in contrast with divine and natural law.[86] For this reason Scotus rejects Aristotle's theory on natural slavery and extends it to other forms of structural oppression wherein another's freedom is externally restricted, stating that this is "that damnable form of servitude, where the slave is like an animal."[87] All humans have an inherent right, by divine and natural law, to exercise their freedom. Ways of conceiving of the human person that justify the dehumanizing of some by means of restricting their potential to exercise their freedom are as untenable as locating the principle of individuation in matter or an accidental attribute.

At least on this topic Scotus's anthropology remains consistent. He argues for inalienable dignity and value rooted not in conformity to an external or ideal form, type, substance, or essence, but in the radical particularity of each creature prior to consideration of any way there might be something identified as shared in common. Furthermore, an existential dimension of personhood is the divinely bestowed metaphysical freedom that is the condition for the possibility of exercising moral or political freedom. Institutions, cultural presuppositions, ecclesial structures, and the like that inhibit or restrict the possibility of human agency in this way—such as one sees overtly in chattel slavery and categorical racism—are an injustice that must be resisted and a violation of God's will that must be named as such. As we saw at the outset of this section, this is why we must interrogate the Aristotelian-Thomistic anthropologies that have grounded such problematic and dehumanizing structures and ways of knowing through the centuries to the present day.

While Scotus, because of his own historical context and social location, might not have anticipated all the anthropological

---

[86] Nielsen, *Foucault, Douglass, Fanon, and Scotus in Dialogue*, 127.

[87] *Ordinatio* IV, dist. 36, q. 1, art. 1, reply (trans. Allan B. Wolter, *Duns Scotus on the Will and Morality*, ed. William A. Frank [Washington, DC: Catholic University of America Press, 1997], 330).

concerns raised in this chapter, he did have something to say about the inherent evil of dehumanizing institutions, ways of knowing, and structures that distinguished him from most of his contemporaries. Imagine if Scotus's arguments about human personhood and freedom had been introduced and defended in the debates between Sepúlveda and Las Casas. It is my hope that broader rediscovery and consideration of his insights today might allow us to reframe our Christian theological anthropology in order to move closer to overcoming the sexism of gender complementarity, recognizing the reality of transgender persons, and resisting the dehumanization of racism that is reinscribed in part due to essentialist views of human personhood.

Chapter 6

What We Have Done,
What We Have Failed to Do

So far we have looked at various themes of theological anthropology through the lens of catholicity. This hermeneutical
approach demands that we raise questions about doctrinal
expressions that bear inherent yet uncritically accepted incompleteness—that is, when the partial is mistaken for or presented
as the whole—while seeking wholemaking responses in understanding and articulating particular theological loci. In order to
understand the human person with any sense of wholeness or
catholicity, we must acknowledge from the outset the simultaneity of our existential goodness and sinfulness. While Western
Christianity has, certainly since the time of Augustine of Hippo
(d. 430 CE), focused a great deal on the reality of humanity's
finitude and sinfulness, far less attention has been given to the
fact that we were created by a loving God as good and lovable
creatures oriented toward justice and mutuality. A significant
paradox of our existence surfaces when we affirm that truth of
original goodness alongside the incontrovertible truth of original
sin. Classically, the concepts of original goodness and original sin
stem from the same divine gift of free will *(liberum arbitrium)*.

Although Augustine would historicize the distinction between
the pre- and post-lapsarian states, suggesting that there existed
a literal time wherein human persons (that is, Adam and Eve)
did not suffer the consequences of original sin *(peccatum originatum)* because the original transgression *(peccatum originans)*

189

had not yet taken place, we do well not to follow that aspect of his fourth-century interpretation today. Instead, we should first make the distinction that theologian Tatha Wiley insightfully describes when she states: "The *concept* of original sin and the *reality* to which the concept refers are different."[1] Augustine's articulation of the *concept* original sin with its emphasis on a historical moment at which what would forever exist as inherited sin originated, with its explanation for the persistence of evil shaped by a Platonic worldview, along with its expression governed by a contentious debate with Pelagius (d. ca. 420 CE) is something of a timepiece that has understandably come under scholarly and pastoral criticism over the centuries. However, as Wiley notes, Christians must reckon with the *reality* of original sin that is experienced by all persons throughout life as both perpetrators and victims. In other words, the reality of original sin is phenomenal as much as it is theological. Each of us, upon reflection, will recognize the quotidian ways that our free will is affected or limited by something—call it temptation or constriction or concupiscence (as Augustine did) or something else—and in this way, we recognize an inherent capacity for sin deep within our heart.

This chapter is, in part, an exploration of this reality of original sin, that inherent capacity for rejecting God's invitation to relationship at the ultimate level that is manifest in the myriad ways we harm or break relationship with one another and with the rest of creation. Given the prominence of the discussion of sin in the Western Catholic Christian tradition (technically called *hamartiology*), this chapter precedes the next on grace and the human capacity for God. In our consideration of sin we are mindful of that concurrent truth of our having been created

---

[1] Tatha Wiley, *Original Sin: Origins, Developments, Contemporary Meanings* (New York: Paulist Press, 2002), 8. This distinction is also anticipated by Paul Ricoeur in the essay "Original Sin: A Study in Meaning," in *The Conflict of Interpretations: Essays in Hermeneutics*, ed. Don Ihde (Evanston, IL: Northwestern University Press, 2007), 269–86. Also see Paul Ricoeur, *The Symbolism of Evil*, trans. Emerson Buchanan (New York: Harper and Row, 1967), esp. 232–78.

very good (Gen 1:31) and the Christian axiom of Christ's final triumph over sin and death. The Trappist monk Thomas Merton, in reflecting on the reality of original sin, notes the counterintuitive truth of the doctrine's paradoxical affirmation of our original goodness. He writes:

> We hate others because we cannot stand the disorder, the intolerable division in ourselves. We are violent to others because we are already divided by the inner violence of our infidelity to our own truth. Hatred projects this division outside ourselves into society. This is not far from the traditional doctrine of the Fathers of the Church concerning original sin! Note of course that the doctrine of original sin, properly understood, is *optimistic*. It does not teach that man is by nature evil, but that evil in him is unnatural, a disorder, a sin. If evil, lying, and hatred were natural to man, all men would be perfectly at home, perfectly happy in evil. Perhaps a few seem to find contentment in an unnatural state of falsity, hatred, and greed. They are not happy. Or if they are, they are unnatural.[2]

In essence, the concept of original sin that arises from the experienced reality always points toward our more fundamental original goodness because it unveils sin and evil as not constitutive of God's desire for creation. It is also worth noting that the condition of the possibility for the good life, as many philosophers have described it, is the existential prospect for exercising one's free will for sin—personal and structural. The choice is indeed ours. In this chapter we explore the capacity for sin, the way we might better understand the phenomenon of personal sin, the reality and persistence of structural sin, and close with a look at the too often overlooked other side of the experience of sin, namely, the situation of the sinned against or what Korean and Korean American theologians refer to as *han*.

---

[2] Thomas Merton, *Conjectures of a Guilty Bystander* (New York: Image Books, 2009), 80–81.

The Capacity for Sin

This book is not directly concerned with the theological subfield known as theodicy, that is, the study of why evil exists or, to put it colloquially as it so frequently is, why bad things happen if God is understood to be absolutely good. The focus of theodicy is really the mystery of God, whereas our focus here is explicitly on the human person.[3] There are numerous excellent volumes that explore this important and complicated area of reflection on the mystery of evil as such.[4] Additionally, we discuss personal sin in the next section of this chapter. The primary question currently at hand is how we might better understand the *capacity* for human sinfulness as a universal experience and an existential phenomenon. How are we to understand better the reality of original sin according to catholicity?

Returning to the astute distinction Wiley names between original sin as concept and original sin as reality, part of our task here is to "deconstruct the concept," as philosopher Paul Ricoeur once argued, in order to recontextualize and therefore express the truth of the reality contained or signified as it were in the *symbol* of original sin.

> I think that the concept must be destroyed as a concept in order to understanding the meaning intention. The concept of original sin is a false knowledge, and it must be broken as knowledge. It involves the quasi-juridical knowledge of the guilt of the newborn and the quasi-biological knowledge of the transmission of a hereditary taint. This false

---

[3] This is an important distinction also made in Susan Ross, *Anthropology: Seeking Light and Beauty* (Collegeville, MN: Liturgical Press, 2012), 110.

[4] For example, see Daniel Castelo, *Theological Theodicy* (Eugene, OR: Cascade Publishing, 2012); David B. Burrell, *Deconstructing Theodicy: Why Job Has Nothing to Say to the Puzzled Suffering* (Grand Rapids, MI: Brazos Press, 2008); Terrence W. Tilley, *The Evils of Theodicy* (Eugene, OR: Wipf and Stock, 2000); and Marilyn McCord Adams, *Horrendous Evils and the Goodness of God* (Ithaca, NY: Cornell University Press, 2000).

knowledge compresses in an inconsistent notion a juridical category of debt and a biological category of inheritance.[5]

Ricoeur and others note that while the Adamic myth cannot be taken in a simple literalist manner, it nevertheless bears a fecundity of meaning situated in the symbols it contains. Indeed, there are a number of immediately recognizable dimensions of the biblical narrative that inspires the classical concept of original sin that Augustine articulates. Among these, we see a narrative reflection on the *experience* or phenomenon of sin. For example, there is a particular, clear, and willful transgression on the part of the humans in Genesis 3 against God's instructions. We also see the *universality* of sin, which is reiterated by several church synods and ecumenical councils over the centuries, culminating with Trent's articulation of the concept in Augustinian and Thomistic terms.[6] It is present in the experiences of all human persons, Adam and Eve, you and me. And we see the *apriority* of sin, the "discovery" as it were of something that is already there before our individual volitional acts. What follows in the primordial myths of Genesis 3 and beyond is that what has gone before us shapes our ability to exercise agency and free will.

If we take for granted the untenable status of a historicized and literal reading of Genesis 3 as the explanatory ground for the universality of humanity's capacity for sin, then we are left with a question about how to account for this simultaneously personal and communal reality.[7] Recognizing the limitations present both here in this particular book and in the broader

---

[5] Ricoeur, "Original Sin," 270.

[6] For the decrees of the Council of Trent, see *Decrees of the Ecumenical Councils*, ed. Norman P. Tanner, 2 vols. (Washington, DC: Georgetown University Press, 1990), 2:660–799. For the "Decree on Justification," see 671–68.

[7] Wiley writes: "Explanations, as well as their breakdowns, have reasons and dates. The breakdown of the patristic and medieval account of the origin of sin has been in process since at least the eighteenth century" (Wiley, *Original Sin*, 206). Here we see expressed plainly the deconstruction of the concept of original sin Ricoeur discusses; it is always already taking place.

theological enterprise—that a complete explication of what is essentially a theological mystery is impossible—several theologians have nevertheless attempted to bring new insight into the ongoing discussion about the capacity for sin. In an effort to consider the human capacity for sin through the lens of catholicity and therefore strive toward ever-greater wholeness, we consider two recent discussions: the role of evolutionary biology and the explanatory proposal of mimetic violence.

As has been a consistent theme throughout this book, a theological anthropology articulated in the key of catholicity must take seriously developments in knowledge and interpretation outside of theology and incorporate them into our theological reflection on the human person when fitting. In recent decades it has become increasingly evident that one such area in need of greater attention is the natural sciences in general and evolutionary biology in particular. While the theory of evolution offers us numerous insights that enrich our understanding of our corporeality and animality, as we saw earlier in this book, several scholars have turned to the biological in order to discover a greater wholeness in explaining the universal human capacity for sin.

Luke Jeffrey Janssen, a professor of medicine, makes an important point that, despite the lapsarian tradition so integral to the Augustinian concept of original sin, evolutionary biology makes it irrefutably clear that human beings never "fell" from a pristine or perfect state of existence. Janssen explains that "humans were never perfect anatomically, intellectually, theologically, or morally."[8] Given what we know scientifically now, we are forced to reconceive the concept of original sin in light of evolution. Our history as a distinct species is intertwined with numerous other species and developed over hundreds of thousands of years into what we recognize as *Homo sapiens* today. Recasting the concept of a "fallen" human state, Janssen believes that we need to look at a kind of "missing the mark,"

---

[8] Luke Jeffrey Janssen, "'Fallen' and 'Broken' Reinterpreted in the Light of Evolution Theory," *Perspectives on Science and Christian Faith* 70 (2018): 38.

and not one judged against an Edenic perfection but one that aspires to align with what divine revelation has conveyed as our actual potential. He states:

> Humans are indeed "fallen," but not in the common sense of that theological term. We have not fallen from perfection, but from potential; not from the ideal, but from what could have been. We are *called toward wholeness* in right relationship with God and one another, and have been given the perfect example to follow [in Christ]. The scientific idea of biological evolution helps us to better see what God is doing.[9]

Janssen's statements further bolster Elizabeth Johnson's work on the role of the Holy Spirit in the world, as we saw in Chapter 2. Rather than a naive and pseudo-nostalgic hope of returning to some earlier perfect state that we once had and have now lost, it is better to consider ourselves as rightly imperfect creatures of a loving God who are called into relationship with that same Creator and are therefore on a personal and communal journey toward a more catholic humanity.

Our experience as creatures on the journey of emerging personhood consists of the capacity for sin or what theologian Stephen Duffy calls a "proclivity to evil."[10] Cautioning us to recall that human creatures are always more than the sum of our parts (a warning to avoid material reductionism), Duffy contends that the very mechanisms of evolution witnessed in our genetic makeup suggest a natural capacity for selfishness or self-preservation, which is alternatively described as the experience of the evolutionary survival of the fittest in popular discourse. That at the genetic and molecular levels we can trace a history of competition and violence—a reality that is witnessed throughout

---

[9] Janssen, "'Fallen' and 'Broken' Reinterpreted in the Light of Evolution Theory," 45, emphasis added.

[10] Stephen J. Duffy, "Genes, Original Sin, and the Human Proclivity to Evil," *Horizons* 32 (2005): 210–34.

the whole of creation at each level and which is not limited to humanity alone—suggests that there is an evolutionary factor that supports claims of a universal human capacity for sin. We see this leading to the slow emergence of a moral sense within humanity, something that appears not instantaneously but over eons of evolutionary history.[11] And yet, if we are to avoid a material reductionism, we must also recognize that we are not merely determined biologically and that sociology and culture also play a role in the presence and persistence of this capacity. "Sin is a compound deriving from the symbiosis of genetic and cultural influences," Duffy explains.[12] "Ours is not a freedom of absolute indetermination. There is a structural instability and fallibility in the human being, who exists at the intersection of freedom and nature, consciousness and body, the voluntary and the involuntary, the individual and the social."[13]

We will continue to learn more about the science of human origins, history, and evolution, which will certainly challenge aspects of our theological assertions about sin. And yet, while no clear consensus about or causal relationship between evolution and theology has been established, this brief consideration of recent engagement between the two areas suggests that while the *concept* of original sin as outlined by Augustine is largely unsustainable today, the *reality* of original sin is anything but disproven by scientific research. Instead, the relationship natural sciences play in our quest for a better understanding of humanity according to catholicity might be best described as situated between a naive concordism and a hostile view of science and theology as non-overlapping magisteria.[14]

---

[11] See Celia Deanne-Drummond, *The Wisdom of the Liminal: Evolution and Other Animals in Human Becoming* (Grand Rapids, MI: Eerdmans, 2014), esp. 122–52.

[12] Duffy, "Genes, Original Sin, and the Human Proclivity to Evil," 227. For more on this point, see Philip Hefner, "Biological Perspectives on Fall and Original Sin," *Zygon* 28 (1993): 77–101.

[13] Duffy, "Genes, Original Sin, and the Human Proclivity to Evil," 231.

[14] J. Richard Middleton, "Reading Genesis 3 Attentive to Human Evolution: Beyond Concordism and Non-Overlapping Magisteria," in

Like those interested in considering what insights evolutionary biology may offer theological reflection on the human person, some scholars have turned to the mimetic theory of social anthropologist and literary critic Réne Girard.[15] Girard's key insight centers on the role of mimesis—a deep, often unconscious, interior form of imitation—that is tied to desire.[16] In fact, the phenomenon of desire is at the heart of what it means to be human for Girard. As James Alison notes, one of Girard's most significant contributions is the discovery that we do not desire "lineally" but "*according* to the desire of the other. . . . All desire is triangular, and is suggested by a mediator or model."[17] Despite the modern depiction of human subjectivity and agency as entirely self-determining and free, our desire is actually conditioned by mimesis; we want to have what others have, to be who others are, and to want what others want. As both a personal and social phenomenon, the unavoidable production of mimetic desire is not inherently bad or dangerous, but in fact it often results in violence arising from rivalry with the mediator or model of our desire. Because we cannot simply destroy everyone who is a mediator or model for our desire—because we live with them, depend on them, are related to them, genuinely love them, and so

---

Evolution and the Fall, ed. William T. Cavanaugh and James K. A. Smith (Grand Rapids, MI: Eerdmans, 2017), 67–97.

[15] James Alison, *The Joy of Being Wrong: Original Sin through Easter Eyes* (New York: Herder and Herder, 1998); and, more recently, Grant Kaplan, *René Girard, Unlikely Apologist: Mimetic Theory and Fundamental Theology* (Notre Dame, IN: University of Notre Dame Press, 2016). The key works of Girard include *Violence and the Sacred*, trans. Patrick Gregory (Baltimore: Johns Hopkins University Press, 1972); *The Scapegoat*, trans. Yvonne Freccero (Baltimore: Johns Hopkins University Press, 1986); *Things Hidden since the Foundation of the World*, trans. Stephen Bann and Michael Metteer (Stanford, CA: Stanford University Press, 1987); and *I See Satan Fall like Lightning*, trans. James G. Williams (Maryknoll, NY: Orbis Books, 2001).

[16] See Alison, *The Joy of Being Wrong*, 12–13. For a general overview of mimetic theory, see Matthew Potolsky, *Mimesis* (London: Routledge, 2006).

[17] Alison, *The Joy of Being Wrong*, 9.

on—there seems to be no end to the escalation of social tensions and violence at both the personal and social levels. Therefore another solution must be sought. As Alison explains:

> This imitative desire leads to conflicts, which are resolved by a group's spontaneous formation of unanimity over against some arbitrarily indicated other who is expelled or excluded, thereby producing a return to peace. In this way we humans create and sustain social order. The mechanism of the creation and maintenance of social order by means of the expulsion of the arbitrarily chosen victim depends for its success on the blindness of its participants as to what is *really* going on: they have to believe in the guilt or dangerous nature of the one expelled.[18]

This last aspect of what Alison describes is what Girard calls the "scapegoat mechanism," the phenomenon of seeking a way to alleviate the escalating tensions and conflict that surfaces as a result of rivalry, jealousy, and anger by means of sacrifice. Societies have, over the course of human history, sought to identify and blame another party for the problems in the community, the breakdown of relationships that comes from the desiring of what the other possesses or desires or is. The result is the identification of a scapegoat who bears the collective burden and responsibility for the violence that arises within the society. A myth then develops that is used to justify the exclusionary or even murderous narratives, which state that if the community were to rid itself of this problematic scapegoat then, and only then, tranquility among relationships in the community will follow. Over time, the practices arising in response to the rivalistic conflict occasioned by mimetic desire become ritualized and serve as the normative means for alleviating the social conflict and violence.[19]

Wilhelm Guggenberger summarizes well the potential contribution of Girard's work for a theology of original sin: "Girard's

---

[18] Alison, *The Joy of Being Wrong*, 9–10.
[19] See Girard, *Violence and the Sacred*, 250–73.

theory might inspire theological anthropology as it faces the challenge to reformulate the concept of original sin in contemporary language while nevertheless retaining the concept's traditional meaning."[20] We can see this take form in several ways. As with the scientific efforts to makes sense of the reality of original sin, those who draw on Girard's mimetic theory argue that the classical concept of original sin that is both dependent on a historical "fall" and the passage of the effects of that fall from one generation to the next through sexual procreation is inadequate. Girard argues that mimetic desire is constitutive of human personhood and is antecedent to any formal human religion. It accounts for the universality of the experience of sin, while also positing a theory about its transgenerational persistence given the rootedness of mimetic theory in social relationships. We learn from imitation and desire, as is so clearly seen in the various stages of early human development, and this continues throughout our lifetimes even though most people are unaware or deliberately conceal (from themselves or others) the source and object of their desire. Girard's work also offers us something of a modern accounting for the relationship between free will and what Augustine called concupiscence. As Grant Kaplan explains, "Girard upholds some measure of human freedom, however truncated, and maintains that human behavior cannot be reduced to biological or neurological predictors."[21] Our exercise of free will is always already curbed by the formation of mimetic desire, regardless of our awareness of that reality in any given moment or particular decision.

Mimetic theory provides some explanation for the dynamic of sin understood as a universal human capacity rather than offering a historical account of sin's origin, as many other theological projects have been preoccupied with over the centuries.

---

[20] Wilhelm Guggenberger, "Desire, Mimetic Theory, and Original Sin," in *Questioning the Human: Toward a Theological Anthropology for the Twenty-First Century*, ed. Lieven Boeve, Yves De Maeseneer, and Ellen Van Stichel (New York: Fordham University Press, 2014), 171.

[21] Kaplan, *René Girard, Unlikely Apologist*, 19.

As with the scientific insights presented in recent decades, the social scientific and anthropological insights of Girard allow us to acknowledge what we call the *reality* of original sin as an incontrovertible truth of Christian faith, while still recognizing that the classic *concept* of original sin falls well short of the veritable mark and needs further consideration. Having briefly surveyed examples of contemporary scientific and anthropological resources for better understanding our human capacity for sin, we now consider personal sin through the lens of catholicity.

Examining Personal Sin

The classical articulation of personal sin has focused on the rebellious, prideful, selfish, and arrogant dimensions of the breaking of relationship between an individual exercising free will and the Creator. William May summarizes the Augustinian influence on two classic definitions: "The first defines sin as 'anything done, said, or desired against the eternal law' *(factum, dictum, vel concupitum contra legem aeternam)*. . . . The second defines sin as a 'turning away from God and turning toward the creatures' *(aversio a Deo, conversio ad creaturam)*."[22] This has been adopted by ecumenical councils and incorporated into magisterial teaching for centuries, including most recently at Vatican II in the *Pastoral Constitution on the Church in the Modern World (Gaudium et Spes)* (see esp. nos. 13–35). On the one hand, this recognition of a divine law or eternal moral norm that God has envisioned for humanity that is violated by individuals who act deliberately in ways contrary to it in what we call personal sin is not inherently problematic. Yet, on the other hand, in order

---

[22] William E. May, "Sin," in *The New Dictionary of Theology*, ed. Joseph A. Komonchak, Mary Collins, and Dermot A. Lane (Collegeville, MN: Liturgical Press, 1987), 957. Also see Piet Schoonenberg and Karl Rahner, "Sin," in *Encyclopedia of Theology: The Concise Sacramentum Mundi*, ed. Karl Rahner (New York: Crossroad Publishing, 1984), 1579–90.

to reflect on the reality of sin in a manner in keeping with a hermeneutic of catholicity or wholemaking, we must pause to reflect on whether this seemingly straightforward definition of sin adequately reflects the reality of sin as experienced by the sinner. To this end it is important to consider the critiques and insights of those whose experience of personal sin does not conform to what we are calling the classical articulation. Here, by way of example, we look at two perspectives.

The first begins in the form of a now-classic essay by theologian Valerie Saiving titled "The Human Situation: A Feminine View."[23] Using the work of well-known male theologians Anders Nygren and Reinhold Niebuhr as emblematic of those who presuppose a certain static or classical articulation of the human experience and therefore of personal sin, Saiving explains that "they represent a widespread tendency in contemporary theology to describe man's predicament as rising from his separateness and anxiety occasioned by it and to identify sin with self-assertion and love with selflessness."[24] This selfishness she critiques is a placeholder for the millennia-old presumption that personal sin is first and foremost about the self-interested turning away from God and God's will. Saiving does not challenge that this is what many Western men experience insofar as that is the case for them and—for some women who conform to certain internalized norms arising from that presumption—some Western women too. Nevertheless, she suggests that too many theologians have overlooked the historical and social conditions that form an androcentric bias in the naming of sin, which has compounding deleterious effects for women in their own relationship to the concepts of sin and love. Saiving explains:

---

[23] Valerie Saiving, "The Human Situation: A Feminine View," *Journal of Religion* 40 (1960): 100–112. For some commentary on the reception and significance of this important essay, see Ann McReynolds and Ann O'Hara Graff, "Sin: When Women Are the Context," in *In The Embrace of God: Feminist Approaches to Theological Anthropology*, ed. Ann O'Hara Graff, 161–72 (Eugene, OR: Wipf and Stock, 1995).

[24] Saiving, "The Human Situation," 100.

It is my contention that there are significant differences between masculine and feminine experience and that feminine experience reveals in a more emphatic fashion certain aspects of the human situation which are present but less obvious in the experience of men. Contemporary theological doctrines of love have, I believe, been constructed primarily upon the basis of masculine experience and thus view the human condition from the male standpoint. Consequently, these doctrines do not provide an adequate interpretation of the situation of women—nor, for that matter, of men, especially in view of certain fundamental changes now taking place in our own society.[25]

The Christian tradition has been too often articulated in an uncritically androcentric mode and therefore does not reflect the experience of at least half of the human population.[26] For men, generally speaking, the classical articulation of sin arising from one's existential anxiety, insecurity, will to power, and selfishness might resonate. The call to Christian conversion, therefore, is a move from pride and selfishness to a loving selflessness, traditionally associated with the christological model of *kenosis*. But, as Saiving insightfully notes, this outlook and understanding of sin and love reinscribes a patriarchal social structure that does not begin to consider the differences in the experiences of Christian women and men:

> For the temptations of woman *as woman* are not the same as the temptations of man *as man*, and specifically feminine forms of sin—"feminine" not because they are confined to women or because women are incapable of sinning in other ways but because they are outgrowths

---

[25] Saiving, "The Human Situation," 101.

[26] While this illustration is gender focused, other theologians have offered complementarily critical assessments of the way we talk about sin and its harmful consequences for marginalized communities. For example, see Stephen G. Ray, *Do No Harm: Social Sin and Christian Responsibility* (Minneapolis: Fortress Press, 2003).

of the basic feminine character structure—have a quality which can never be encompassed by such terms as "pride" and "will-to-power." They are better suggested by such items as triviality, distractibility, and diffuseness; lack of an organizing center or focus; dependence on others for one's own self-definition; tolerance at the expense of standards of excellence; inability to respect the boundaries of privacy; sentimentality, gossipy sociability, and mistrust of reason— in short, underdevelopment or negation of the self.[27]

Saiving's occasional gender-essentialist discourse notwithstanding, her point is one that challenges the hubris of ubiquitous descriptions of sin that do not account for the significant differences in experience that exist within the human community. For men, for whom "sin is the self's attempt to overcome that [existential] anxiety by magnifying its own power, righteousness, or knowledge," resulting in a man knowing "that he is merely a part of the whole, but he tries to convince himself and others that he *is* the whole. He tries, in fact, to become the whole," the notion of love as selfless and *kenotic* makes sense and can be viewed as a behavioral and spiritual corrective.[28] But for women, for whom social norms, the act of child rearing, and other internalized principles contribute to an expectation of selflessness and a prioritization of the other and community over oneself, to say that prioritizing self-assertion or self-actualization is inherently sinful is to reinforce an unjust double bind. Context and experience matter, especially when we are talking about sin. It is important to note that explorations of the *particularity* of context and experience have been the focus of theologians who have followed Saiving's foundational work.[29]

---

[27] Saiving, "The Human Situation," 109.

[28] Saiving, "The Human Situation," 100.

[29] For example, among many others, see Judith Plaskow, *Sex, Sin, and Grace: Women's Experience and the Theologies of Reinhold Niebuhr and Paul Tillich* (Washington, DC: University Press of America, 1980); Emilie Townes, *A Troubling in My Soul: Womanist Perspectives on Evil and Suffering* (Maryknoll, NY: Orbis Books, 1993); Mary McClintock

The second perspective comes from Native American experiences. In their chapter on sin and ethics Clara Sue Kidwell, Homer Noley, and George "Tink" Tinker examine the Christian notion of sin as it was received by (or better, forced upon) the native peoples of North America within the context of Western colonization.[30] The history of the colonial imposition of European Christianity on the indigenous peoples of the Americas reveals some of the inadequacies of the classical articulation of personal sin. For example, Kidwell, Noley, and Tinker note that the concept of sin is itself a foreign abstraction from the perspective of most Indian traditions. The gap between the European Christian notion of personal sin and longstanding spiritual traditions of North American native peoples is witnessed in the untranslatability of the concept of sin itself. "The difficulty of imposing the Christian notion of sin upon Indian people is apparent in the native words that missionaries have used to try to convey the meaning of sin. These words generally mean to make a mistake, or to be lost, which implies non-willful behavior. . . . These terms hardly equate with Christian ideas of depravity and original sin."[31]

Fulkerson, *Changing the Subject: Women's Discourses and Feminist Theology* (Minneapolis: Fortress Press, 1994); Ann E. Carr, *Transforming Grace: Christian Tradition and Women's Experience* (New York: Continuum, 1996); Serene Jones, "Women's Experience between a Rock and a Hard Place: Feminist, Womanist, and *Mujerista* Theologies in North America," in *Horizons in Feminist Theology: Identity, Tradition, and Norms*, ed. Rebecca S. Chopp and Sheila Greeve Davaney (Minneapolis: Fortress Press, 1997), 33–53; and Kwok Pui-Lan, "Feminist Theology as Intercultural Discourse," in *The Cambridge Companion to Feminist Theology*, ed. Susan Frank Parsons (New York: Cambridge University Press, 2002), 23–39.

[30] Clara Sue Kidwell, Homer Noley, and George E. "Tink" Tinker, *A Native American Theology* (Maryknoll, NY: Orbis Books, 2001), 100–112. Also, see George E. "Tink" Tinker, *American Indian Liberation: A Theology of Sovereignty* (Maryknoll, NY: Orbis Books, 2008), 84–111.

[31] Kidwell, Noley, and Tinker, *A Native American Theology*, 100–101. Also, see George Tinker, "Decolonizing the Language of Lutheran Theology: Confessions, Mission, Indians, and the Globalization of Hybridity," *Dialog* 50 (2011): 193–205, esp. 199–201.

From the outset it is clear that a view of human pride, selfishness, and self-assertion expressed in a deeply individualistic key from the European Christian context does not find a comparable analog semiotically—both terminologically and conceptually—in the lived experiences of local, traditional cultures. If personal sin is tied to the willful breaking of relationship or the deliberate violation of God's will or eternal moral law, then the guilt and blame associated with that transgression will be perplexing to a Choctaw hearer when a European missionary uses *aiashachi* or *aiyoshoba* as a way to translate "sin." The former term means "to make a mistake or err"; the latter conveys the sense of "getting lost, wandering, or losing one's sense of direction or way."[32] What kind of God would threaten eternal damnation because of one's unintended mistakes or accidentally getting lost? Even according to the European Christian context this would be categorized in terms of invincible ignorance and lack of moral culpability.

That the concept and terms associated with the *sin* part of personal sin do not have adequate counterparts in the various Native American languages is revelatory in that, yet again, we see a presumption of universal experience—not only gendered, but also culturally and ethnically—tied to Western European priorities, principles, and worldviews. But it is not only that sin is not easily translated across cultural divides, it is also the notion of *personal* in personal sin. Ethical value systems that are tied to a strong sense of community and interdependence, such as that found in many Native American contexts, resist the individualistic focus of classical articulations of personal sin. "In Christianity, sin has become a privatized personal matter. For Indian people it is a matter of responsibility to community."[33] This is not to suggest that Christianity has no sense of sin against community or even the rest of creation; it most certainly does. This is especially seen in the age of Pope Francis's encyclical letter *Laudato Si'*. Rather, when trying to make sense of a classical

---

[32] Kidwell, Noley, and Tinker, *A Native American Theology*, 101.
[33] Kidwell, Noley, and Tinker, *A Native American Theology*, 110.

understanding of personal sin as tied primarily to the rejection of God and eternal laws, the lived experience of peoples who have an intimate understanding of interrelationship and community with one another and the whole of creation that is unfamiliar to the modern Euro-American imaginary sheds light on yet another instance of incomplete theological reflection. This understanding of the theology of sin fails to take into consideration non-male, non-Euro-American cultural contexts, histories, traditions, languages, and modes of relationship. Kidwell, Noley, and Tinker reiterate: "The idea of sin as willful behavior that transgressed laws dictated by a supreme being contrasted sharply with the moral values of obligation and responsibility to one's family and community."[34]

This brief study of the problems with the classical articulation of the doctrine of personal sin from a Native American perspective shows both a challenge and an opportunity. The challenge has been expressed in terms of the potential inadequacies of our current discourse around the doctrine of sin and the need we have to reevaluate what we mean and how we express it that better reflects the manifold experiences of peoples around the world. The opportunity, though it exceeds the limit and scope of this particular chapter, is the possibility of a robust event of intercultural communication. This requires deliberation and openness, an awareness of operative biases, social locations, and hermeneutics, as well as a humility that has not often been associated with Christian theological reflection, particularly from within a Euro-American context. But it may be possible.

These insights from feminist and Native American theologians help us to approach the doctrine of sin, especially the part pertaining to personal guilt and culpability, with an eye toward greater catholicity and wholemaking. We now move from the personal to the collective, the individual to the institutional, as we consider the persistence of structural sin.

---

[34] Kidwell, Noley, and Tinker, *A Native American Theology*, 112.

The Persistence of Structural Sin

Understanding the reality of original sin as a universal experience of human existence and recognizing that, albeit articulated imperfectly, there is some sense in which our exercise of free will is personally impaired and leads to individual transgressions, we shift our focus now to an understanding of sin from a structural or social perspective. Such an understanding of sin according to a hermeneutic of catholicity takes into account the interrelatedness of sin. As John Paul II made clear in his 1984 apostolic exhortation *Reconciliatio et Paenitentia (RP)* and his 1987 encyclical letter *Sollicitudo Rei Socialis (SRS),* the church teaches that sin is not merely an individual matter but is manifest socially and structurally too.

John Paul II talks about three types of social or structural sin. The first he describes in terms of the way personal sins affect others. A sense of sin that considers God as the only one offended is untenable. This is because we are interrelated, connected, and called to solidarity and communion. With "greater or lesser violence, greater or lesser harm," every sin has repercussions on the entire ecclesiastical body—the church—and the whole human family (*RP,* no. 16). The second type has to do with the way a given society, institution, or structure affects sins against an individual or is the collective victim of such a transgression. This may consist either of an individual versus the community or, as is more typically the case, the community against an individual, which we see manifested in instances of sexism, racism, homophobia, and anti-Semitism, among others. The third is seen in the sinful actions and attitudes between various communities. Here, John Paul II is referring to violations against the way God intends societies to exist in the promotion and protection of the common good, according to which justice, freedom, and peace among individuals, groups, and peoples is maintained. He explains that this sort of social sin is at times difficult to trace explicitly because it appears anonymously and unconsciously, it is written into the fabric of social relations, laws, and cultural practices. Here we get a clear sense in magisterial teaching of what most theologians refer to as structural sin.[35]

The very structures of our institutions and societies are affected by sin, which typically benefits a particular group while simultaneously oppressing another. As Eleazar Fernandez explains, "These sinful constructions are embedded in our ideologies, cultural rules, and practices."[36] We are shaped by and shape the societies and social institutions into which we were born, reared, and continue to live. Fernandez reminds us that

> society and its social institutions, while creations of human beings, outlast the lives of individuals. [For this reason,] institutions acquire a status or life of their own; they are bigger than the sum of all individuals; and they transcend the individuals in space and time. This point is crucial in understanding how we become inheritors of previous acts and how our collective acts influence and shape coming generations.[37]

It is not only within the individual human heart that sin takes root but also within the collective systems, institutions, and manners of ordering our societies and even our churches that sin can and does take hold. This has different implications depending on one's social location. And yet, those who unwittingly benefit from and those who are oppressed by the structural sin are united in relationship, like two sides of the same coin. For example, the structural sin of racism is deeply embedded in the society of the United States of America. Even if a particular white person does not consciously harbor anti-black racist animus, that person is nevertheless intertwined in a structure that simultaneously

---

[35] This reality is also named by the Second Vatican Council in *Gaudium et Spes*, nos. 25–26.

[36] Eleazar S. Fernandez, *Reimagining the Human: Theological Anthropology in Response to Systemic Evil* (St. Louis: Chalice Press, 2004), 65.

[37] Fernandez, *Reimagining the Human*, 65.

advantages him or her and disadvantages people of color. The nature of the structural sin is such that while complicit in the perpetuation of the structural sin and even perhaps visibly aware of some of its particular deleterious manifestations against persons of color more broadly, those who benefit from unjust systems, societies, and institutions are blinded to their own advantage and often also blinded to the simultaneous disadvantage or oppression of others. Fernandez explains that this dynamic is true across the spectrum of structural sin, including racism, sexism, classism, and others.[38]

Canadian theologian Gregory Baum outlined the dynamic way institutions get "corrupted" or become sinful in four levels, which can be seen in various instances (racism, sexism, and so on).

First Level: Structural sin is made up of unjust and dehumanizing trends that are built into various societal institutions. The destructive trends corrupt the individuals and dehumanize them.

Second Level: Structural sin refers to cultural and religious symbols that legitimize and reinforce unjust social institutions.

Third Level: Structural sin refers to false consciousness that institutions have created and perpetuated.

Fourth Level: Structural sin refers to collective decisions, generated by distorted consciousness, which exacerbate the injustices in society as well as intensify the power of the dehumanizing trends.[39]

A theological understanding of the human person in general and of the doctrine of sin in particular that seeks a spirit of

---

[38] Fernandez, *Reimagining the Human*, esp. 68.

[39] Here I have adapted Fernandez's summary of Gregory Baum's four levels (see Fernandez, *Reimagining the Human*, 66–67). The original source is Gregory Baum, *Religion and Alienation: A Theological Reading of Sociology* (New York: Paulist Press, 1975).

wholemaking and catholicity cannot just consider personal sin and personal conversion as sufficient to the Christian task of transformation. As the Catholic bishops at their 1971 synod made clear: "Action on behalf of justice and participation in the transformation of the world fully appear to us as a constitutive dimension of the preaching of the Gospel, or, in other words, of the Church's mission for the redemption of the human race and its liberation from every oppressive situation."[40] Sin must be considered at the personal and the structural levels, recognizing the relationship between the two and the simultaneous call to transformation of both related spheres. While acknowledgment and consideration of the persistence of structural sin is important, it nevertheless continues to focus predominantly on the perpetrators of sin, whether the individual or the collective community. A truly catholic theology of sin must also take into consideration the victims or, as some theologians have put it, the "sinned against."

Han and the Sinned Against

Christian theology of sin is generally concerned with the sinner. But what about those who have been sinned against?[41] Where are the victims, the survivors, those who have endured abuse or harm and continue to strive toward human flourishing while suffering—where are they in our theology of sin? Committed to understanding better the human person from a perspective of catholicity, it becomes clear that a theological anthropology that takes into consideration only the victimizers (the sinners or oppressors) without adequate reflection on the victims (the sinned against or the oppressed) replicates the partial and inadequate theological reflections on the human person that have already

---

[40] Synod of Bishops, *Justice in the World*, no. 6 (1971).
[41] One of the earliest contemporary uses of "sinned against" appears in Raymond Fung, "Compassion for the Sinned-Against," *Theology Today* 37 (1980): 162–69.

come before. In response, we turn to the recent work of Korean and Korean American theologians who have, over the last several decades, suggested that the concept of *han* offers Christian theologians an insightful resource in naming the reality and experience of the sinned against.[42] What follows here is in no way exhaustive but rather an initial foray toward restoring an overlooked and avoided part of sin that must be considered in a theological anthropology that seeks to be wholemaking.

The Korean term *han* is incredibly difficult, if not impossible, to translate into English. It is a polyvalent concept that is deeply tied to Korean culture and identity,[43] though it also speaks beyond Korean communities to all those who suffer or are oppressed.[44] Theologian Andrew Sung Park has offered a

---

[42] For example, Andrew Sung Park, "Theology of Han (The Abyss of Pain)," *Quarterly Review* 9 (1989): 48–62; Andrew Sung Park, *The Wounded Heart of God: The Asian Concept of Han and the Christian Doctrine of Sin* (Nashville, TN: Abingdon Press, 1993); Grace Ji-Sun Kim, "Oppression and *Han*: Korean Women's Historical Context," *Journal of Asian and Asian-American Theology* 3 (1999): 55–70; Andrew Sung Park, *From Hurt to Healing: A Theology of the Wounded* (Nashville, TN: Abingdon Press, 2004); Wonhee Anne Joh, *Heart of the Cross: A Postcolonial Christology* (Louisville, KY: Westminster John Knox Press, 2006); Andrew Sung Park, *Triune Atonement: Christ's Healing for Sinners, Victims, and the Whole of Creation* (Louisville, KY: Westminster John Knox Press, 2009); Kevin P. Considine, "*Han* and Salvation for the 'Sinned Against,'" *New Theology Review* 26 (2013): 87–89; Kevin P. Considine, "Kim Chi-Ha's *Han* Anthropology and Its Challenge to Catholic Thought," *Horizons* 41 (2014): 49–73; and Kevin P. Considine, *Salvation for the Sinned-Against: Han and Schillebeeckx in Intercultural Dialogue* (Eugene, OR: Pickwick Publications, 2015).

[43] Kim Sang-Yil notes that *han* is so tied to Korean identity that the Japanese colonizers sought to eradicate it from Korean culture during the Japanese occupancy. See Kim Sang-Yil, "*Hanism*: Korean Concept of Ultimacy," *Ultimate Reality and Meaning* 9 (1986): 17–36. For a historical overview of the term *han*, see Considine, *Salvation for the Sinned-Against*, 98–113.

[44] See Park, *The Wounded Heart of God*, 20–30; and Jae Hoon Lee, *The Exploration of the Inner Wounds—Han* (New York: Oxford University Press, 1994).

constellation of descriptors to help orient the sense or meaning of *han* including "frustrated hope," "the collapsed feeling of pain," "letting go," "resentful bitterness," and "the wounded heart."[45] It is more than momentary or even extended suffering; it is better likened to the enduring experience and combined effects of trauma.[46] As theologian Kevin Considine explains, "Suffering is too thin to account for the full complexity of woundedness. *Han* points to the interconnected levels of woundedness in human beings, their communities, and all of creation. *Han* is a festering wound and frozen energy in need of unraveling. The question is not *if* it will unravel, but *when* and *how* it will unravel and what the consequences will be."[47] *Han* is that aspect of human existence that signifies the "deep wounds carried by oppressed and violated individuals, groups, and peoples."[48]

Whereas sin is the experience of the transgressor or oppressor, *han* is the experience of the sinned against. Much of our collective Christian attention has been focused on the source and effects of sin in our world without adequate consideration of the enduring *effect* of sin or *han*. The cause of *han* is sin or injustice,

---

[45] Park, *The Wounded Heart of God*, 15–20.

[46] It should also be noted that, concurrent to the retrieval of *han*, a number of European and North American theologians have been working in and drawing from the area of trauma studies in order to provide a similar focus on victim survivors, the suffering, and the wounded in theological anthropology. For examples, see Wendy Farley, *Tragic Vision and Divine Compassion: A Contemporary Theodicy* (Louisville, KY: Westminster John Knox Press, 1990); Elaine Scarry, *The Body in Pain: The Making and Unmaking of the World* (New York: Oxford University Press, 1985); Jennifer Beste, *God and the Victim: Traumatic Intrusions on Grace and Freedom* (New York: Oxford University Press, 2007); Serene Jones, *Trauma and Grace: Theology in a Ruptured World* (Louisville, KY: Westminster John Knox Press, 2009); Shelly Rambo, *Spirit and Trauma: A Theology of Remaining* (Louisville, KY: Westminster John Knox Press, 2010); and Shelly Rambo, *Resurrecting Wounds: Living in the Afterlife of Trauma* (Waco, TX: Baylor University Press, 2017).

[47] Considine, "*Han* and Salvation for the 'Sinned Against,'" 87.

[48] Considine, "*Han* and Salvation for the 'Sinned Against,'" 88.

which means that *han* is the reverse side of sin, its complement. As Park explains, "Where sin is committed, *han* arises as its corollary. The victims of sin develop *han*, a deep agonizing pain. They bear excruciating agony and humiliation under oppression, exploitation, abuse, mistreatment, and violation. If their situations do not allow them to change such conditions, they further deepen their *han*."[49]

A wholemaking theology of the human person must take both the experience and perspective of sin and the experience and perspective of the sinned against as part of a singular reality that ties together the oppressor and the oppressed. Park and others note that while personal sin is often the cause of another's *han*, we must also consider the structural forms of sin that also cause *han*.[50] Among these structural sins we can count patriarchy, sexism, racism, homophobia, xenophobia, and economic inequality, among others.

Whereas oppressors and oppressive structures need redemption from their sins, the oppressed seek liberation from their *han*.[51] Our work in developing a theological anthropology of catholicity requires looking at the ways sin and *han* are processed in terms of healing. Drawing on Park's work, Considine offers the following parallel but different sequential processes:

Sin → guilt → guilt anger → repentance → forgiven-ness → justification by faith → holiness/sanctification → Christian perfection.

---

[49] Andrew Sung Park, "The Bible and *Han*," in *The Other Side of Sin: Woundedness from the Perspective of the Sinned-Against*, ed. Andrew Sung Park and Susan L. Nelson (Albany, NY: SUNY Press, 2001), 48.

[50] Park, *The Wounded Heart of God*, 45–67.

[51] Andrew Sung Park explains that his starting point is different from Latin American liberation theologians such as Gustavo Gutiérrez in that a distinction needs to be made between the salvation/redemption of the sinner/oppressor and the *liberation* of the oppressed from their *han* (see Park, *From Hurt to Healing*, 4).

Han ➞ shame ➞ shame anger ➞ resistance ➞ forgivingness ➞ justice by faith ➞ healing/wholeness ➞ jubilee.[52]

There are both theological implications and practical consequences for developing a sense of sin in theological anthropology that takes both of these processes into consideration. Theologically, it challenges us to reconsider heretofore "universal" notions of sin and salvation that further contribute to the *han* of the oppressed through occlusion or marginalization. Viewed through a hermeneutic of catholicity, one cannot reflect on the reality of sin—personal or structural—without also recognizing the resulting *han*. Practically, it challenges us to reexamine our pastoral ministry and perhaps even our liturgical practices. In terms of ministry, bringing the reality of *han* to the forefront of our pastoral outreach and programming could dramatically affect how we reconceive ministries of reconciliation and justice.[53] Regarding liturgical practices, the acknowledgment and incorporation of *han* as a particular or collective reality within a worship community necessitates a delicate reflection about how we celebrate the sacrament of penance, provide resources for an examination of conscience, and offer referral opportunities or bring in expert support for personal, family, and community care. Perhaps our intercessory prayer or the prayer of the faithful at the celebration of the Eucharist could better reflect the twofold reality of sin and *han*—perhaps also the language that introduces our penitential act.

In conclusion, there are many aspects of our Christian doctrine of sin that require further inquiry and reevaluation. From understanding better the human capacity for sin to the reconsideration of the manifold experiences of personal sin and the persistence of structural sin to the need for greater recognition of *han* and the experience of the sinned against, a theological

---

[52] Considine, *Salvation for the Sinned-Against*, 137, drawing on Park, *From Hurt to Healing*.

[53] For example, see Robert J. Schreiter, *The Ministry of Reconciliation: Spirituality and Strategies* (Maryknoll, NY: Orbis Books, 1998).

anthropology conceived in terms of catholicity challenges us to rethink the reality of sin. Despite the focus of this chapter it is important to note that we are more than sinners. In fact, we are created with a sense of original goodness as much as original sin. In the next chapter we consider how God has created us precisely for grace, which is the divine gift of God's self to us.

Chapter 7

Grace and the Capacity for God

The theme of grace has haunted the entirety of this book so far, even if its spectral presence has not always been clearly discernible. Grace is the subject that most directly focuses our attention on the reason for our being, the purpose of life (insofar as one might be ascertainable through faith), and what God's intention for creating us (and anything) actually is. In discussing what it means for us to be creatures or to have (or not have) a human nature presupposes the reality of grace when exploring these themes from the Christian perspective. When we discussed sin—the capacity to sin and the reality of sin—the subject of grace was in the shadows, unnamed but nevertheless present by implication, for it is the other side of the anthropological coin.[1]

---

[1] For as significant and central the theme of grace is to any study of theological anthropology, there were both methodological and historical reasons for addressing it head on last. First, at the risk of slipping into an extrinsicism that could suggest a radical break between the created world and the gift of grace, I felt it necessary to begin with the truth of our creatureliness and animality as the fitting grounding for considering the human person today. God works through time, space, matter, and history. There is no other way. Second, the history of Christianity has, in some part thanks to Augustine's weighty influence over the last millennium and a half, paid disproportionate heed to the condition, reality, and effects of sin at the expense of a robust consideration of grace. While not desiring to repeat this approach, the historical predominance of sin talk begged addressing. Delaying such consideration would potentially distract readers who might dismiss the talk of grace that follows

We have seen that while a hermeneutic of catholicity is central to Christian theology, the manner in which theological reflection has unfolded over the centuries has often strayed from an approach to wholemaking. The history of the doctrine of grace is yet another example of this. As with other instances of dualistic and hierarchical thinking that undermine catholicity, the history of the theology of grace has shifted in ways that have produced an incomplete vision of who we are and how God relates to us. And yet, the tradition has always offered alternative ways of thinking about grace more holistically. This is where the modern retrieval and interpretation of ancient understandings of grace provide us with a constructive opportunity. Additionally, as we will see, a more catholic approach to grace is important not only for a renewal of theological anthropology, but also for the development of a spirituality of catholicity that invites us to see the world and ourselves in a new light.

In this chapter we explore the reality of grace, its meaning, and its implications. First, we consider what grace means in a technical, theological sense. Second, we examine what it means to assert that every human person has the capacity for God, what twentieth-century Jesuit theologian Karl Rahner calls the "supernatural existential." Finally, in light of this universal dimension of human existence, we shift our attention to consider how we might see the world in a new way, a world always already shaped by the presence of grace. With a renewed sense of ourselves, our world, and God, we can strive to become "everyday mystics" whose experience of reality is informed by this divine gift of grace.

---

in this chapter as unduly optimistic as long as the locus of sin continued to loom as of yet unaddressed, providing a potential distraction from this important subject. Furthermore, the Western Christian doctrine of grace is deeply indebted to the work of Augustine, whose theology of grace was worked out against the backdrop of sin and wounded free will (*concupiscence*). Therefore, it was necessary in the spirit of catholicity to address the ways in which such sin-related foci have lacked adequate consideration of the interlocutors and themes engaged in the last chapter.

What Is Grace?

Few theologians have described the challenge facing discussions of grace better than Jesuit theologian Roger Haight. He succinctly articulates the paradoxical task of explicating the meaning of grace:

> The word "grace" is one of the most common in the Christian vocabulary. At the same time, it is probably the most slippery word to define. Of all Christian terms, the word grace is the simplest, and at the same time it is the most complicated. Grace refers to the most basic and fundamental of Christian realities since it indicates the presupposition of all Christian spirituality. And yet the word has acquired so many different secondary meanings in technical theology, in doctrine and in common understanding, that it is almost impossible to say what exactly the word grace means. In fact, grace means many different things to different Christians; it corresponds to many different Christian experiences and understandings. But in all of them, there should be some inner core that remains the same.[2]

Haight is correct to name the multivalent quality of the word *grace,* particularly at this point in Christian history. Most readers will be familiar with at least the colloquial usage of the word *grace,* such as when one describes a day or a particular experience as graced. We might also describe the performance of a dancer or the handling of a delicate debate as graceful. When flying on a long-haul flight, the airline might provide wine and beer to us gratis. And when we see a particularly gory movie, our assessment might conclude that the violence was gratuitous. While these grace-based terms and usages are related, at the very least etymologically, to the theological concept, they do not generally help us ascertain what we mean by the theological reality of grace and its relationship to human personhood.

---

[2] Roger Haight, *The Language and Experience of Grace* (New York: Paulist Press, 1979), 6.

Apart from the popular invocation of grace and grace-related terms, the theological history of the development of the doctrine of grace reveals a diverse and at times complicated trajectory. Its origins are found in the Old and New Testaments. The Latin word *gratia*, from which we get the English term *grace*, is a translation of the Greek *charis*, which itself is a translation found in the Septuagint for the Hebrew word *hen*. *Hen* originally had two valences; it could mean either (a) goodwill, the favor one finds from another, or (b) charm or beauty that would occasion the favor one found. But *hen* was not the only Hebrew word translated into Greek as *charis*. Another common term in the Old Testament translated this way was *hesed*, which is extraordinarily difficult to translate. Various English biblical translations render it as "steadfast love" or "covenantal loyalty" or some other form of "fidelity." In truth, it is best rendered as a concept rather than in a term. It is used to describe God's disposition toward creation, particularly toward humanity, when the covenant is broken. It is that undeserved, unmerited, unearned mercy that is bestowed to (sinful) humanity by means of inexplicable divine gratuity.

In the New Testament, the term *grace (charis)* appears most frequently in the writings of Saint Paul. Its meaning follows closely the Hebrew origins, best understood as pertaining to God's desire or will to save. This is a completely unmerited and unearned disposition of the Creator toward creation. The fullness of God's *charis* is seen in the life, death, and resurrection of Jesus Christ.[3] Paul discusses the grace or *charis* of God as effecting communion with God, calling us to a new way of being-in-the-world, which is seen in his regular use of the phrase "adoption" in Christ Jesus. Essential is the pneumatological dimension of God's grace. In the New Testament grace is primarily understood in terms of the Holy Spirit; the Spirit is God's gift of God's self to us in a truly immanent way. The experience of the life, death,

---

[3] For a survey of the development and meaning of grace in the New Testament, particularly as it pertains to Christ, see Edward Schillebeeckx, *Christ: The Experience of Jesus as Lord*, trans. John Bowden (New York: Crossroad Publishing, 1980), 463–538.

and resurrection of Jesus Christ brings about a new awareness in the Christian community of the immanent presence of God's grace among us.

The early Christian communities, both East and West, had an understanding of grace that was deeply indebted to this New Testament understanding of the role of the Spirit and God's gift of self to creation.[4] The early theologians of the Eastern church focused on two key aspects of grace. First, that grace is identified primarily with the Holy Spirit and that grace signified divine indwelling. Unlike what would become commonplace in the medieval Western context with an emphasis on so-called created grace, the Eastern theologians held strongly to the New Testament view that grace was *God's very self* as gift to us. Borrowing the Pauline imagery, the notion of indwelling was tied to the adoption that has taken place in the Spirit, making us daughters and sons of God. The indwelling of grace—the Spirit—is a process of *huiopoiesis* ("Christoformation"), making us "like the Son" through baptism. This led the Eastern church's second primary focus on grace, which is known as *deification*. If divine indwelling is what grace is about, then deification answers the question, "What does grace *do*?" The Eastern theologians explained that through the indwelling of grace we experience *theosis* ("divinization"), which restores us to our original nature as God intended and therefore makes us more like Christ so as to share in the divine life.[5] The early Christian theologians Irenaeus of Lyons and later the Cappadocian fathers summarized this reality with the now-classic line: God became like us so that we might become like God.

By the fourth century differences in what would become Western or Latin Christianity and the thought and writings

---

[4] See Stephen J. Duffy, *The Dynamics of Grace* (Eugene, OR: Wipf and Stock, 1993), 43–74.

[5] For more, see Michael J. Christensen and Jeffrey A. Wittung, eds., *Partakers of the Divine Nature: The History and Development of Deification in the Christian Traditions* (Grand Rapids, MI: Baker Academic, 2008).

of theologians in the Christian East would begin to depart. Emblematic of this shift is the influential work of Augustine of Hippo (d. 430 CE). Whereas the Eastern approach to the theology of grace remained focused on the gratuity of God's gift of self and its effects in terms of participation in the divine life, the Western approach increasingly focused on human freedom, sin, and the relationship of grace to those realities. Augustine's preoccupation with the reality—and later his particular concept—of original sin surfaces from a twofold source: his own experience of Christian conversion and, more important, his debate with the British theologian Pelagius (d. 418 CE).[6]

Augustine maintains that grace is primarily the gift of God's self to us as Spirit, but Pelagius argues that grace is not this indwelling of God's self but the divine gift of our human nature, which for him centers on free will or the capacity to choose freely. This has significant implications for the reality of original sin. For Pelagius, the effects of original sin are not debilitating in the manner Augustine contends. Instead, in an effort to maintain the reality of human freedom, Pelagius argued that the originating sin *(peccatum originans)* of Adam and Eve was theirs alone and that there was no quasi-genetic passing down of the effects of the original sin *(peccatum originatum)* apart from a bad example—albeit an influential one—for human behavior and exercise of free will. The value Pelagius wished to uphold was the validity of human free will; his thought is that if our will is inhibited by what Augustine would call concupiscence in such a powerful manner as to be *a priori* disposed toward sin, our free will is not free at all. Augustine, however, maintained an absolute dependence on God's grace, particularly its healing effect *(gratia sanans)*, which is necessary in order for human beings to

---

[6] Pelagius does not often receive the credit his careful thought deserves, particularly after his writings and his followers were condemned. For more on Pelagius, see Robert F. Evans, *Pelagius: Inquiries and Reappraisals* (New York: Seabury Press, 1968); and B. R. Rees, *Pelagius: A Reluctant Heretic* (Wolfeboro, NH: Boydell and Brewer, 1988).

exercise their will for the good at all.[7] Augustine's views would be largely adopted by both the Council of Carthage (418 CE) and later, in response to the so-called semi-Pelagians, the Synod of Orange (529 CE).

Notable here is that while Augustine maintained the primacy of grace as the gift of the Holy Spirit, the focus shifted in the Christian West from *what* grace is (divine gift of self) to the question of what it *does*. Augustine earned the title Doctor of Grace in part because of his detailed parsing of the effects of grace almost always understood from the starting point of sin and its crippling effects.

Following the Synod of Orange little development takes place concerning the theology of grace in the West until the important synthetic work of Thomas Aquinas (d. 1274 CE).[8] As is well known, Thomas was one of the main beneficiaries of the thirteenth-century rediscovery of Aristotle through Islamic and Jewish commentaries on the ancient philosopher's writings. One of the aspects of Aristotelianism that became central to Thomas's thought, as we have already seen in earlier chapters, is the notion of nature, in particular, the teleological character of a given thing's nature. Put simply, an Aristotelian nature is understood as that which makes a thing what it is and, at the same time, governs how it acts in accord with what that thing is. Everything that is necessary for a given thing to reach its intended end or goal *(telos)* is contained within its nature. It is also understood that a particular thing's end or goal is concomitant with its nature. We noted in previous chapters how this view of nature has facilitated essentialism and other problems in the history of theological anthropology. This philosophical framework has

---

[7] For a sampling of the key Pelagian and Augustinian texts, see the translations in *Theological Anthropology*, ed. J. Patout Burns (Minneapolis: Fortress Press, 1981), esp. 39–56, 61–108.

[8] The primary sources from which the following summary is derived are found in Thomas Aquinas, *Summa Theologica*, I–II, qq. 109–14, trans. Fathers of the English Dominican Province, vol. 2 (Notre Dame, IN: Ave Maria Press, 1948), 1123–61.

certain metaphysical implications that become significant for Thomas's understanding of grace.[9]

First, Christian faith claims a supernatural end that is not concomitant with a creaturely nature. What Thomas and others will call the beatific vision (or what the early Christian theologians referred to as participating in the divine life) is not on par with the created world. How could it be? From this a problem arises. It would appear that we are naturally lacking something necessary to reach our intended end or goal. Furthermore, because we are creatures, we do not, at least at first glance, appear to have the capacity to receive what the early theologians (including Augustine) identified as the primary meaning of grace: the gift of God's very self to us as Spirit. So grace must mean something else as it pertains to our human experience. This is where Thomas shifts emphasis from grace understood primarily as the Holy Spirit toward what he calls "created grace," which is tied to divine gratuity but is distinct from God.

Second, the focus of the Scholastic period moves away from the moral quandary presented by Augustine to an apparent metaphysical problem: how do we, creatures with a created nature, attain our divinely intended end or goal, which is supernatural? As Roger Haight explains by way of contrasting Augustine and Thomas, "Instead of being understood as the power and force of God working in human personality, in a person's willing and action, grace began to be thought of in the technical metaphysical and ontological categories of nature and habit."[10] Whereas Augustine argued that before the Fall the first humans were, with the assistance of grace, naturally able to choose the good and attain God's intended end or goal because their free will was not affected by the effects of original sin, Thomas argues that Adam and Eve were never capable of achieving their end because what is necessary is not contained within their created human nature. They, like every human creature, need something else.

---

[9] See Jean-Marc Laporte, "The Dynamics of Grace in Aquinas: A Structural Approach," *Theological Studies* 24 (1973): 203–26.

[10] Haight, *The Experience and Language of Grace*, 73.

Thinking of this dilemma in spatial terms, imagine that you are standing on the first floor of a building and that the purpose and goal of your life is getting to and living on the second floor. But there are no stairs, ladders, ropes, elevators, or any other natural means to get there. You simply cannot get there on your own no matter how high you try to jump or wish your way there. Thomas's understanding of grace, "created grace," is like a divine ladder or elevator (in fact, in Latin he refers to this is as *gratia elevans*—"elevating grace"), which allows you to get to that second floor that you had no natural way of reaching. For Thomas, the concern is an ontological or metaphysical one that launched generations of debate about whether or not and how a creature can have a divinely intended supernatural end without the inherent capacity to attain it.[11]

Thomas contends that this created grace elevates our nature and resides in us as a *habitus* or permanent disposition that raises us to a supernatural level and therefore allows us to fulfill the natural desire for our supernatural end. This perspective has had a deep and lasting influence on the understanding of grace. Over the centuries less and less attention was paid to what Thomas called "uncreated grace," which is God, and increasing emphasis was placed on the "created grace" that was needed—not to restore us to some original nature, but to add on top of the nature we were given at a creation. Thomas's Aristotelian synthesis resulted in the Scholastic expression that grace perfects nature or, alternatively, grace builds on nature. This attempted solution to the perceived metaphysical problem of humanity's supernatural end was notably dualistic and hierarchical, positioning nature apart from and subservient to the need for and work of grace. This dualistic view and hierarchical approach to imagining the relationship between God and creation persisted to and

---

[11] For an overview of this history, see Edward T. Oakes, *A Theology of Grace in Six Controversies* (Grand Rapids, MI: Eerdmans, 2016). Also, see Bernard Lonergan, *Grace and Freedom: Operative Grace in the Thought of St. Thomas Aquinas*, ed. Frederick E. Crowe and Robert M. Doran, *Collected Works of Bernard Lonergan*, vol. 1 (Toronto: University of Toronto Press, 2000).

through the Reformations, at which point the Council of Trent (1545–63 CE) sought to articulate a hybrid view of grace that acknowledged the *uncreated* grace of Augustine and the early Christian community and the necessary role of *created* grace as presented by Thomas.[12]

What followed the Council of Trent and intensified in the wake of the ecumenical fracturing of the Christian churches was a nearly exclusive focus on "created grace" for the next four centuries. This led to a view of grace as something "out there," apart from or extrinsic to nature, which humans had to collect by deliberate means. With an increased emphasis on created grace as a thing one needs and acquires to obtain our supernatural end, there emerges a pastoral approach to ministry that centers on the means, locations, and times wherein one can acquire this grace so as to have a finite share in the divine Life. The post-Trent Roman Catholic Church generally focused on valid participation in the sacramental life of the church as the means of access grace. It became an increasingly rarefied concept that was reserved for a few and excluded the vast majority of the human community (to say nothing of the rest of creation). The faithful were urged to participate in the sacraments in order to "get" the grace that is necessary to reach their supernatural end.

The prevailing shift to a nearly exclusive focus on created grace in adopting the Thomistic view of nature and grace has led to an incomplete understanding of who we are and how God the Creator relates to us as creatures. Grace conceived as a limited resource in some kind of cosmic zero-sum game of salvation still remains a popular understanding, even if it is not easily articulated by the average person of faith. In previous chapters we noted how dualistic and hierarchical thinking has undermined catholicity in theological anthropology. It compromises the characteristic of wholemaking that constitutes a truly Christian theological sensibility. What we see in this brief history

---

[12] See Council of Trent, "Decree on Justification," in *Decrees of the Ecumenical Councils*, ed. Norman P. Tanner, vol. 2 (Washington, DC: Georgetown University Press, 1990), 671–83.

of the doctrine of grace is a gradual but lasting and significant movement away from catholicity and toward a dualistic and hierarchal relationship between nature and grace that has significant implications for our understanding of the relationship between human nature and God.

While Trent and the Scholastic theological approach that grounds its articulation of grace continue to cast a long shadow over the contemporary church, there were significant developments in the twentieth century that led to a renewed articulation of grace at the Second Vatican Council that helps us to understand the human person with an eye toward greater catholicity or wholemaking.[13] A closer look at the contributions of one of the key theological architects of the Second Vatican Council will help us recognize the church's efforts to restore a more catholic understanding of grace and the significance it has for our understanding of the human person today.

Capax Dei and the Supernatural Existential

The Second Vatican Council's *Dogmatic Constitution on Divine Revelation (Dei Verbum)* opens with a claim to be "following in the footsteps of the Council of Trent and the First Vatican Council" in its articulations.[14] However, in truth the proclamation departs in several notable ways from its predecessors, offering instead a clear if understated corrective to the style and content of the previous ecumenical councils rather than proceeding

---

[13] Though it exceeds the scope of this chapter, it is worth noting that the most significant (and controversial) historical reexamination and constructive articulation of a theology of grace is Henri de Lubac, *Surnaturel: Etudes Historiques* (Paris: Desclée de Brouwer, 1991). See also idem, *The Mystery of the Supernatural*, trans. Rosemary Sheed (New York: Crossroad Publishing, 1998).

[14] "Therefore, following in the footsteps of the Council of Trent and of the First Vatican Council, this present council wishes to set forth authentic doctrine on divine revelation and how it is handed on, so that by hearing the message of salvation the whole world may believe, by believing it may hope, and by hoping it may love" (*DV*, no. 1).

by way of the footsteps laid down during the previous four centuries. The primary shift directly relates to our efforts to understand better the human person. Whereas the councils of Trent and Vatican I embrace a propositional view of revelation, arguing that what God communicates to humanity is essentially static, universal, and unchanging in nature, Vatican II returns to the ancient sources *(ressourcement)* in order to update our theology *(aggiornamento)*. What results is a renewed understanding of revelation that recognizes its dynamic, particular, historical, and, most important, *relational* characteristics.

Revelation is first and foremost understood as God's self-disclosure, the revealing or unveiling of not only the divine will but also of God's very self, culminating with the incarnation of the Word, which is the fullness of divine revelation.[15] *Dei Verbum* reaffirms that God reveals God's self to us in history and in a manner understandable to humanity, even if the fullness of the mystery of God always exceeds human comprehension. What is especially significant about this conciliar teaching, which lays the theological foundations for understanding scripture and tradition, is that it presupposes something about the human person that was not present in the propositional view of revelation expressed at Trent and Vatican I, namely, if revelation is first and foremost the self-disclosure of God to us, then there has to be something about us that makes the dynamism possible in the first place.

A question once posed by one of the primary theological architects of *Dei Verbum*, Karl Rahner, addresses the human capacity for God directly: "What kind of hearer does Christianity anticipate so that its real and ultimate message can be heard?"[16] Rahner, a *peritus* (theological adviser) to the bishops

---

[15] "In His goodness and wisdom God chose to reveal Himself and to make known to us the hidden purpose of His will (see Eph. 1:9) by which through Christ, the Word made flesh, man might in the Holy Spirit have access to the Father and come to share in the divine nature (see Eph. 2:18; 2 Peter 1:4)" (see *DV*, esp. no. 2).

[16] Karl Rahner, *Foundations of Christian Faith*, trans. William V. Dych (New York: Crossroad Publishing, 1982), 24.

at Vatican II, understood the importance of exploring the other side of the revelation coin; that is, what about us makes it possible for us to receive God's self-disclosure in the first place? If we claim that "God speaks a word" to creation, what conditions make it possible to hear or recognize that revelation?[17] This is where Rahner serves as an exemplary model of someone who takes the ancient Christian understanding of the primacy of grace seriously. Furthermore, his work offers a constructive and *catholic* response to the incomplete theology of revelation and grace emphasized at and after Trent. A wholemaking approach to the human person has to take into consideration the very structures that make revelation possible at all. Essentially, Rahner's theological work shows that Christianity presupposes that human beings are created *capax Dei*, with the "capacity for God," from the beginning. God's intention from all eternity was to enter into relationship with creation in general and humanity in particular, and in order to do so, God created us with the ability to receive the gift that is God's very self: grace.

Rahner's work returns to the early Christian theological sources, as witnessed in both the East and West, in order to correct for disproportionate focus on so-called created grace. In his summary article on grace he explains that the starting point for a theology of grace is a fundamental theological anthropology; one cannot understand grace without understanding the human person and vice versa. Furthermore, in response to the Tridentine emphasis on the partial understanding of grace articulated by Thomas and other Scholastics, Rahner writes: "God does not confer on man merely created gifts as a token of his love. God communicates *himself* by what is no longer simply efficient causality. He makes man share in the very nature of God."[18] With language evoking the Eastern Christian emphasis on *huiopoiesis*,

---

[17] See Karl Rahner, *Hearer of the Word: Laying the Foundation for a Philosophy of Religion*, trans. Joseph Donceel (New York: Continuum, 1994).

[18] Karl Rahner, "Grace—II. Theological," in *Encyclopedia of Theology: The Concise Sacramentum Mundi*, ed. Karl Rahner (New York: Continuum, 1984), 588.

he continues: "He constitutes man as co-heir with the Son himself, called to the eternal life of God face to face, called to receive the direct vision of God, called therefore to receive God's own life."[19] In an earlier article Rahner explains:

> God wishes to communicate himself, to pour forth the love which he himself is. That is the first and the last of his real plans and hence of his real world too. Everything else exists so that this one thing might be: the eternal miracle of infinite Love. And so God makes a creature whom he can love: he creates man. He creates him in such a way that he *can* receive this Love which is God himself, and that he can and must at the same time accept it for what it is: the ever astounding wonder, the unexpected, unexacted gift.[20]

What Rahner does in returning to the ancient Christian understanding of grace being first and foremost the gift of God's self to us is shine a light on the other side of that coin we call revelation or God's self-disclosure, namely, that there must be something intrinsic to the human person that provides the condition of the possibility for hearing this word of God or, better put, receiving this gift of God's self in the first place. Rahner says that humanity "should be *able* to receive this Love which is God himself; he must have a congeniality for it. He must be able to accept it

---

[19] Rahner, "Grace—II. Theological," 588.

[20] Karl Rahner, "Concerning the Relationship between Nature and Grace," in *Theological Investigations*, vol. 1, trans. Cornelius Ernst (Baltimore: Helicon Press, 1961), 310. This article was original published as "Über das Verhältnis von Natur und Gnade," *Orientierung* 14 (1950): 141–45. More than ten years earlier the eventual full restoration of grace as primarily "uncreated" appears in his study on the Scholastic concept of uncreated grace in "Zur scholastischen Begrifflichkeit der ungeschaffenen Gnade," *Zeitschrift für katholische Theologie* 63 (1939): 137–57. This is reemphasized a decade later by Rahner in an article originally published in 1960: "Nature and Grace," in *Theological Investigations*, vol. 4, trans. Kevin Smyth (Baltimore: Helicon Press, 1966), 177: "Grace is God himself, the communication in which he gives himself to man as the divinizing favor which he is himself."

(and hence grace, the beatific vision) as one who has room and scope, understanding and desire for it. Thus he must have a real 'potency' for it. He must have it *always*."[21] He goes on to add that "the capacity for the God of self-bestowing personal Love is the central and abiding existential of man as he really is."[22] This leads us to one of Rahner's most innovative and significant contributions to the theology of grace: the supernatural existential.

In affirming the universality of humanity's capacity for God (*capax Dei*), Rahner introduces the "supernatural existential." Borrowing the term *existential* from the phenomenologist Martin Heidegger, a concept referring to an *a priori* and inalienable structural aspect of human existence, Rahner argues that there is an intrinsic dimension of human existence that is always already open to the divine and capable of receiving the gift of grace. While it is indeed, by virtue of being an existential, a dimension of the whole human person, Rahner is clear that this supernatural existential is not simply a natural element of human existence owed to persons but instead a completely free and unexacted gift from God.[23] Theologian John Galvin summarizes this notion well: "The divine offer of self-communication forms a constant dimension of human existence, always present, yet not part of human nature as such, affecting the whole of our being and directing us toward unsurpassable nearness to the triune God of grace and eternal life."[24] This suggests that there is also a primordial relationship between God and humanity, even prior to an individual's conscious reflection on such a relationship (if one ever considers it thematically at all). Theologian Stephen

---

[21] Rahner, "Concerning the Relationship between Nature and Grace," 312.

[22] Rahner, "Concerning the Relationship between Nature and Grace," 312.

[23] See Daniel P. Horan, "A Rahnerian Theological Response to Charles Taylor's *A Secular Age*," *New Blackfriars* 95 (2014): 32.

[24] John P. Galvin, "The Invitation of Grace," in *A World of Grace: An Introduction to the Themes and Foundations of Karl Rahner's Theology*, ed. Leo O'Donovan (Washington, DC: Georgetown University Press, 1955), 72.

Duffy notes that "even in the absence of reflexive awareness of the existential, humans remain, nonetheless, always graced by an inner dynamism thrusting toward the God who calls and gives God's self."[25]

Rahner's insight, as expressed in the magisterial teaching of *Dei Verbum* at the Second Vatican Council and elsewhere, offers two important implications from the perspective of catholicity. First, it responds to the incomplete and atrophied theology of grace that began to decline with the Scholastic prioritization of *created* grace and continued through the Council of Trent until the contemporary era. Instead of some extrinsic concept of a created thing bestowed by God as an elevating gift to remedy an insufficient human nature, the return to the ancient Christian prioritization of *uncreated* grace—the free gift of God's very self—restores the theology of grace to a better sense of wholemaking that presupposes an inherent and intimate relationship freely initiated by God between the Creator and creation. Second, the articulation of the supernatural existential locates the condition of the possibility of receiving a possible divine revelation squarely in human experience. Additionally, given that this *capax Dei* is recognized as an existential of human existence, it is universal and inalienable. God's grace, the free gift of God's self to humanity, is not limited to Christians alone but is the very foundation of all human freedom, knowing, and action. In terms of a theological anthropology focused on wholemaking, this commonality shared across race, gender, class, orientation, religious tradition, and so on, offers a note of

---

[25] Stephen J. Duffy, "Experience of Grace," in *The Cambridge Companion to Karl Rahner*, ed. Declan Marmion and Mary Hines (New York: Cambridge University Press, 2005), 47. Given the universality of the supernatural existential, this also applies to nonbelievers and atheists, among others. Rahner addresses this in the following two essays: "Atheism and Implicit Christianity," in *Theological Investigations*, vol. 9, trans. Graham Harrison, 145–64 (New York: Herder and Herder, 1972); and "Anonymous Christianity and the Missionary Task of the Church," in *Theological Investigations*, vol. 12, trans. David Bourke, 161–78 (New York: Seabury Publishing, 1974).

hope in a recognizably fractured world. Each and every person has the same capacity for God.

A World of Grace and Everyday Mysticism

There are important implications that surface from a view of God and the world that recognizes the universal and free gift of grace, which is accessible always and everywhere to all people. For as technical and esoteric as some of the debates about nature and grace may appear in general over the centuries, and in Rahner's modern writing in particular, there is always present that practical concern, the pastoral concern, the concern for what it means to live a Christian life with a renewed understanding of ourselves as human. We close this chapter with a brief reflection on precisely such implications, drawing from Rahner's own articulation of the connection between the theology of grace and the lived experience of Christian faith. These insights offer us some practical strategies for developing a more catholic way of everyday living.

Rahner understood the limitations and at times the problematics of institutional religion. While a faithful and devout Jesuit and Roman Catholic priest, he nevertheless recognized that, over the years, theology had been taught in a manner that reduced faith to catechetics and that religious instruction was inadequate for the task of navigating one's lived faith in a complicated world. In response, his seemingly abstract theological reflection on the human person as always already experiencing God by virtue of the supernatural existential, that we are always already oriented to God who is both our ground and goal, actually serves as the foundation for a spirituality of Christian life that is tenable in these increasingly uncertain and complex times. Anticipating this, he wrote: "The devout Christian of the future will either be a 'mystic,' one who has 'experienced' something, or he will cease to be anything at all. For devout Christian living as practiced in the future will no longer be sustained and helped by the unanimous, manifest, and public convictions and religious customs of all, summoning each one from the outset to a personal experience and a personal decision."[26] Rahner was not arguing for a monadic or individualistic Christianity, for he frequently stated in his writings and interviews that there could be no such thing given that Christianity is inherently about relationship—the relationship of God to the world, and the relationships we share among ourselves. Instead, Rahner was addressing the challenge that he often referred to as "faith in a wintry season."[27] Those social and institutional markers and presuppositions previously taken for granted in striving to live out one's Christian faith were no longer present or sustainable. Another foundation needed to be found, a new or renewed sense of grounding needed to be uncovered. To this end Rahner calls for a genuine Christian mysticism.

Typically, mystics are seen in popular contexts as extraordinary individuals who have been chosen by God to receive a special experience of the Divine. Rahner argues that, while there are certainly those who are extraordinary for their life of courage and exemplary living that might be counted as great mystics, the opportunity to become a mystic is not given only to a relatively limited number.[28] Instead, given his work of theological *ressourcement* in the area of grace, "Rahner seemingly identifies mysticism as the primordial experience of God in every human life."[29] As historian of mysticism Harvey Eagan explains, "From a Rahnerian perspective, therefore, the human person is *homo mysticus* . . . because the person is the addressee of God's

---

[26] Karl Rahner, "Christian Living Formerly and Today," in *Theological Investigations*, vol. 7, trans. David Bourke (New York: Seabury Press, 1977), 15.

[27] See Paul Imhof, Harvey D. Eagan, and Hubert Biallowons, *Faith in a Wintry Season: Interviews and Conversations with Karl Rahner in the Last Years of His Life—1982–1984* (New York: Crossroad Publishing, 1990).

[28] This is addressed in Karl Rahner, "Mystical Experience and Mystical Theology," in *Theological Investigations*, vol. 17, trans. Margaret Kohl, 90–99 (New York: Crossroad Publishing, 1981).

[29] Harvey D. Eagan, *Karl Rahner: Mystic of Everyday Life* (New York: Crossroad Publishing, 1998), 57.

self-communication, all personal experiences contain at least an implicit, yet primordial experience of God."[30] All persons have an equal opportunity to bring to consciousness or thematic awareness the experience of God they always already have but may not be conscious of for a variety of reasons. True mysticism is the bringing to awareness that which is already present, the free gift of God's self to us that occasions our recognition of God's constant proximity to creation.[31]

For Rahner, because grace "is a grace which always surrounds man, even the sinner and the unbeliever, as the inescapable setting of his existence,"[32] the entire cosmos is a world of grace. The Christian mysticism that such a reality calls for is the continual attuning of our hearts and minds to the presence of the Spirit always already in our midst. This is certainly challenging, particularly during those periods in our lives when loss, suffering, or tragedy strike. And yet, this theology of grace also beckons a spirit of Christian hope, calling us to practice what Rahner invariably calls the mysticism of everyday life. "This mysticism of everyday life encompasses even the most humble aspects of our daily routine, such as our working, sleeping, eating, drinking, laughing, seeing, sitting, and getting about."[33] Becoming an everyday mystic—that is, attuning ourselves more and more to the world of grace in which we live and move and have our being—is what we might call a spirituality of catholicity. The idea that wholemaking is not merely a theological abstraction, concerned as it is with the theoretical and systematic catholicity of doctrinal articulation and theological reflection. Instead, a spirituality of catholicity invites us to reimagine the parameters of the holy, the divine, or the presence of the Creator in creation. A world of grace presupposes a God who draws near to us, not

---

[30] Eagan, *Karl Rahner*, 57.

[31] Rahner, "Mystical Experience and Mystical Theology," 2. Also see Karl Rahner, "Experience of the Holy Spirit," in *Theological Investigations*, vol. 18, trans. Edward Quinn, 189–210 (New York: Crossroad Publishing, 1983).

[32] Rahner, "Nature and Grace," 181.

[33] Eagan, *Karl Rahner*, 58.

only in the person of Jesus Christ as the incarnate Word, but also and still as Spirit—the divine Spirit that moves "throughout the whole," is present to all, and is not confined by the limited scope of institution or ritual.

The task before us is connecting our increasing appreciation for emerging personhood in the key of catholicity with the lived experience of everyday mysticism, which calls us to a new awareness of the mysteries of who God is and who we are. We can take a clue from Rahner himself, who, though he was the consummate academic theologian, wrote several accessible and disarmingly simple essays on the theology and spirituality of everyday experiences such as sleeping, eating, working, and laughing.[34] His outlook was one shaped by a sense of catholicity found in his recognition that grace is always already present and operative in all moments of existence. Practicing this everyday mysticism could take the form of our pausing daily to reflect on what makes possible our life, safety, and growth in sleep or recognizing the multitude of little ways God's presence breaks through the banal and mundane realities of office work or parental tasks. The more we attune ourselves to the continual and ongoing presence of God in the world, the more the quotidian and ordinary will begin to appear more extraordinary. In this way we might pursue a path toward becoming everyday mystics.

---

[34] See Karl Rahner, *The Mystical Way of Everyday Life*, trans. Anne Marie Kidder (Maryknoll, NY: Orbis Books, 2010).

Conclusion

What does it mean to be human? While a complete answer to the question will always remain elusive because of the mystery that is at the heart of creation in general and humanity in particular, we can nevertheless work toward deeper knowledge and appreciation for who we are. Throughout this book we have examined the question through a lens of catholicity, seeking to address key themes in the field of theological anthropology with an eye toward resources and articulation that aims to be more wholemaking than many earlier efforts. As a result, we have presented a contemporary theological anthropology that may serve as a starting point for further inquiry and elucidation about the meaning of human personhood.

Any venture into greater understanding of what it means to be human must begin with an acknowledgment of our creaturely origins and persistent animality. While off-putting to many modern people, the embrace of our creatureliness—loving the dust we are, as I like to say—is a reflection on the profound truth of our collective identity and inescapable interrelatedness with the rest of creation. This reality is bolstered not only by sources in scripture and the theological tradition, but also by the discoveries made in the natural and social sciences. For example, the theory of evolution presents both challenges and promises to theological anthropology. The challenge is to the incomplete answers, often articulated in universal and static frames, about what it means to be human that have been presented as irrefutable truths or foundations for a Christian understanding of human exceptionalism. Charles Darwin, Pierre Teilhard de Chardin, and many contemporary scholars have shown that human distinctiveness can be maintained alongside the cosmological truth of the emergence of our species and its development with other creatures over eons. The promise of evolution reveals that we are stronger because of our shared creaturely origins and ongoing interdependence, not weaker or less significant.

With a renewed sense of our creaturely origins, interrelatedness, and human animality, questions surface about the presuppositions we have reinscribed around the doctrine of the *imago Dei*. For centuries this term has served as a valuable placeholder for human dignity and value, which, in itself, is not problematic. The problem arises when we consider that the manner in which the *imago Dei* has been invoked to refer to human beings alone has perpetuated the false narrative of human separatism. This has further reinforced the mistaken view of absolute human uniqueness that relies upon a hierarchal dualism that has deleterious consequences for the whole of creation. Once one begins to consider these problems with the notion of the *imago Dei*, it does not take long to discover the ambiguity of the term itself and the history of projecting meaning into it in order to create a doctrine that begs the question of human uniqueness in the first place. Considered from the point of catholicity and wholemaking, a new articulation of *imago Dei* that does not merely replicate the inadequate and human-separatist approach becomes necessary, one that maintains both an inclusive understanding that all creation images the Creator in some way and that there exists a real distinction among the species in bearing the *imago Dei*.

In considering the history of theological reflection on the human person, it is clear that a major contribution to the impasses and challenges in Christian anthropology is the nearly exclusive reliance on a singular philosophical and theological framework from the thirteenth century, namely, the Aristotelian-Thomistic approach to theology. It is not that Thomas Aquinas is some kind of historical villain or erroneous thinker. Rather, this historically situated and contextually limited way of understanding the human person—scientifically and metaphysically—is not sufficient for grounding a contemporary theological anthropology, particularly in light of the discoveries that have emerged in the natural sciences, philosophy, and theology over the last eight centuries.

Alternative philosophical and theological approaches to understanding the world, such as those found in the work of John Duns Scotus, offer more fecund foundations for contemporary theological reflection. Accordingly, the concept of *haecceitas* provides an orthodox yet alternative starting point for metaphysical reflection on the human person that prioritizes the particularity of each creature over the commonplace tendency to describe humanity in general and abstract terms. This approach offers us a renewed sense of intrinsic relationality that is made possible by radical particularity, thereby providing a stronger sense of wholemaking in the understanding of the human person. By way of illustration, we looked at how the adoption of *haecceitas* as the philosophical foundation provides a constructive response to the sexism of gender complementarity, a correction to the contemporary erasure of transgender experiences and persons, and an alternative starting point that responds to the dehumanization of racism under the current Aristotelian-Thomistic approach to theological anthropology. Much more work still needs to be done in these three areas, among others. The aim of engaging these cases in this book is to begin the conversation and initiate a process by which we might think the human person anew, looking for renewed foundations and new dialogue partners for developing a theological anthropology that responds to the complexity of human existence now realized.

This brings us to sin and grace, themes that the Christian theological tradition has reflected on for millennia. As with the other theological anthropological loci explored in this book, approaching the human person with a hermeneutic of catholicity raised questions about the way in which sin and grace have been considered and articulated. While no one denies the reality of sin, the concept of original sin and other facets of the doctrine have widely been recognized as untenable in their classical articulations. In the spirit of wholemaking we sought to maintain the reality of our universal human capacity for sin, while also accounting for the incompleteness in which particular sin and structural sin have been previously addressed. Furthermore, most reflections on the doctrine of sin have focused on the sinner, the perpetrator, or the oppressor, to the exclusion of the victims, survivors, and sinned against. A theology of sin according to the hermeneutic of catholicity must consider both sides of this coin, which led us to explore the Korean concept of *han* as one resource in this effort. Historically, the theology of grace has likewise been considered and articulated in an incomplete manner. Whereas the earliest Christian understandings of grace were tied to the divine gift of God's self to creation, over time—especially since the High Middle Ages—theological reflection on grace and the human person has focused on so-called created grace. This emphasis has consequently presented humanity as insufficient for its divinely intended end or goal, which demeans human beings while further distancing the Creator from creation. A theology of grace rooted in catholicity restores the primacy of God's gift of self to creation, which reveals the universal human capacity to receive that very gift. Here, the insights of theologian Karl Rahner are invaluable, especially because they encourage us to change not only our abstract understanding of God and creation, but also because they challenge us to live our faith and see the world in a significantly renewed way with practical implications.

The work of addressing the question of what it means to be human continues. What has begun here is merely the beginning of reconsideration of classicist approaches to complex realities and impartial answers to robust questions seeking wholeness. Indeed, the hermeneutic of catholicity necessitates this ongoing work. The Christian theological tradition fails to actualize catholicity when it takes particular truths as universal absolutes. Lest we repeat this tendency, we must embrace theological reflection on the human person as an ongoing and perennial task in which the normative truths of our time are always reconsidered with care but also with an eye toward wholeness. As such, the work inaugurated in this book also gestures toward other themes regarding facets of the human person not considered here, such as what this vision of catholicity means for the human person's embrace of our universal call to holiness or how we might understand death and eschatology in a new light. There is much that remains to be addressed, but I hope this foray into considering the human person through the lens of catholicity and wholemaking encourages others to likewise reconsider our theological approaches to what remains our emerging person-hood.

Select Bibliography

Abram, David. *The Spell of the Sensuous: Perception and Language in a More-Than-Human World*. New York: Vintage Books, 1997.

James Alison, *The Joy of Being Wrong: Original Sin through Easter Eyes*. New York: Herder and Herder, 1998.

Anderson, Victor. *Beyond Ontological Blackness: An Essay on African American Religious and Cultural Criticism*. New York: Bloomsbury, 1995.

Aquinas, Thomas. *Summa Theologica*, trans. Fathers of the English Dominican Province, 5 vols. Notre Dame, IN: Ave Maria Press, 1948.

Bauckham, Richard. *The Bible and Ecology: Rediscovering the Community of Creation*. Waco: Baylor University Press, 2010.

Bergson, Henri. *Creative Evolution*, trans. Arthur Mitchell. New York: Dover Publications, 1998.

Buchanan, Brett. *Onto-Ethologies: The Animal Environments of Uexküll, Heidegger, Merleau-Ponty, and Deleuze*. Albany: SUNY Press, 2008.

Clough, David L. *On Animals: Volume 1, Systematic Theology*. London: T & T Clark, 2012.

Considine, Kevin P. *Salvation for the Sinned-Against: Han and Schillebeeckx in Intercultural Dialogue*. Eugene, OR: Pickwick Publications, 2015.

Copeland, M. Shawn. *Enfleshing Freedom: Body, Race, and Being*. Minneapolis: Fortress Press, 2010.

Cunningham, David S. "The Way of All Flesh: Rethinking the *Imago Dei*." In *Creaturely Theology: On God, Humans, and Other Animals*, edited by Celia Deane-Drummond and David Clough, 100–20. London: SCM Press, 2009).

Darwin, Charles. *On the Origin of Species by Means of Natural Selection*. New York: Bantam Books, 2008.

———. *The Descent of Man*. Edited by Michael Ghiselin. New York: Dover Publications, 2010.

Delio, Ilia. *Making All Things New: Catholicity, Cosmology, Consciousness*. Maryknoll, NY: Orbis Books, 2015.

———. *The Emergent Christ: Exploring the Meaning of Catholic in an Evolutionary Universe*. Maryknoll, NY: Orbis Books, 2011.

———. *The Unbearable Wholeness of Being: God, Evolution, and the Power of Love*. Maryknoll, NY: Orbis Books, 2013.

Duffy, Stephen J. *The Dynamics of Grace*. Eugene, OR: Wipf and Stock, 1993.

———. "Genes, Original Sin, and the Human Proclivity to Evil," *Horizons* 32 (2005): 210–34.

Dulles, Avery. *The Catholicity of the Church*. Oxford: Clarendon Press, 1985.

Fernandez, Eleazar S. *Reimagining the Human: Theological Anthropology in Response to Systemic Evil*. St. Louis: Chalice Press, 2004.

Fung, Raymond. "Compassion for the Sinned-Against," *Theology Today* 37 (1980): 162–69.

Gilkey, Langdon. "Nature as the Image of God: Signs of the Sacred," *Theology Today* 51 (1994): 127–41.

Gonzalez, Michelle A. *Created in God's Image: An Introduction to Feminist Theological Anthropology*. Maryknoll, NY: Orbis Books, 2007.

Gregersen, Niels Henrik. "The Cross of Christ in an Evolutionary World," *Dialog: A Journal of Theology* 40 (2001): 192–207.

Haight, Roger. *The Language and Experience of Grace*. New York: Paulist Press, 1979.

Hopkins, Dwight N. *Being Human: Race, Culture, and Religion*. Minneapolis: Fortress Press, 2005.

Horan, Daniel P. *All God's Creatures: A Theology of Creation.* Lanham, MD: Lexington Books/Fortress Academic, 2018.

———. "Beyond Essentialism and Complementarity: Toward a Theological Anthropology Rooted in *Haecceitas*," *Theological Studies* 75 (2014): 94–117.

———. "Light and Love: A Franciscan Look at the 'How' and 'Why' of Creation." In *Francis of Assisi and the Future of Faith: Exploring Franciscan Spirituality and Theology in the Modern World*, 145–57. Phoenix: Tau Publishing, 2012.

———. *Postmodernity and Univocity: A Critical Account of Radical Orthodoxy and John Duns Scotus.* Minneapolis: Fortress Press, 2014.

Ingham, Mary Beth. *The Harmony of Goodness: Mutuality and Moral Living according to John Duns Scotus.* Second edition. St. Bonaventure, NY: Franciscan Institute Publications, 2012.

———. *Understanding John Duns Scotus: 'Of Realty the Rarest-Veined Unraveller.'* St. Bonaventure, NY: Franciscan Institute Publications, 2017.

Ingham, Mary Beth, and Mechthild Dreyer, *The Philosophical Vision of John Duns Scotus: An Introduction.* Washington, DC: CUA Press, 2004.

Johnson, Elizabeth A. *Ask the Beasts: Darwin and the God of Love.* New York: Bloomsbury, 2014.

———. "Creation: Is God's Charity Broad Enough for Bears?" In *Abounding in Kindness: Writings for the People of God*, 97–123. Maryknoll, NY: Orbis Books, 2015).

———. "Does God Play Dice? Divine Providence and Chance," *Theological Studies* 57 (1996): 3–18.

Kaplan, Grant. *René Girad, Unlikely Apologist: Mimetic Theory and Fundamental Theology.* Notre Dame, IN: University of Notre Dame Press, 2016.

Las Casas, Bartolomé de. *A Short Account of the Destruction of the Indies.* Translated by Nigel Griffin. New York: Penguin Classics, 1999.

Meyer, Eric Daryl. *Inner Animalities: Theology and the End of the Human*. New York: Fordham University Press, 2018.

Middleton, J. Richard. *The Liberating Image: The Imago Dei in Genesis 1*. Grand Rapids, MI: Brazos Press, 2005.

Moritz, Joshua M. "Evolution, the End of Human Uniqueness, and the Election of the *Imago Dei*," *Theology and Science* 9 (2011): 307–39.

Muray, Leslie A. "Human Uniqueness vs. Human Distinctiveness: The *Imago Dei* in the Kinship of All Creatures," *American Journal of Theology and Philosophy* 28 (2007): 299–310.

Nielsen, Cynthia R. *Foucault, Douglass, Fanon, and Scotus in Dialogue: On Social Construction and Freedom*. New York: Palgrave Macmillan, 2013.

Newman, John Henry. *An Essay on the Development of Christian Doctrine*. Notre Dame, IN: University of Notre Dame Press, 1989.

Noone, Timothy. "Individuation in Scotus," *American Catholic Philosophical Quarterly* 69 (1995): 527–42.

Oliver, Kelly. *Animal Lessons: How They Teach Us to Be Human*. New York: Columbia University Press, 2009.

Park, Andrew Sung. *The Wounded Heart of God: The Asian Concept of Han and the Christian Doctrine of Sin*. Nashville, TN: Abingdon Press, 1993.

Prevot, Andrew. "Sources of a Black Self? Ethics of Authenticity in an Era of Anti-Blackness." In *Anti-Blackness and Christian Ethics*, edited by Vincent W. Lloyd and Andrew Prevot, 77–95. Maryknoll, NY: Orbis Books, 2017).

Rahner, Karl. *Foundations of Christian Faith*, trans. William V. Dych. New York: Crossroad Publishing, 1982.

———. *Hearer of the Word: Laying the Foundation for a Philosophy of Religion*. Translated by Joseph Donceel. New York: Continuum, 1994.

Ross, Susan. *Anthropology: Seeking Light and Beauty*. Collegeville, MN: Liturgical Press, 2012.

Saiving, Valerie. "The Human Situation: A Feminine View," *Journal of Religion* 40 (1960): 100–112.

Schreiter, Robert J. *The New Catholicity: Theology between the Global and the Local.* Maryknoll, NY: Orbis Books, 1997.

Scotus, John Duns. *Opera Omnia: Studio et Cura Commissionis Scotisticae ad fidem codicum edita.* Edited by Carlo Balíc et al. 21 volumes. Vatican City: Typis Polyglottis Vaticanis, 1950– .

Southgate, Christopher. *The Groaning of Creation: God, Evolution, and the Problem of Evil.* Louisville, KY: Westminster John Knox Press, 2008.

Teilhard de Chardin, Pierre. *Christianity and Evolution: Reflections on Science and Religion.* Translated by René Hague. New York: Harcourt Brace, 1971.

———. *Man's Place in Nature: The Human Zoological Group.* Translated by René Hague. New York: Harper and Row, 1966.

———. *The Heart of Matter.* Translated by René Hague. New York: Harcourt Brace, 1978.

———. *The Phenomenon of Man.* Translated by Bernard Wall. New York: HarperCollins, 2008.

Tinker, George E. "Spirituality, Native American Personhood, Sovereignty, and Solidarity," *Ecumenical Review* 44, no. 3 (1992): 312–24.

Uhl, Christopher. *Developing Ecological Consciousness: The End of Separation.* Second edition. Lanham, MD: Rowman and Littlefield Publishers, 2013.

Uexküll, Jakob von. *A Foray into the World of Animals and Humans* and *A Theory of Meaning.* Translated by Joseph O'Neil. Minneapolis: University of Minnesota Press, 2010.

———. *Theoretical Biology.* Translated by D. L. McKinnon. New York: Harcourt Brace, 1927.

Wiley, Tatha. *Original Sin: Origins, Developments, Contemporary Meanings.* New York: Paulist Press, 2002.

Wood, Bernard. *Human Evolution: A Very Short Introduction.* New York: Oxford University Press, 2005.

Zimmer, Carl. *The Tangled Bank: An Introduction to Evolution.* Greenwood Village, CO: Roberts and Co. Publishers, 2010.

Index

Summa Theologica (Thomas), 150
supernatural existential, 20, 218, 231–33
Swimme Brian, 38–39
Synod of Orange, 223
systematic theology, 7–8, 11, 156

Taylor, Charles, 180
Teich, Nicholas, 158
Teilhard de Chardin, Pierre
    anthropocentric outlook of, 69–70
    Bergson, expanding evolutionary insights of, 68
    Christogenesis proposal, 71–73
    Christological reflection, building on, 75
    in hermeneutics of catholicity, 6
    human distinctiveness. on the maintenance of, 237–38
teleological worldview, 127, 129
theodicy, 76, 79–80, 192
theology of creation, 32, 34, 82
theology of election, 98–99
theology of the body, 147
Theoretical Biology (Uexküll), 114
Theory of Meaning (Uexküll), 116
theosis (divinization), 221
Thomas Aquinas, Saint
    Aristotelian framework of, 127, 161–66, 223
    Catholic theology, Thomistic presuppositions in, 18, 149, 238–39

as the Common Doctor, 126
on created grace, 224–26, 229
on the diversity of creatures, 26
divine causality theory, Johnson expanding on, 62
essence and existence in metaphysics of, 128, 139
negative principle in theology of, 137
Scotus, differing sense of common nature, 132
social norms, arising from Thomistic essentialism, 152–53
Thomistic worldview as problematic, 144
top-down approach to anthropology, 129, 153
women, skewed views on, 149-51
    See also Aristotelian-Thomistic anthropology
Tillich, Paul, 11
Tinker, George
    Christian creation doctrine, critique of, 32–34
    kinship of creation, recognizing, 36
    on the reign of God, 34–35
    sin, on indigenous responses to, 204–6
transgender persons
    gender dysphoria and, 159–60, 161, 163, 165
    gender reassignment surgery (GRS), 164
    haecceitas concept, applying to, 167–68, 170–71, 239